OF 4

INTERGOVERNMENTAL COOPERATION

COMPARATIVE POLITICS

Comparative Politics is a series for students, teachers, and researchers of political science that deals with contemporary government and politics. Global in scope, books in the series are characterised by a stress on comparative analysis and strong methodological rigour. The series is published in association with the European Consortium for Political Research. For more information visit www.essex.ac.uk/ecpr

The Comparative Politics series is edited by Professor David Farrell, University of Manchester.

OTHER TITLES IN THIS SERIES

Cabinets and Coalition Bargaining
The Democratic Life Cycle in Western Europe
Edited by Kaare Strøm, Wolfgang C. Muller, and Torbjörn Bergman

Redistricting in Comparative Perspective
Edited by Lisa Handley and Bernard Grofman

Democratic Representation in Europe
Diversity, Change, and Convergence
Edited by Maurizio Cotta and Heinrich Best

Party Politics in New Democracies
Edited by Paul Webb and Stephen White

Democratic Challenges, Democratic Choices
Russell J. Dalton

Democracy Transformed?
Edited by Bruce E. Cain, Russell J. Dalton, and Susan E. Scarrow

Environmental Protest in Western Europe
Edited by Christopher Rootes

Social Movements and Networks
Edited by Mario Diani and Doug McAdam

Delegation and Accountability in Parliamentary Democracies
Edited by Kaare Strøm, Wolfgang C. Müller, and Torbjörn Bergman

The Presidentialization of Politics
Edited by Thomas Paguntke and Paul Webb

Losers' Consent
*Christopher J. Anderson, André Blais, Shaun Bowler,
Todd Donovan, and Ola Listhaug*

Elections, Parties, Democracy
Michael D. McDonald and Ian Budge

Extreme Right Parties in Western Europe
Piero Ignazi

The Performance of Democracies
Edeltraud Roller

Political Parties in the New Europe
Edited by Kurt Richard Luther and Ferdinand Müller-Rommel

The European Voter
Edited by Jacques Thomassen

Intergovernmental Cooperation

Rational Choices in Federal Systems and Beyond

NICOLE BOLLEYER

UNIVERSITY PRESS

OXFORD
UNIVERSITY PRESS

Great Clarendon Street, Oxford OX2 6DP

Oxford University Press is a department of the University of Oxford.
It furthers the University's objective of excellence in research, scholarship,
and education by publishing worldwide in

Oxford New York

Auckland Cape Town Dar es Salaam Hong Kong Karachi
Kuala Lumpur Madrid Melbourne Mexico City Nairobi
New Delhi Shanghai Taipei Toronto

With offices in

Argentina Austria Brazil Chile Czech Republic France Greece
Guatemala Hungary Italy Japan Poland Portugal Singapore
South Korea Switzerland Thailand Turkey Ukraine Vietnam

Oxford is a registered trade mark of Oxford University Press
in the UK and in certain other countries

Published in the United States
by Oxford University Press Inc., New York

© Nicole Bolleyer 2009

The moral rights of the author have been asserted
Database right Oxford University Press (maker)

First published 2009

All rights reserved. No part of this publication may be reproduced,
stored in a retrieval system, or transmitted, in any form or by any means,
without the prior permission in writing of Oxford University Press,
or as expressly permitted by law, or under terms agreed with the appropriate
reprographics rights organization. Enquiries concerning reproduction
outside the scope of the above should be sent to the Rights Department,
Oxford University Press, at the address above

You must not circulate this book in any other binding or cover
and you must impose the same condition on any acquirer

British Library Cataloguing in Publication Data
Data available

Library of Congress Cataloging in Publication Data
Bolleyer, Nicole.
Intergovernmental cooperation : rational choice in federal
systems and beyond / Nicole Bolleyer.
    p. cm.—(Comparative politics)
Includes bibliographical references.
ISBN 978–0–19–957060–7
1. Federal government. 2. Central-local government relations.
3. Decentralization in government. 4. Comparative government. I. Title.
JC355.B65 2009
320.4'049—dc22   2009016653

Typeset by SPI Publisher Services, Pondicherry, India
Printed in Great Britain by the MPG Books Group, Bodmin and King's Lynn

ISBN 978–0–19–957060–7

1 3 5 7 9 10 8 6 4 2

Für Ingrid und Andreas,
wer sie kennt, der weiss warum

Contents

Acknowledgements ix
List of Figures xi
List of Tables xiii
List of Abbreviations xv

1. Intergovernmental Relations and the Puzzle of Institutional Choice 1
2. A Rationalist Account of Intergovernmental Institution-Building 29
3. Intergovernmental Institutionalization in Canada 61
4. Intergovernmental Institutionalization in Switzerland 93
5. Intergovernmental Institutionalization in the United States 111
6. Intergovernmental Integration in Canada, Switzerland, and the United States 137
7. Intergovernmental Institutions and the Nature of Intergovernmental Agreements 171
8. Rational Choices in Federal Systems and Beyond 203

References 229
Index 243

Acknowledgements

This book is based on my doctoral dissertation defended at the European University Institute in Florence in May 2007. It owes its existence to many people. First of all, I would like to thank Peter Graf Kielmansegg, my first teacher back in Mannheim, who taught me that 'reality' is not disorderly – we simply tend to look at it the wrong way. Throughout my Ph.D. period, I could not have been better supervised than by Adrienne Héritier. Her enthusiasm for my dissertation project and her support for all kinds of professional activities have been a constant motivation. Special thanks also go to Tanja Börzel, an important source of support, professionally and privately. Her professional input is most visible in the EU case study in this book which draws on a common paper. Peter Mair and Alberta Sbragia were always ready to push me in the right direction, not only during my Ph.D. but also after. Many other people commented on ideas, papers, or chapters, among them André Bächtiger, Keith Banting, Stefano Bartolini, Arthur Benz, Matthijs Bogaards, Daniel Bochsler, Liesbet Hooghe, Michael Keating, B. Guy Peters, Richard Simeon, Lori Thorlakson, Sonja Wälti, and Ronald L. Watts. Many thanks go also to the numerous interviewees, without whom this book would not have been possible.

In terms of 'external' crisis management, Diana Panke as well as my brother Andreas have been most active over the years. In Florence, Natalia Ajenjo, Judith Ay, Hanna Bäck, Sandra Eckert, Zsolt Enyedi, Andrea Herrmann, Christian Kascha, Luis Leal, Anna Müller-Debus, and Christine Reh were always there to support and, equally important, to distract me. Atina Krajewska, Thomas Morton, Karl O'Connor, and Lise Storm helped me to settle in Exeter, where this book was completed. In the very final phase, I owe most to Jonathan. Despite my root- and restlessness, he made Exeter my home. The book is dedicated to my mother Ingrid and my brother Andreas.

Nicole Bolleyer

Exeter
November 2008

List of Figures

7.1. Institutionalization as major impact on agreements' constraining capacity   181
7.2. Intragovernmental incentives and institutionalization as simultaneous impacts on agreements' constraining capacity   181

List of Tables

1.1. Three dimensions of intergovernmental relations	21
1.2. Levels of intergovernmental institutionalization	25
1.3. Levels of integration between intergovernmental arrangements	27
2.1. Characteristics of lower level governments in three federal systems	57
3.1. Classifying intergovernmental arrangements	69
3.2. Intergovernmental arrangements in Canada, Switzerland, and the United States	70
3.3. Intergovernmental institutionalization in Canada in eight policy fields	84
4.1. Intergovernmental institutionalization in Switzerland in eight policy fields	95
5.1. Interstate compacts and compact commissions until 1998	126
5.2. Main functions of generalist arrangements on the national level	134
6.1. Institutionalization and integration of ministerial councils	144
6.2. Intergovernmental integration in Canada, the United States, and Switzerland	169
7.1. Agreements in Canada, Switzerland, and the United States[b]	176
7.2. Intergovernmental arrangements and their level of institutionalization	185
7.3. Percentages of precise and substantial agreements issued by generalist intergovernmental arrangements in 2004–5	187
7.4. Percentages of precise and substantial agreements in education in 2004–5	192
7.5. Precise and substantial agreements in Canadian policy-specific intergovernmental arrangements in 2004–5	195
8.1. Dominant patterns of institutionalization and integration in three federal systems	205
8.2. Dominant modes of policy coordination and configurations of institutionalization and integration	207
8.3. Types of power sharing and territorial representation	216
8.4. Modes of policy coordination in four multilevel polities	223

List of Abbreviations

CSG	Council of State Governments
EU	European Union
FMC	First Ministers' Conference
IGA	Intergovernmental arrangement
IGR	Intergovernmental relations

1

Intergovernmental Relations and the Puzzle of Institutional Choice

Over the last few decades, boundary-crossing problems in federal systems have become increasingly pronounced, blurring formally separate jurisdictions and creating incentives for interaction across different spheres of authority. Europeanization and globalization have been identified as major 'external' forces which motivate political actors to establish denser cooperation structures. Expanding state responsibilities, in contrast, are a major 'internal' force which intensify boundary-crossing policy-interdependencies. As a consequence, scholars have observed the strengthening of intergovernmental channels in federal systems and multilevel systems beyond the nation state (see, among others, Simeon 2001: 145–7; see also Hooghe 1996; Börzel 2000, 2001, 2002; Hooghe and Marks 2001; Peters and Pierre 2001; Kincaid 2003; Benz 2004a; Benz and Papadopoulos 2006).

Despite the widely confirmed observation that policy interdependencies across separate jurisdictions have become more and more pronounced – and indeed that actors respond to these – the way in which exchanges are channelled, how these channels are structured, and why their institutional development varies across polities remain widely neglected issues. This book starts out from the finding that political actors increasingly respond to coordination pressure and attempts to account for *how they* do so across the variety of federal polities and multilevel systems assessing patterns of intergovernmental institution-building. Both theoretically and empirically, *the puzzle of institutional choice* reflected by the variety of arrangements in which intergovernmental cooperation takes place inside individual countries and across their borders remains surprisingly underexplored.[1] To solve this puzzle, the book tackles the following questions: why are the arrangements governments set up to deal with boundary-crossing problems so different? To what extent do these institutional differences affect the effectiveness of intergovernmental problem-solving?

The creation of intergovernmental arrangements (IGAs) is – like intergovernmental cooperation itself – voluntary. These arrangements can range from

---

[1] Note that intergovernmental cooperation presupposes the explicit interaction between governments. Since governments can also coordinate activities unilaterally, the term 'coordination' will be used to cover the whole range of ways governments in multilevel systems can relate to each other.

irregular ad hoc coordination between ministries, as in Canada and Spain, to intergovernmental secretariats with dozens of employees, as in Switzerland and the United States. While individual cases are analysed in depth, this issue is hardly addressed by systematic comparative research. Nor has there yet appeared a theoretical framework able to reveal the causal mechanisms underlying these structural choices across a wider range of settings. A comparative study explaining these divergent patterns of informal institution-building in multilevel systems and assessing their impact on intergovernmental policy-making is missing. To close this gap, this book adopts a deductive, rationalist approach to institution building. It argues that the type of *executive–legislative relations within the interacting governments* explain the nature of institutions set up to channel intergovernmental processes. The incentives generated by the executive–legislative relations in governments, which constitute a multilevel system, define *corridors of adaptation* systematically delimiting the scope for the institutional development of IGAs in a system. By disaggregating individual government units, the theoretical approach reveals how micro-incentives drive the macro-dynamics in multilevel systems and reveals the rationale underlying the institutional choices of governments.

Drawing on Benz, who convincingly emphasized the relevance of *intragovernmental* relations for intergovernmental relations (IGR) (2004a: 133, 2004b), the internal life of lower level governments, the book demonstrates how the institution-building capacity of governments varies according to the *degree and type of power sharing generated in their executive–legislative relations*. Furthermore, it examines how these institutional choices shape the effectiveness of intergovernmental agreements to cope with shared problems. Most fundamentally, it argues that the degree of power sharing (depending on the cabinet type) and their type of power sharing (the constitutional separation of powers as opposed to voluntary power sharing) explain the choice of particular IGAs set up to facilitate political negotiations and policy coordination.

By putting forward this argument, the book attempts to direct attention to a neglected dimension in the literatures on comparative federalism and multilevel governance. Interstate relations, the horizontal relations between lower level governments, have received astonishingly little attention so far. Studies on centralization and decentralization in multilevel systems quite naturally concentrate on the vertical dimension of federal–state interaction. The power relations between federal government and lower level governments are indeed crucial to understand the overall dynamics of a multilevel polity. Horizontal relations, however, are equally relevant. In part, their neglect is rooted in the perception of federal systems as '*multilevel* settings', a term prominent in federalism research as in European studies dealing with the interplay between several layers of government (Swenden 2006: 18–20). Most prominently, Hooghe and Marks identify the *individual government* as the core unit in federal governance, yet define the latter as a governance system composed of *governmental levels* (2003: 236–7). In so doing, they shift the unit of analysis towards a system's constituent levels and systematically blind out the internal life of the lower level composed of a multitude of governments. In contrast, the internal life of this 'lower level' plays a central role in this study.

While existing scholarly work still recurs frequently to constitutional features of multilevel systems to understand their overall dynamics (e.g. Filippov, Ordeshook, and Shvetsova 2004), a number of recent studies have emphasized the role of 'politics' underlying intergovernmental bargaining and conflict – the informal dimension of IGR (Wibbels 2005: 9). Political dynamics are necessarily located within interacting governments and their consideration has advanced the analysis of intergovernmental policy-making in areas such as fiscal policy or economic reform (Wibbels 2005; Rodden 2006). However, federal–state relations in a bilateral sense remain the primary focus of these analyses. The degree of partisan disharmony between the federal government and individual Argentine provinces accounts for the likelihood of market reform being successfully implemented on both levels of a federal system (Wibbels 2005). In a similar manner, only if the federal government and lower level units are governed by the same party, do we see fiscal discipline in federal systems (Rodden 2006), an argument following up on Riker's seminal study (1964). The degree of disagreement between the subunits themselves, however, is taken into account only indirectly although this factor crucially affects the capacity of lower level governments to oppose federal reforms. If the former are divided along partisan lines, it is much easier for the federal government to impose its policies on lower level units even if the latters' competences are affected and lower level governments in principle oppose such action.

This book argues that the analysis of vertical federal relations profits from an understanding of horizontal relations as generated by the internal political dynamics of the governments constituting a federal system. Centralization is accelerated by, if not rooted in, the incapacity of lower level governments to unify, oppose federal plans, and coordinate policy without central intervention. Emphasizing the need to understand the forces underlying federal dynamics, Coglianese and Nicolaidis conceptualize the changing power distribution between constituent governments in multilevel settings as a delegation of competences from one governmental level, the principal who formally holds authority in a certain sphere, to another level, the agent. Given centralizing tendencies in many federal systems, lower level governments play most often the role of the principal. They face a core problem theorized in principal–agent theory: to ensure that the agent - the federal government - acts in their interest. IGAs, whose institutional development this book accounts for, are understood as monitoring mechanisms avoiding 'agency loss', mechanisms which help to assure that intergovernmental agreements are implemented (Coglianese and Nicolaidis 2001: 289–91).

Structures able to facilitate monitoring are not only crucial to check upon the federal government, but are equally important to check whether individual lower level governments comply with horizontal intergovernmental agreements or not, since such agreements allow for horizontal harmonization making federal intervention unnecessary, thus more difficult to justify. While Coglianese and Nicolaidis, as very common in federalism research, deliberately conceptualize each governmental level as a 'unitary actor' (2001: 282–3), this study emphasizes the coordination problem among lower level governments which form the 'subnational level' and thereby constitute a collective principal. This perspective has two important implications. Lower level governments do not necessarily agree on whether to delegate power (e.g. whether to accept national regulations which are potentially beneficial to lower level governments but touch upon their competences), a situation which the federal government can easily exploit through pursuing a 'divide-and-rule' strategy. To give a concrete example, depending on their economic situation, some lower level governments might favour national regulations in certain areas of economic policy, while others reject it. Even different institutions within lower level governments might disagree. In the United States, for instance, governors tend to be less averse against national regulations as long as they consider them as econcomically beneficial. The state legislatures, however, not being directly in charge of 'running the state' as state executives are, in principle, oppose federal intrusion into areas of state competence. Furthermore, conflicts among or within lower level governments often allow the federal government to act outside its jurisdiction irrespective of lower level governments' individual or collective preferences, which makes collective monitoring of the federal government all the more important. The threat of federal intrusion into areas of lower level competence also implies that while authority migration towards the centre within a multilevel system can be the result of deliberate decisions on behalf of the governments concerned (as implied by Coglianese's and Nicolaidis' principal–agent perspective), authority migration can also be the simple result of inefficient collective resistance. While (vertically and horizontally directed) 'monitoring' tends to be a function of IGAs, to overcome differences between lower level governments is equally important. This book argues that whether IGAs support this range of functions effectively crucially depends on their institutional infrastructure which varies considerably from one federal system to the other.

Shifting our perspective from vertical to horizontal federal relations helps us to solve the puzzle of these very diverse intergovernmental infrastructures existing across federal polities and multilevel settings, a diversity which shapes the capacity of lower level governments to push for collective interests and to deal with coordination demands across individual jurisdictions. In order to account for intergovernmental actors' readiness (or disinclination) to set up strongly developed and mutually integrated IGAs when facing the need to coordinate, it is necessary to understand the overall logic of a composite polity. This 'overall logic' is shaped by the internal nature of those governments constituting a multilevel system.

As a consequence, the study rejects a general convergence of multilevel systems towards 'cooperative federalism' in domestic policy domains. Case study research illustrates that growing interaction should not simply be equated with institutional convergence. Most federal systems have adapted to global and regional integration without any major institutional transformations (Lazar, Telford, and Watts 2003: 1). For instance, Kincaid points out in his analysis of American federalism that: '... intergovernmental responses to globalization have been consistent with intergovernmental responses to other challenges' (2003: 37–8). Thus, adaptation processes have been clearly shaped by the pre-established system-specific patterns of interaction in the intergovernmental arena. Although this is not surprising, the literature makes little of this finding. It primarily looks at individual cases in isolation but does not climb up the 'ladder of abstraction' (Sartori 1970) to integrate case-specific observations into a comparative and explanatory framework. In contrast, this book attempts to climb up the 'ladder of abstraction' to the point of a middle-range approach on intergovernmental institution-building instead of remaining in the realm of understanding the complexities of individual cases in an encompassing manner (Lijphart 1971).

In theoretical terms, the study specifies the institution-building strategies of governments by substantiating typologies of democracy (Lijphart 1999) through a rationalist and actor-centred underpinning (e.g. Scharpf 1997; Tsebelis 2002; Wibbels 2005). It refers to positive and negative incentives generated within the constituent governments of a federal system as major determinants of actor behaviour, hence relies on a rational choice perspective – a logic of consequentialism (March and Olsen 1995; Hall and Taylor 1996) – in which intragovernmental incentive structures drive actors' choices in favour of or against institutionally strong IGAs. Thereby, it provides a proper micro-foundation which often remains implicit in the mostly empirically oriented and inductively pursued research on federal systems and IGR. This is paramount since only a micro-foundation allows for the systematic development of hypotheses on how individual rationales display themselves on the meso and the macro level of a federal polity (Scharpf 1997).

The empirical analysis is directed towards this goal. Based on over eighty semi-structured interviews with intergovernmental actors, the study captures the motives of intergovernmental actors to invest in certain types of IGAs. The study deliberately combines the rigorous deduction of hypotheses based on rational choice theory and the precision and specificity of in-depth case studies, two strategies often considered as incompatible in current research. It thereby tries to create doubts about the trend in scholarly work to associate rational choice approaches with quantitative methods. It implies that in order to examine rational choice hypotheses rooted in methodological individualism (thus, micro-dynamics), qualitative methods can deliver information that quantitative methods often miss due to the need to rely on proxies and aggregate data – the immediate link between actors' interests, their choices, and these choices' structural outcomes.

In contrast to many studies relying exclusively on structural analyses, the approach is able to show how micro-incentives drive macro-dynamics. It traces back the features of *intergovernmental* structures – institutional choices with *long-term consequences* – to the *short-term interests* of federal and lower level actors generated by *intragovernmental* dynamics. In contrast to March and Olsen's logic of appropriateness (1989: 160–2), actors do not invest in cooperation structures in the intergovernmental arena (or refrain from such) because it is 'socially appropriate'. They invest in an infrastructure facilitating exchanges when the costs 'at home' are sufficiently low and, as a consequence, the 'outside gains' can be expected to reimburse the initial investment. The empirical analysis of Swiss IGR as the prototype of a 'power-sharing polity' will be particularly telling. Voluntary party cooperation inside the cantons lowers the cooperation costs in the intergovernmental sphere considerably. Correspondingly, intergovernmental bodies and inter-institutional linkages are strong reflecting the best strategy to defend individual (governmental or institutional) self-interests (for an alternative conceptualization, see Börzel 2002: 28–31). Just to mention one of the underlying mechanisms: when constituent governments expect vote losses from intergovernmental cooperation, they will not engage in it even if they could profit from it in the long run. Swiss parties, in contrast, rarely face this problem. Due to the formation of oversized coalitions, competitive pressure is low and investments in IGAs are therefore profitable. Summarizing the overall rationale, the first core hypothesis of the book accounts for institutionalization – the institutional development of IGAs:

> Power-concentrating governments undermine the institutionalization of intergovernmental arrangements, while power-sharing governments support it.

The four mechanisms generated by power concentration or power sharing in lower level governments respectively are the following. The first mechanism refers to the (in)stability of the interest configuration among these governments. Given mostly one-party majority cabinets, government turnover frequently alters the interest configurations among governments. This raises the costs for actors to maintain strong IGAs. Ad hoc coordination, in contrast, allows politicians to adapt to these changing configurations. They participate in a profitable agreement when interest convergence is given with a certain group of partners, and if not, they resort to unilateralism. A strongly institutionalized arrangement would delimit this flexibility. As soon as coalitions come into play, alternation is less probable as a potential force of change because complete turnovers become less likely. Power-sharing coalition governments generate opposite incentives since government interests remain fairly stable. A second aspect related to the interest configuration among lower level governments is its ideological congruence. The expectation is that the conflict potential between governments should be lower, given parties of similar ideological profile in office. If party systems are similar across lower level governments (i.e. none or only few regional parties are in office), congruence is most likely when oversized governments are formed. In this case, the same parties tend to participate in coalitions within different governments; hence, coalitions across the different jurisdictions are likely to overlap in composition. Given mainly one-party governments in office, the share of overlapping governments should decrease. Third, given a high likelihood of alternation (again measured by the alternation rate), the immediate threat of electoral loss motivates regional politicians to shift blame onto the other governments. Mutual distrust is fostered because each actor is aware of the pressure on the other to focus on the short-term goal of electoral victory at the cost of the long-term goal of fruitful intergovernmental exchanges. Finally, when engaging in intergovernmental interaction, autonomy losses are higher for parties which govern alone than for parties which govern in a coalition. If power sharing is a part of daily decision making in the domestic arena, the relative autonomy losses are comparatively minor. In summary, incentives generated by 'majoritarian dynamics' within lower level governments easily undermine institutionalization processes among them, while power-sharing governments create more favourable conditions for institutionalization.

The second core hypothesis accounts for the integration of IGAs within a system – the links between them. Different from institutionalization, the level of integration is not only affected by the degree of power sharing but also by its type. Drawing on the neo-institutionalist literature on veto points (Birchfield and Crepaz 1998), the approach distinguishes between compulsory (constitutionally defined) power-sharing (e.g. presidentialism) and voluntary power-sharing (e.g. coalition governments). In contrast to voluntary power-sharing (favourable both to institutionalization and integration), compulsory power-sharing fragments individual governments internally and thereby weakens the links between IGAs. Compulsory power-sharing undermines the representation of coherent government units in the intergovernmental arena. It sets incentives for governmental branches to push for their (institutionally defined) interests separately, which thereby weakens intergovernmental integration. This rationale underlies our second hypothesis:

> Compulsory power-sharing undermines integration between intergovernmental arrangements, while voluntary power-sharing supports it.

The two core hypotheses are empirically examined in a comparative study of Canada, Switzerland, and the United States. These three federal systems reflect the core configurations, namely power concentration, voluntary power-sharing, and compulsory power-sharing, in their constitutive governments – those features expected to underpin the structuring of IGR. They can be expected to display the effects of intragovernmental incentives on IGR most clearly. In Canada, one-party majority cabinets usually dominate lower level governments. In Switzerland, oversized coalitions – voluntary power-sharing – are the rule. Finally, in the United States, one finds constitutionally defined, compulsory power-sharing unbridged by party ties in all government units – constituting a division between state executives and legislatures.

Reflecting the two hypotheses, the empirical analysis assesses first the *institutionalization* of IGAs such as the Council of the Federation in Canada, the

National Governors' Association in the United States, or the Conference of Cantonal Executives in Switzerland. These bodies' institutional features are assessed one by one. In a second step, it explores the *integration* of the whole system of IGR defined by the types of linkages between IGAs in each system. The distinction between institutionalization and integration is paramount – substantially and analytically. Institutionalization refers to the institutional development and the internal functioning of IGAs and has important implications for the member governments' capacity to form collective positions and to agree on shared solutions to boundary-crossing problems. Yet to understand fully the coordination dynamics and the functional orientations of intergovernmental bodies in a system, we need to know how IGAs interact, whether they are mutually supportive, backed up by stable institutional linkages, or whether they compete for influence. The interplay of institutionalization and integration helps us to gauge the coordination capacity among lower level governments supported by the respective intergovernmental infrastructure. It also reveals the driving forces underlying the power distribution within the intergovernmental arena analysed.

Comparing patterns of institutionalization simultaneously across three polities and eight policy areas, the book further demonstrates that incentives generated by the respective executive–legislative configurations are more important than the nature of the individual policy area, e.g. the respective intensity of redistributive conflicts, a finding at odds with a considerable part of the literature emphasizing the policy-specific character of IGR. Also the mode of constitutional competence distribution in individual policy fields cannot account for the cross-sectoral patterns of institutionalization which reconfirms the approach relying on government dynamics. The latter finding, in particular, challenges accounts of intergovernmental cooperation which rely heavily on constitutional classifications of federal polities (Hueglin and Fenna 2006: 51; Swenden 2006: 189–32). IGR are established within the framework of the given constitutional rules which can either correspond to constitutional predispositions or contradict them. While intragovernmental dynamics are indeed influenced by constitutional variables,[2] the study shows that the constitutional make-up is not an immediate force driving patterns of institution building in the intergovernmental arena of a polity.

These patterns of institution building are immediately policy-relevant. Institutionalization and integration shape whether and how effectively governments can deal with coordination pressure. To give a concrete example, the theoretical framework helps explain why the power-sharing Swiss cantons manage to create strong IGAs and enter detailed agreements to tackle collective policy-problems, while the power-concentrating Canadian provinces regularly fail to do so. A comparative analysis of intergovernmental agreements in Chapter 7 shows that high

---

[2] For instance, Neidhart (1970) argued that facultative referenda are one important factor motivating the set-up of oversized coalitions in the cantons.

institutionalization favours the drafting of precise and substantial agreements. Moreover, the interplay of institutionalization and integration indicates towards which tasks intergovernmental processes are directed, most importantly, whether policy coordination (not only position taking) can be pursued effectively. More generally, by driving institutionalization and integration, intragovernmental incentives affect the potential for institutional reforms to be successful. Even if, in special circumstances, intergovernmental actors deliberately ignore intragovernmental incentives when attempting to reform intergovernmental processes, internal constraints will continue to shape day-to-day processes in actors' home arenas. The capacity of intergovernmental bodies to counteract these internal constraints is likely to be limited.

Political dynamics, which systematically undermine intergovernmental cooperation as one possible path of action, weaken lower level governments whenever cooperation could strengthen their position towards the federal government (e.g. in the form of collective opposition against certain federal actions or the collective solutions of policy problems by lower level governments to avoid federal intervention). Note that this empirical observation may not be equated with the claim that intergovernmental cooperation is generally desirable, neither in normative nor functional terms. Collective action or nationwide harmonization, for that matter, are not per se functionally superior or necessarily preferable from a lower level government's perspective. Especially bigger, economically strong governments quite regularly find it more beneficial to 'fend for themselves' and strive for special deals with the federal government. Furthermore, depending on the policy issue at stake, competition between lower level governments and locally specific measures might be superior to policy harmonization and intense intergovernmental cooperation (Breton 1985). What is claimed, however, is that we find regular instances in which lower level governments can or could increase their weight in intergovernmental negotiations through cooperation and, given such instances, the nature of intergovernmental structures becomes relevant since they affect how successfully governments can work together. Only if the effectiveness of policy coordination is applied as a yardstick, can institutionalization and intensified intergovernmental cooperation be considered as something 'good'. And again, this does not mean that policy coordination provides always the best solution with regard to every issue at stake. It only implies that strong IGAs can facilitate such endeavours whenever governments decide to engage in cooperation (while they are usually unable to impose cooperation since they are, as understood in this book, voluntarily created structures).

Moving away from considerations of efficiency towards considerations of legitimacy, if the need for transparent decision-making is applied as a major yardstick, intense intergovernmental cooperation becomes problematic since it easily undermines democratic accountability of the participating governments towards their citizens. Furthermore, executives tend to dominate intergovernmental processes inside and outside the nation state. This tendency weakens the role of parliaments as the locus of democratic legitimation – a central issue brought up when engaging in normative debates on the role of modern parliaments not only in federal but also in democratic systems more generally (e.g. Auel 2005; Auel and Benz 2007; O'Brennan and Raunio 2007). In a nutshell, since the criteria underlying normative assessments are distinct from those criteria used to analyse the structures and patterns of intergovernmental cooperation, the normative repercussions of intensifying intergovernmental processes are deliberately kept separate from the empirical assessments which form the core of this book.

This deliberate restriction does not imply that normative arguments are empirically irrelevant. Intergovernmental actors in all three systems analysed below are well aware of the trade-offs between the benefits in terms of policy making which effective cross-jurisdictional cooperation can generate and the normative costs it might involve. Trade-offs between efficiency and legitimacy are present in any political system and different types of actors in a system (e.g. executive vs. legislative, elected vs. unelected, or national vs. lower level actors) tend to bring up particular normative arguments to redirect debates in their favour or to justify own actions. But whether actors in a system set up a strong intergovernmental infrastructure, supporting intense intergovernmental cooperation or not, however, can be traced back more directly to the incentives structures prevalent within their governments.

One major challenge for the theoretical framework presented in this book – as for all theoretical frameworks – relates to its scope of applicability. Since federalism is regularly used as a template to discuss multilevel governance outside the nation state (e.g. Scharpf 1988; Sbragia 1993; McKay 2001; Nicolaidis and Howse 2001; Börzel 2002; Hooghe and Marks 2003; Kelemen 2004; Menon and Schain 2006), the final chapter of this book discusses the implications of the theoretical framework for modes of policy coordination in the European Union (EU). Unlike the three federal systems of Canada, Switzerland, and the United States, this polity mixes power-concentrating and power-sharing member states and different types of power sharing across its constitutive levels. The approach reveals core similarities of the EU with national federal systems, while helping to identify those peculiarities rooted in its origins as an international organization. Furthermore, it helps to account for the different repertoires of modes of cross-jurisdictional policy-coordination which lower level governments resort to in the four multilevel systems which re-emphasizes its policy relevance. Facing an already immense and continuously growing literature on multilevel governance in the EU and beyond (e.g. Hooghe and Marks 2001; Börzel 2002; Bache and Flinders 2004; Schmidt 2006), this application can only be 'suggestive' pointing out further directions of research rather than providing final answers. Nonetheless, it highlights the comparability of multilevel systems inside and beyond the nation state and the urgent need to engage in an ongoing dialogue between comparative politics research and EU scholarship.

Intergovernmental Relations and the Puzzle of Institutional Choice 11

The overall structure of the book is as follows. The remainder of this introductory chapter will present the core concepts upon which the study rests, most importantly, the two explananda: institutionalization and integration. Chapter 2 provides a rationalist framework able to account for the institutional make-up of IGR in federal systems. It presents the two main hypotheses on institutionalization and integration in detail and concludes with a comparative analysis of the degree and type of power sharing characterizing lower level governments in Canada, Switzerland, and the United States, laying out how they are expected to affect institutional choices in the intergovernmental arena. The four mechanisms driving these institutional choices are the programmatic differences between lower level governments, changes in government interests over time, incentives for blame-shifting, and the relative autonomy losses for governments caused by intergovernmental cooperation.

Chapters 3 through 6 present an empirical analysis of IGAs in Canada, Switzerland, and the United States. Based on extensive interview material and document analysis, institutional choices can be traced back to the incentives generated within lower level governments described in Chapter 2. All of these chapters look at nationwide arrangements (e.g. the Council of the Federation, the Conference of Cantonal Executives, and the National Governors' Association) and their regional pendants. Furthermore, in each system, policy-specific IGAs are compared across eight policy fields. Thus, these chapters demonstrate that – within one polity – similar patterns of institutionalization and integration show irrespective of governmental level and policy field. Chapter 3 shows that the institutionalization of IGAs in Canadian federalism is low. The interaction between power-concentrating Canadian provinces evolves in a largely ad hoc manner. In contrast, oversized coalition governments in the Swiss cantons (voluntary power-sharing) invest in highly institutionalized IGAs generating stable interaction patterns (Chapter 4). Despite the compulsory nature of power sharing, intergovernmental infrastructures in the United States are also highly developed (Chapter 5). Turning to integration, Chapter 6 demonstrates that power concentration in the Canadian provinces leads to weak integration, while voluntary power-sharing in the cantons favours strong links between IGAs. In the United States, as this chapter underlines, compulsory power-sharing between state executives and state legislatures as well as within state executives undermines integration. Although this type of power sharing invites investments in highly institutionalized IGAs, none of these represent the 'states' as coherent units. Instead, they compete for influence in the federal arena and therefore integration remains weak. Chapter 7 demonstrates that the nature of these arrangements affect the precision, substantial depth, and function of intergovernmental agreements, and thereby the effectiveness of intergovernmental cooperation. Finally, Chapter 8 applies the theoretical framework to the EU and reveals parallels and peculiarities of the European polity as compared to federal systems in terms of the ways in which coordination demands between governments are handled.

INTERGOVERNMENTAL RELATIONS AND FEDERALISM: CONCEPTUAL DISCREPANCIES AND OVERLAPS

IGR and federalism are so closely intertwined that at first sight the attempt to locate research on IGR within federalism research seems quite futile. Yet the concept of IGR is usually so broadly defined that it can easily be applied to any political system – be it a federal or a non-federal one. Thus, the explicit focus on federal systems narrows the scope of the analysis to a considerable extent and therefore requires justification.

Formal–legal versus behavioural definitions of federalism

Looking at the wide array of definitions of federalism put forward in the literature, formal–legal definitions tend to be the most prominent. This study will rely on one such definition since it has a range of methodological advantages with regard to the phenomenon studied – patterns of IGR and their underlying infrastructure – as laid out below. In formal terms, federal systems presuppose (at least) two levels of government to which substantial authority is assigned (Lijphart 1999: 186; Thorlakson 2003) which constitutes a first core element. The term 'substantial' already implies that the operational specification of a cut-off point is problematic. A more specific standard is the assignment of legislative competences to at least two governmental levels. Although the power to implement federal legislative is by no means irrelevant, only explicitly assigned legislative authority allows both levels of government to genuinely generate their own answers to policy problems. Legislative competences increase the leeway for autonomous government action on each level to a much wider extent than implementation power does. Systematically comparing the different types of competences assigned to governmental levels in federal systems we find that also in classical cooperative federal systems such as Germany's – where the *Länder* governments mainly deal with the implementation of federal law – these governments indeed possess legislative competences (Thorlakson 2003; Bolleyer and Thorlakson 2008).

As a second core element, in order to classify a system as federal, the unilateral withdrawal of competences attributed to one governmental level by the other governmental level needs to be constitutionally prohibited (Watts 2005: 235). Authority cannot be surrendered without the explicit consent of each tier. This assures the constitutional equality of the interacting governments. Federal systems – in contrast to decentralized unions – realize the strictest form of vertical power-dispersion, a constellation which is currently realized in twenty-three national polities (Watts 2005; see also Hueglin and Fenna 2006).

As classificatory criteria, the *prohibition of unilateral withdrawal and the attribution of legislative competences* to government units located on different levels have the advantage of being parsimonious and fairly precise. Moreover, they are behaviourally neutral descriptors of *formal elements* characterizing a polity. Of course, this strategy has its downsides: Spain, for instance, does not belong to the group of federal systems although one might consider it as fully 'federalized'.[3] Like the United Kingdom, Spain has been classified as regionalized state with strong regional tiers of government, which, however, remain constitutionally subordinate to the centre (Swenden 2006: 14). One still might consider it to be federal. De facto, unilateral withdrawal of territorial competences is unfeasible for the centre since it directly depends on territorial votes. Although the possibility to do so exists through constitutional amendment, the weakening or even the abolition of the Autonomous Communities would be unacceptable from the point of view of citizens who strongly identify with their regional government. Based on this line of reasoning, one can consider the Spanish system as 'functionally equivalent' to a constitutionally federalized system because the coexistence of the federal government and the Power level governments in place – though not formally – is de facto constitutive for the Spanish polity (Moreno 1999).[4] The constellation corresponds to the logic underlying the formal definition introduced. In this sense, as long as the rationale behind such classifications is maintained and conceptual stretching is avoided (Sartori 1970), such problems are minor compared to flaws related to *looser concepts* or to concepts introducing *behavioural properties* as constitutive elements.

This brings us to a variety of other definitions which have more far-fetching implications for the power relations in federal systems. Wheare (1951), for instance, defines federalism as a political arrangement in which neither level of government is constitutionally subordinate to the other, and each is independent within its sphere of authority. While the first criterion – the absence of constitutional subordination – corresponds to the definition just introduced, the second criterion refers to 'independence' which is problematic for several reasons. Indeed, one might understand independence only in a formal sense referring to governments' formal capacity to handle the authority assigned to them. This, however, forms part of the absence of constitutional subordination and does not deliver additional information. Instead, one can interpret independence as 'de facto autonomy' on the process level, the extent to which lower level governments actively use the leeway they formally have in terms of unilateral action. Then the criterion becomes problematic since the degree of independence of the constitutive governments most likely varies considerably from one federation to the other – even if lower level governments possess a similar range of formal competences.

---

[3] Hueglin and Fenna define federalism as a system of government, in which 'sovereignty is shared and powers divided between two or more levels of government each of which enjoys a direct relationship with the people' (2006: 32–3). According to their definition, they classify Spain as federal.

[4] For a detailed account see Agranoff (1999*b*) and Swenden (2006).

Independence understood as 'autonomy' needs to be conceptualized as an *output* of the interplay of constitutional, fiscal, and processual aspects, not as an element constituting a federal system. Lower level governments in some federal systems might prefer to set up strong intergovernmental structures which facilitate mutual exchange and thereby voluntarily reduce their degree of individual independence or autonomy. Intergovernmental competition is not the natural outcome of a federal constitution (Chapman 1993: 75–6; Heinmiller 2002). Yet the reference to 'de facto independence' already implies an orientation towards autonomy protection, and, with it, competition. Competition is only one end of the behavioural continuum, along which the nature of IGR can vary across the range of federal systems – cooperation is the other. Vice versa, one should avoid assuming that the coexistence of constitutionally equal governments necessarily implies cross-jurisdictional cooperation. Accordingly, it is problematic to include processes and institutions to facilitate intergovernmental collaboration in those areas where governmental responsibilities are shared or inevitably overlap as a defining criterion for federalism. Where, on a continuum of competition versus cooperation, a federal system is located is a puzzle challenging federalism research, a puzzle which needs to be addressed explicitly.

IGR come in as a response to the very nature of a federal constitution since governments need to relate to each other in one way or the other. Following Agranoff:

> Self-rule can be formally introduced in a government's arrangement but cannot be maintained without the working connections that tie central governments to those constituent units that enjoy measures of independent and interdependent political power. (2004: 26)

IGR further includes the working connections between lower level governments. As mentioned above, IGR can be analysed in any type of polity. It does not presuppose federalism, since even in unitary systems we find at least local governments. However, the more powerful lower level governments are, the broader the range of behavioural patterns we can find in IGR. Furthermore, the restriction to federal systems helps to specify the core actors upon which a study on IGR focuses. Without being conceptually explicit, it is commonly held that federal dynamics can be captured reasonably well referring to *federal–state* or *interstate interaction* only (Rosenthal and Hoefler 1989: 2). This focus is plausible for two reasons closely tied to our formal definition of federalism. First, local governments have comparatively limited legislative authority and tend to be preoccupied with the implementation of policy (Wright 1982; Bächtiger and Hitz 2006). And, second, whenever lower level governments are able to compete with the federal government as major foci for citizen identification, those governments tend to be regional rather than local. Hence, the analysis of federal–state and interstate relations can be justified from a formal–legal as well as from a societal point of view.

The study of intergovernmental relations: linking policy-oriented and systemic perspectives

Like the federalism literature, the work on IGR is extremely rich. Nonetheless, there are still gaps to fill which can be identified by briefly systematizing the existing scholarly production. This systematic overview also reveals the basic methodological requirements for the comparative study of IGR. It helps to justify basic conceptual choices since substantial foci and their methodological implications are closely intertwined. The literature can be divided into two strands which use different analytical lenses through which they analyse IGR, and are characterized by different strengths and weaknesses. Roughly speaking, IGR is analysed from a *policy-oriented* or from a *systemic* viewpoint. Depending on the given viewpoint the methodological status of IGR tends to change. The policy-oriented lens perceives IGR as a factor which helps to account for the formation or the implementation of policy across a range of separate jurisdictions. From a systemic viewpoint, IGR is the phenomenon to be accounted for. Discussing these strands of the literature simultaneously and specifying their analytical and empirical foci allows us to arrive at a research design capable of uniting both their advantages.

When looking at IGR from a *policy-oriented* perspective, scholars usually question how intergovernmental actors arrive at cross-jurisdictional policy-harmonization or, put differently, why such efforts fail in some policy areas but not in others. Here, the focus necessarily rests on those arrangements which channel interstate or federal–state relations directed towards policy coordination. IGAs which do not directly serve this function – those for political position-taking of lower level governments towards the federal government or intergovernmental lobbying of federal legislation – are not crucial in these analyses. This explains, for instance, why American studies on intergovernmental policy-making hardly mention bodies such as the National Governors' Association: the latter are not involved in policy coordination.

In terms of their analytical scope, these studies tend to be restricted either to one individual policy field in several federal systems or to different policy fields in the same system in order to understand the detailed mechanisms underlying intergovernmental processes, policy formation within the units, and harmonization across them. They usually embrace the political and the administrative level and deliver detailed information on their interplay (e.g. Hocking 1993; Leibfried and Pierson 1995; Rich and White 1996; Cattoir 1998; Lazar and McIntosh 1998; Fafard and Harrison 2000; Banting and Corbett 2001; Rothmayr, Varone, and Montpetit 2003; Wälti 2004; Wibbels 2005; Rodden 2006). Methodologically, in these studies, IGR usually play the role of an independent or intervening variable. IGR are interesting insofar they affect the choice of instruments and strategies applied in particular policy fields aiming at cross-jurisdictional policy-harmonization and these instruments' and strategies' effectiveness. Some particularly fruitful studies on intergovernmental policy-making try to develop conceptual tools to capture the particular intergovernmental dynamics present in their cases which can be applied to different contexts later on (e.g. Painter 1998; Brown 2002; see for an overview, Heinmiller 2002).

What policy-oriented studies often fail to provide is an overall picture of the patterns of IGR in a particular political system – a picture of the 'structural logic of the system' assumed to be considerably stable in its basic patterns and tendencies (see for example Simeon 1972; Lehmbruch 1976, 1978; Esman 1984; Czada 2003). Such a picture is the answer to a completely different question than policy-oriented studies on IGR attempt to address in the first place. *Systemic approaches* respond to the question of why IGR are organized and work in a particular way, implicitly or explicitly assuming that there are commonalities in the working of intergovernmental processes across the range of policy fields. Certain dynamics might be more pronounced in one policy area than in another, or be particularly pronounced in certain periods. Nevertheless, they are interpreted as general dispositions of a political system understood as a specific configuration of formal and informal institutions. Examples are the strong fragmentation of American IGR (Wright 1982; O'Toole 2000; Trench 2006) or the ad hoc character of Canadian and Spanish IGR (Börzel 2000; Grau I Creus 2000; Lazar and McLean 2000; Simmons 2004).[5] These features are perceived as reflecting the very nature of these composite polities constituted by a structural connection between micro-incentives and macro-dynamics, a connection which cross-cuts the nature of individual policy fields.

Comparing policy-oriented and systemic approaches, the willingness to abstract from micro-level processes differs considerably, pointing to a crucial conceptual and methodological trade-off inherent in comparative politics per se. Due to the goal to identify an 'overall logic', systemic approaches tend to be located well 'above' the micro level. Yet, while convincingly systematizing the dominant dynamics resulting from a configuration of macro-level institutions, their micro-foundation often remains implicit. Such a tendency is visible in the literature not only on federalism but also on power-limiting or power-sharing democracies more generally. This literature often rests on the implicit assumption that different power-limiting structures tend to be compatible or even mutually supportive.[6] And even if approaches point to disinclinations between different types of power-sharing structures (Lehmbruch 1978, 1991, 2003; Czada 2003), they necessarily remain descriptive as long as they state tensions on the macro level without identifying the mechanisms underlying them.

---

[5] Looking at the literature on Germany, one finds insightful studies about the tensions between party competition and joint-decision making in federalism and corporatism (Lehmbruch 1978, 2003). Other works discuss the logic of joint-decision making which in the context of German federalism is thought to lead into a joint-decision trap (Scharpf 1985, 2005).

[6] Lijphart's construction (1999) of consensus democracy is one of the most famous examples.

The opposite problem is equally severe. It appears with particular clarity in works on American IGR. Here, a behaviourally driven focus on administrative micro-level processes has replaced the formerly dominant constitutional approach of dual federalism. Unfortunately, this shift widely undermined any hope for systematization feeding the critique that the unit of analysis could be virtually anything in IGR studies which have become indistinguishable from American politics per se (Rosenthal and Hoefler 1989: 5–7). The low level of abstraction led to a considerable fragmentation of the literature along policy lines reinforcing the attitude that efforts to pinpoint *durable* and *constitutive* features of American IGR are futile (see for one of the exceptions, Derthick 2001). Consequently, students of IGR became more and more reluctant to place the role of 'structure' in their approach which would require them to specify the behavioural rules flowing from them (Rosenthal and Hoefler 1989: 20). The broader implications for comparative and cross-national research are as clear as they are destructive: American, Canadian, or German IGR are perceived as completely different sets of relations (Hueglin and Fenna 2006: 50) without serious efforts to sort out their conceptual and empirical boundaries so essential for systematic comparative research.

The fundamental challenge this book tries to address through the framework developed in Chapter 2 is to find middle ground between the description of macro-dynamics without specifying a micro-foundation and the description of micro-processes buried in detail, making it impossible to identify any overall patterns of IGR characteristic for a federal system as a whole. To find a proper balance, this book tries to link both lenses as laid out above within one research design. This is possible since the two lenses and their respective empirical foci reflect a conceptual distinction between two types of IGAs: the distinction between *generalist* (cross-sectoral) arrangements (corresponding to a systemic perspective) and *policy-specific* arrangement (corresponding to a policy-oriented perspective) which will shape the later analysis both theoretically and empirically.

Starting from a policy-oriented viewpoint, arrangements or instruments for cross-jurisdictional policy coordination are of major interest. In contrast, a systemic view aims to analyse the linkage between processes on a micro and macro level to account for the fundamental nature of IGR, focusing on all major IGAs irrespective of their function. While *generalist* IGAs tend to be directed towards information exchange and position taking, the coordination of particular policies – the most demanding function – is often channelled through *policy-specific* IGAs. Including both types of structures in the empirical analysis and thereby looking at IGAs from a cross-system as much as from a cross-sectoral perspective allows for an encompassing assessment of intergovernmental interaction capturing variance across and within federal systems. Simultaneously, this strategy unites the endeavour inherent in systemic perspectives to account for the overall logic of IGR in a system with the policy-oriented endeavour to specify the micro-processes underlying it.

CORE CONCEPTS: INTERGOVERNMENTAL RELATIONS, INTERGOVERNMENTAL ARRANGEMENTS, AND CORRIDORS OF ADAPTATION

To engage in such an analysis, we need to specify the central concepts of this study: intergovernmental relations (IGR) and intergovernmental arrangements (IGAs). Necessarily, IGR and IGAs overlap conceptually and need to be separated out. Beginning with the former, we return to Agranoff who defines IGR as 'those transactional activities and interactions between government units and with the nongovernmental sector of all types and levels' (2004: 29). It captures the multiplicity of ways in which one government unit can 'relate' to and 'interact' with the other, and thus IGR – and its sub-category, IGA – in all their complexity. A strong emphasis on complexity, however, easily undermines the capacity to formulate clear-cut expectations about which type of IGR we find where, under which conditions, and the consequences it might generate. If hypothesis generation is our purpose rather than thick description (which is an equally valid endeavour), it is useful to restrict the boundaries of the two concepts from the start.

Three dimensions of intergovernmental relations

In existing analyses of IGR, the term 'relations' can refer to *exchanges* (e.g. the intensity of communication or the density of meetings), to *patterns of interaction* (e.g. the regularity of meetings in general, the regularity of meetings between particular partners, or dominant modes of interaction), and to *structures* (e.g. the decision-making rules or number of intergovernmental staff). Empirically speaking, all three dimensions coexist and interact. Studies often refer to all three at once without trying to separate one from the other, which is problematic since each has distinct implications for the way IGR are theorized and operationalized.

Exchange is the broadest understanding of IGR. It embraces communication via phone, emailing, and unofficial or official meetings between politicians and administrators belonging to distinct jurisdictions or governments.[7] To analyse IGR as intergovernmental 'exchanges' implies a considerable fluidity and irregularity of processes. To measure the density of exchanges, there are two core strategies which reflect a basic trade-off. Either the conception of 'exchange' needs to be narrowed down, for instance, to face-to-face meetings of officials or politicians in certain arenas or on certain levels, or its scope must be assessed in in-depth interviews to cover the range of intergovernmental exchanges – if possible, in their entirety. While the first strategy implies a considerable impoverishment of the originally targeted phenomenon during the process of operationalization, the second makes it extremely difficult to develop cross-nationally applicable indicators able to reliably quantify exchanges.

---

[7] Note that the concept of exchange used here is much broader than the understanding of exchange (or transaction) referred to in contract theory (Greif 2006).

At the same time, looking at exchanges per se means ignoring the *qualitative dimension* of exchanges. In his study on inter-agency collaboration within the American federal bureaucracy, Bardach convincingly points out that not all collaborative activities are equal. Some are preparatory to others rather than useful in themselves. Taking these 'activities' as major dependent variable would make it necessary to weight different sorts of activities (1998: 20). The observation of an increase of inter-ministerial email-exchanges, for instance, does not indicate that the way IGR are managed in a particular country has changed in any meaningful sense. Since changes are interesting if they have visible implications for the overall working of intergovernmental processes, it is useful to narrow down the concept, which brings us to a second perspective on IGR.

Speaking of *patterns* of IGR presupposes greater regularities in IGR than an analysis of exchanges and, in empirical terms, implies a greater resistance towards change. Regularities can be observed in a multiplicity of dimensions: regarding official meetings between state officials and federal officials or regarding the type of actors that tend to meet more often. A pattern might also find expression in the incapacity or unwillingness to set up regular meetings in particular arenas or in a federal system. Most crucial is that this perspective implies a basic consistency in behavioural choices in the intergovernmental arena over time. Thus, a focus on 'patterns' blinds out those exchanges contradicting what is considered as 'regular' or 'normal'. Following up on the need to reduce complexity to formulate comparatively applicable hypotheses, this book concentrates on patterns rather than exchanges, more precisely, the predominant interaction mode shaping the working and set-up of IGAs within different multilevel systems as one core dimension of IGR.

One can distinguish four intergovernmental interaction modes which help to characterize the pattern of IGR in a political system: (1) unilateral adaptation; (2) ad hoc coordination; (3) co-decision; and (4) the supragovernmental mode. *Unilateral adaptation* denotes a government's unilateral adoption of a measure observed in another jurisdiction unrelated to any intergovernmental agreement, a measure further governments might copy. Adaptation is the result of a series of *individual, independent* decisions. *Ad hoc coordination*, in contrast, captures the *mutual adjustment* of policies on an ad hoc basis. In contrast to unilateral adaptation, coordination is the result of direct governments' *interaction*. Still, governments coordinate only whenever it serves their individual interest, otherwise they refer to unilateral action. *Co-decision* denotes regular joint decision-making. Finally, *supragovernmentalism* directly corresponds to the concept of *supranationalism* in International Relations. It refers to the voluntary creation of collective authority by some or all governments in a federal system which – as long as this authority is in place, thus, governments do not formally exit – supersedes the authority of the individual governments in the sphere of responsibility assigned to it (Elazar 1991; Cameron 2001; Scharpf 2001: 4–9). With each of the four categories, the constraints imposed on individual government autonomy increase.

Each form of interaction is expected to go hand in hand with a particular set of *structures* which leads us to the third reading of 'relations' and to the concept of 'IGA', the second core concept in this book. Following Greif's definition of institution encompassing norms *and* the organizational infrastructure in which rules become manifest and through which various capacities are acquired (2006: 17), IGAs refer to the latter component, hence the structural dimension of IGR: institutions voluntarily set up in the intergovernmental arena.

The focus on voluntarily established structures does not imply that intergovernmental institutions cannot be formally or even constitutionally prescribed. We find such mechanisms in a wide range of countries such as Belgium, Spain, South Africa, the United States, or India (e.g. Lehmann 2002; Majeed, Watts, and Brown 2006; Swenden 2006). However, such formally prescribed mechanisms are not necessarily used by intergovernmental actors. In the opposite, actors might deliberately bypass them. Thus, formal mechanisms – especially in federal system in which IGR tends to be conflict-prone rather than cooperative – might not give a good indication of how intergovernmental processes work in practice. The 1981 law introduced by the Spanish government which constituted policy-specific intergovernmental conferences is one example. The law was challenged by regional governments in front of the Constitutional Court since it was perceived as an instrument of control (Máiz Beramendi and Grau 2002: 404). Despite endeavours to favour multilateral cooperation, IGR in Spain still evolves ad hoc and mostly on a bilateral basis (Bolleyer 2006: 398–400). A similar situation could be observed in Belgium where, among other formal mechanisms, special tribunals designed to resolve intergovernmental disputes related to cooperation agreements have been introduced already in the 1980s but remained unused (Jans and Tombeur 2000; Poirier 2002: 42–8). The creation of informal structures, in contrast, presupposes a certain willingness to cooperate and the degree to which they are institutionalized tends to express the extent of such willingness. This is why structural characteristics of voluntarily established bodies are more likely to give a good indication of the interaction patterns dominant in the system and are targeted by this study.[8]

Structures of IGAs and intergovernmental interaction patterns are expected to be linked in the following way. The dominance of unilateralism and ad hoc coordination is expected to reflect in loose intergovernmental structures allowing for maximal flexibility and autonomy of the participating parties with regard to bargaining, coalition formation, and unilateral withdrawal. It does so at the price of

---

[8] One might argue that formal–legal or constitutional reform is equally voluntary and often presupposes even more cooperation. However, thinking of who participates in these reforms, lower level governments are not necessarily directly involved. Often the second (supposedly territorial) chamber of the national parliament has a veto, but this chamber is ususally not composed of government representatives but of elected representatives or otherwise appointed (the German *Bundesrat* is an exception). This means that often territorial interests dominated by partisan or other considerations (Tsebelis and Money 1997; Lijphart 1999; on second chambers see also Chapter 2).

Intergovernmental Relations and the Puzzle of Institutional Choice 21

the reliability that usually accompanies strong institutionalization. Such reliability presupposes regular meetings, a bureaucratically supported and internally differentiated secretariat, and a formal decision-making rule (Arnold and Plant 1994; Cameron 2001; Opeskin 2001: 130; Simmons 2004). These are the empirical features of an institutionalized embedding facilitating co-decision. In the case of supragovernmentalism, the most constraining mode, pattern and structure are most closely tied. Indeed, they are hardly separable since supragovernmentalism presupposes the transferral of the voluntary coordination of, in principle, free government units into collective authority whose violation by individual governments can be answered by litigation against the latter. The remaining element of individual choice lies in the possibility of each member government to exit along a formally prescribed procedure. While unilateral adaptation resolves the tension between individual choice and collective action in favour of the former, supragovernmentalism does so in favour of the latter. The two middle categories – ad hoc coordination and co-decision – try to establish a balance: ad hoc coordination with an emphasis on individual government autonomy and co-decision with an emphasis on the collective decision-making. These interaction modes are expected to be reflected in the divergent levels of institutionalization.

Comparing corridors of adaptation

While the examination of intergovernmental exchanges forms the most inclusive perspective of IGR, the approach put forward here assumes that *specific patterns* find expression in a *dominant mode of interaction* between intergovernmental actors which again is linked to a set of *structural properties* (further specified below in the two dependent variables, institutionalization and integration). The analysis of intergovernmental interaction patterns and structures directly complement each other. Table 1.1 visualizes the three dimensions of IGR and how they express themselves empirically.

This study looks at Table 1.1 from a cross-country perspective, that is, from the right to the left. If the institutional development of IGR is considerable, we also would expect a particular interaction mode (e.g. co-decision rather than ad hoc coordination) and a high interaction density. On the whole, actors should have more contact than they would have if only weakly institutionalized structures were in place since, given a structural back-up, collaboration is less vulnerable to changes in the momentary interests of individual actors.

TABLE 1.1. *Three dimensions of intergovernmental relations*

Exchange	Patterns	Structure
Interaction density	Mode of interaction (unilateral adaptation, ad hoc coordination, co-decision, or supragovernmentalism)	Institutionalization (development of individual arrangement) Integration (linkages between arrangements on system level)

If, alternatively, one links the dimensions in Table 1.1 chronologically – from the left to the right – increasingly intensive interaction is expected to precede the development of certain patterns and structures. To prioritize cross-national and cross-sectoral differences over long-term changes in intergovernmental patterns involves costs. But these costs remain limited due to the following reasons substantiated further in the empirical analysis below. First, the basic institutional features of IGR are aspects which tend to be sticky, hence usually do not change too frequently. Second, the likelihood that the set-up of a highly institutionalized infrastructure will be initiated as a response to a particular event is in principle low when facing unfavourable intragovernmental incentives that shape day-to-day processes.[9] Third, even if in such an unfavourable context critical events lead to the creation of a structurally strong intergovernmental body, the latter's likelihood to effectively counteract incentive structures rooted within the interacting governments themselves is limited.

Being interested in the dominant patterns and structures of IGR in different federal systems, most fundamentally it is argued that the constraints within the individual lower level governments create *corridors of adaptation*. These corridors of adaptation indicate actors' relative potential to engage in institution building as a response to an environment marked by coordination pressure.[10] Simply put, they define an 'upper limit' for institutional development which might imply a lower institutionalization of IGR than adequate to cope with certain coordination demands in an efficient manner. Since intragovernmental constraints differ across the range of federal systems, these corridors are bigger in some polities than in others depending on the incentives created by the dominant type of executive–legislative relations. Simply put, these incentives impose costs on actors' intergovernmental choices. And as laid out later, majoritarianism in lower level governments restricts these corridors considerably, while power sharing creates the leeway for wider-reaching institutional developments.

The theoretical construct of such *system-specific corridors of adaptation* can be conceptually linked to the three dimensions of IGR as exchange, as pattern, and as structure and indicates each dimension's disposition towards change. With regard to the overall interaction density, the corridors are wide. Hence, the capacity for adaptation is considerable since the *density of exchanges* is driven by the momentary choice of intergovernmental actors and can be changed easily on a demand basis (e.g. to exchange emails, to set-up video conferences more frequently, or to meet more often if necessary). Correspondingly, temporary ups and downs in interaction density often hardly affect the overall patterns or structures

---

[9] On the weakness of the 'shadow of the future', hence long-term orientations, as impacts on institutional design, see Pierson (2000: 481–2).

[10] In principle, coordination pressure can vary across policy fields and across federal systems. However, it is shown later that while different coordination pressure (e.g. due to shared competences) helps to account for cross-sectoral differences within the same systemic context, it does not convincingly account for differences across systems (for alternative explanations see also Chapter 2).

of IGR. Talking about *patterns* of interaction, in contrast, the corridors are more restrictive and adaptation becomes more demanding. If behavioural regularities have been maintained by the majority of actors in a system over a certain period of time, change presupposes a more far-fetching behavioural reorientation than just engaging in more intense exchanges for a while. Finally, the potential for structural adaptation can be expected to be lowest since the costs to set up or reform such structures tend to be considerable and the consequences of such changes are most pronounced.

This book focuses deliberately on the structural features of IGAs, thus institution building, and compares corridors of adaptation as generated by political constraints in different federal systems. Institution building is expected to vary across different federal systems more than across the different policy fields within them – a claim examined later. Furthermore, the study prioritizes a cross-national over a cross-temporal perspective, which involves trade-offs. To minimize the resulting disadvantages, when examining the set-up of IGAs in the three cases, their respective age, major leaps of institutionalization, and the respective triggers for their creation are taken into consideration. Finally, the way institutionalization is measured will help to capture crucial stages in an IGA's development. Its operationlization is laid out in the following section.

THE INSTITUTIONALIZATION AND INTEGRATION OF INTERGOVERNMENTAL ARRANGEMENTS: DEFINITION AND OPERATIONALIZATION

The book examines intergovernmental structures along two dimensions. First, it looks at the institutionalization of the individual IGAs. Second, it looks at the integration of the whole system of IGR shaping federal dynamics as defined by the types of linkages set up between IGAs. Throughout the study, the concept of institutionalization will be used with reference to individual IGAs as the unit of analysis, while integration will be used with reference to the system level. This allows us to see under which conditions a strong institutionalization of the individual arrangements goes hand in hand with a strong integration of the intergovernmental system, and under which conditions this is not the case. Accordingly, the analysis starts out from individual bodies and moves on to inter-institutional dynamics and thereby captures and links the micro, meso, and macro level of intergovernmental processes.

Attempting to measure the institutionalization and integration of IGAs, a first, crucial decision is whether to conceptualize the two phenomena as *categorical or continuous.* While a categorical conceptualization allows for a more clear-cut characterization of IGAs, a continuous one leads to a more differentiated measurement. Regarding integration, the assessment of inter-institutional linkages, the phenomenon itself points towards a categorical solution. Linkages are either in place or not, be it in the form of regularized contacts or formal rules. In the case of institutionalization, the choice between *structure-based* (*categorical*) or *resource-based* (*continuous*) indicators for institutionalization is less obvious. A resource-based approach could refer to the number of full-time staff or the money attributed to IGAs by the various governments embedded in a system which would provide a fine-grained measure of changing institutionalization both across systems and over time. Yet the question is which conclusions could be derived from such a measure. It is reasonable to argue that the more willing governmental actors are to invest in these bodies, the more valuable these bodies are to them. This, however, may not be equated with the capacity of IGAs to provide the infrastructure to represent its members as a 'collective' and to generate results transcending the sum of individual interests. Lower level governments might invest considerable resources in a policy-specific IGA because interdependencies make information exchange particularly valuable to them. However, as long as this body does not engage in the drafting of collective agreements, the amount of resources only indicates that lower level units appreciate the expertise. Vice versa, a body might have comparatively little money and still actively engage in forming collectively shared positions or even negotiating agreements on cross-jurisdictional policy-harmonization, and hence be politically very relevant.

This is why the study expects institutional properties (e.g. the decision-making rule or statutes) to be more telling because they more reliably indicate IGAs' capacity to involve governments into collective decision-making and policy coordination, a claim which I will return to in the later empirical part. A categorical measure is further advantageous since it helps to identify the major steps in an IGA's development. Being less fine-grained than a resource-based measure, it can identify important changes in the institutional status of an arrangement. This focus helps to examine those intragovernmental pressures which define corridors of adaptation shaping the overall patterns of institutionalization within a system rather than measuring fluctuations in resource access.[11]

Having settled on a structure-based conceptualization, the level of institutionalization of an IGA becomes visible, on the one hand, in a process of *internal institutional development*, which is directed towards a more complex functional distribution of tasks to different offices or subunits. On the other hand, it becomes visible in a process of *external differentiation* – in the *boundedness* of an arrangement, which develops boundaries towards other arrangements in terms of own functions as well as material resources (Judge 2003: 500–1; Greif 2006: 31). The 'strength' or 'weakness' of the institutionalization of IGAs is indicated by a set of features which reflect these two processes and tend to be mutually related.

---

[11] To substantiate this conception the empirical part will provide complementary information on resources and staff.

TABLE 1.2. *Levels of intergovernmental institutionalization*

Regularity of meetings	Weak institutionalization
Autonomous institution	Medium institutionalization
• Own secretariat	
• Clearly defined functions	
• Formal basis (e.g. statutes)	
Majority rule	Strong institutionalization
Internal functional differentiation	
• Specification of offices	
• Specification of subunits/bodies	
Legal status of agreements	
Precision of agreements	

Their order in Table 1.2 implies the increasing degree of institutionalization that is assumed to be linked to each feature's presence. Note that while the elements are assumed to cluster, one element is not necessarily a condition for the other.[12]

Even if the density of exchanges is quite high at times or regular meetings are set up between the prime ministers and the ministers responsible for particular policy fields, institutionalization is considered to be weak as long as it is organized directly by the governmental departments without a separate intergovernmental body in place. A medium institutionalization, which involves setting up a separate 'intergovernmental institution', demands the 'boundedness' of an arrangement. This does not mean that boundaries are de facto closed; neither needs exit of a government to be extremely costly nor (re)entry extremely difficult. Instead, 'boundedness' becomes visible through the assignment of specific competences, resources, and staff to a particular infrastructure.

Institutionalization is important because the higher the degree of institutionalization, the more likely it is that intergovernmental transactions no longer exclusively express the momentary interest convergence of a group of individual actors. The stronger it is, the more likely an informal institution is capable of affecting the behaviour of the involved actors as an independent force and the higher the changes to achieve a voluntary deviation from their isolated interests. Only then is more than a lowest common denominator solution a likely result. Also the degree of institutionalization tends to have an impact on whether intergovernmental processes are heavily influenced by changes in the specific group of government representatives in office.

In this sense, *institutionalization* is *absent* when the relations between intergovernmental actors remain completely contingent on the momentary configurations of individual government interests without being structured by any common rules.

---

[12] For instance, it can well be imagined that an IGA with its own secretariat fulfils mainly advisory functions and its members meet only ad hoc. Such combinations, however, should not occur too frequently, since ad hoc contacts are equally possible and less costly without a secretariat.

A body is *weakly institutionalized*, when meetings are regular, yet interaction is still easily affected by changes in individual actors' interests due to a lacking infrastructure. Institutional resources of an IGA in terms of permanent staff, in contrast, can counterbalance such fragility. Stable personnel provides for continuity and the experience required to moderate conflicts between the current officials (who might have started to deal with intergovernmental issues only very recently). Moreover, experienced staff provides for the expert knowledge to discuss issues on a rather factual basis which might weaken ideological tensions or political conflicts which otherwise would easily dominate IGR. Therefore, when we find an autonomous infrastructure (e.g. a secretariat), we speak of *medium institutionalization*.

Regarding *high institutionalization*, the most crucial sign is a formal decision-making rule which deviates from unanimity. The capacity to bind the lower level units to positions or agreements to which they did not agree indicates most strikingly that the IGA represents more than the sum of its parts. Another indicator for a high institutional development is the internal differentiation into offices or organs that have their own formally assigned tasks. Differentiation and formalization are likely to go hand in hand since internal differentiation increases complexity which makes a formal assignment of competences in the form of written statutes more valuable. To get a precise idea about how internal differentiation shows empirically, highly developed generalist IGAs might run policy-specific committees reflecting important areas of lower level legislation in order to cover the range of issues discussed by the members more efficiently. To speak of internal differentiation, this should be stable. At some point, a policy committee might be fused with another one or might be newly established. But the basic structure should remain in place. This is not the case with regard to ad hoc working groups of administrative officials set up by an IGA since they usually work on a particular issue and are dissolved afterwards. Both examples represent different forms of distribution of labour. Only the first is interpreted as internal differentiation of an IGA when assessing its degree of institutionalization. Furthermore, it is crucial whether agreements struck within IGAs can have a legally binding character or not. A legal foundation usually increases the likelihood that an agreement will be transferred into legislation or otherwise implemented. Hence, the legal status of agreements provides an additional indicator (Simeon 2001: 148; Simmons 2004).

The last indicator listed in Table 1.2, the precision of agreements, is crucial since it refers to the degree to which an agreement is targeting a particular policy problem and specifies concrete measures to tackle it. It captures whether an agreement provides the basis to solve a cross-jurisdictional policy-problem by formulating standards for either lower level legislation or federal measures. Hence, precision is a proxy for the constraining character of agreements different from agreements simply making general proclamations. Talking about agreements addressing harmonization problems, a very high degree of precision is certainly not a sufficient condition for the individual agreement partners to adopt a measure. Yet the vaguer an agreement is, the more difficult it is to detect non-compliance in the first place. Facing a very precise agreement on the basis of which non-compliance is easily identified, it is much easier for a government not to sign it when it does not agree with its contents. The same can be said where a government expects strong resistance of its parliament at home (given the agreement demands the latter's ratification). Most likely, it will not sign the agreement to avoid quarrels. As a consequence, if a very precise agreement is signed, a considerable willingness of the participants to implement it can be assumed. According to this line of argument, the degree of precision most likely has immediate implications for cross-jurisdictional policy-harmonization. If agreements are always of a low precision, it indicates that agreements tend to be mere window dressing. In case of highly precise agreements, it is likely that it has implications for how the agreement partners will handle the policy concerned at home, even if the agreement is not legally binding (Poirier 2004: 430–4). If more than two of the four properties of high institutionalization listed in Table 1.2 are present, an IGA is classified as highly institutionalized.

After having specified how to pin down the level of institutionalization, we need to capture the theoretical and empirical specification of integration, the institutional 'linkages' between IGAs (Table 1.3). Accordingly, the unit of analysis is no longer the individual arrangement but the system of IGR as a whole. There is *no integration* when IGAs (staff and members) actively avoid contact. Alternatively, relations might be characterized by disinterest. Again, the inter-institutional relations are considered as not integrated. If, in contrast, voluntary meetings occur on an ad hoc basis, *weak integration* is given. When meetings are organized regularly, it is considered to be *medium* because regularity indicates an active and continuous interest of the involved IGAs in maintaining a channel of communication. Integration is considered to be *strong* when IGAs' responsibilities are distributed based on statutes agreed upon by the IGAs concerned. Such statutes stabilize their mutual cooperation and reduce conflicts since they clarify each body's sphere of authority. The following table sums up the chosen indicators used for the later analysis. As with institutionalization, overall, the properties are assumed to cluster empirically.

TABLE 1.3. *Levels of integration between intergovernmental arrangements*

Contacts with other IGAs	Weak integration
Regularized meetings with other IGAs	Medium integration
No coexistence of IGAs with similar scope and similar functions	Strong integration
Formal statutes about respective responsibilities and meetings	

Chapter 2 will now present a theoretical framework which attempts to account for the institutionalization and integration of IGAs. It will specify under which conditions (i.e. the incentive structures within lower level governments) we expect the corridor of adaption in a federal system to be wide, and under which conditions we expect intragovernmental incentives to constrain intergovernmental institution-building. After having derived a set of hypotheses, the chapter justifies the selection of Canada, Switzerland, and the United States as cases, and considers potential alternative explanations. In the concluding section, the incentive profiles generated by the intragovernmental dynamics in Canadian, Swiss, and American lower level governments are laid out and the institutional choices (in terms of institutionalization and integration expected as a response to them) are specified.

2

A Rationalist Account of Intergovernmental Institution-Building

Having conceptualized the institutionalization and the mutual integration of IGAs, this chapter moves on to the theoretical foundation of the approach developed to account for these phenomena. To explain the institutional differences of intergovernmental patterns and structures, we need to understand the internal nature of governments which systematically spill over to their external relations. Lower level and central governments constituting federal systems are institutionally delimited interaction contexts to which specific tasks and competences are assigned (Benz 2003). They define and delimit the respective political actors' home arenas where politicians have to regularly participate in elections in order to enter or remain in office – whether they necessarily have to 'win' these elections, in the narrow sense of reaching a majority of seats, to achieve this goal, is a different story. This depends on the type of government we are talking about. In any case, *intragovernmental* and *intergovernmental processes* are expected to be linked (Benz 2004*a*: 133, 2004*b*). Whenever particular types of intergovernmental interaction reduce politicians' chances of pursuing internal goals, this has immediate consequences for the institutionalization and integration of IGR. Since institutions constrain and regulate behaviour in the long run, they are only set up if they still allow actors to pursue their respective goals (Scharpf 1997; Héritier 1998). Put differently, strongly developed and integrated IGAs are only established and maintained if the actors involved profit from it or, at least, are not confronted with short-term costs in their home arenas.

WHY RATIONAL CHOICE, NOT NORMS OR CULTURE?

The approach developed in the following section is based on the premise that self-interested actors can consider institutions as constraining but also as windows of opportunity. Most fundamentally, institutions generate mutual predictability among participating actors. This is essential when facing an uncertain environment such as the intergovernmental arena, which is much less structured by formal rules and established routines than the individual government units are internally, since interaction is foremost voluntary. The underlying 'calculus approach' (Hall and Taylor 1996: 939) does not imply that actors necessarily have sufficient information to cope with new challenges efficiently. This is particularly the case when they have to act outside their usual environment: their immediate home arena. Furthermore, there is not necessarily only one benefit-maximizing strategy. Yet, whenever actors confront particular problems for which several solutions exist, it is a plausible assumption that they resort to the solution whose effects they can estimate most accurately. Favouring predictability, they act in a risk-minimizing manner. Sociological institutionalists refer to these behavioural paths as 'standard operating procedures' (Olsen 1998: 89–92). The application of these procedures can be interpreted as an unconscious reaction to a stimulus. In this context, by contrast, it is considered as an actor's conscious choice under uncertainty: choices are rational, yet rationality is context-bound and therefore necessarily limited (Héritier 1998). Thereby we also avoid the concept of 'institutional culture' since for the purposes of this study, the latter does not sufficiently distinguish between the concept of institution and the behavioural responses to it, as will be laid out later.

The core actors on the micro-level constituting intergovernmental patterns are elected officials who are expected to respond to the threat of immediate sanctions (such as losses at the next election) more readily than to long-term demands such as more reliable IGR. If short- and long-term goals conflict, short-term goals are assumed to dominate actors' choices and actors expected to discount future benefits. The second major group of actors are intergovernmental officials who conduct the daily business of intergovernmental management. Clearly, administrators are less affected by potential electoral punishment, and political and administrative intergovernmental exchanges can be conceptualized as separate arenas. Depending on the system analysed, political dynamics feed into administrative processes more or less forcefully. Nonetheless, the latter are not immune to political dynamics and the empirical analysis will substantiate that the working level of IGR is shaped by the same systemic dynamics as 'intergovernmental politics'.

In recent years, political science has experienced a proliferation of rational choice approaches, a trend which has also affected research on federalism and IGR. While Filippov, Ordeshook, and Shvetsova (2004) – building on Riker's seminal book on federalism (1964) – look at constitutional bargaining in federal systems from a rational choice perspective, Wibbels (2005) and Rodden (2006) analyse intergovernmental negotiations in particular policy areas along the same lines. A comparative approach following a rationalist logic to the overall patterns of informal institution-building in the intergovernmental arena across distinct federal systems and across a range of policy fields has not been introduced so far (see, however, for 'rationalist perspectives' on German federalism in particular Benz 1985 and Scharpf 1988).

Overall, the federalism literature most commonly employs cultural approaches or historical accounts exploring individual cases in depth (e.g. Steiner 1974;

Linder 1994; Agranoff 1999a; Moreno 1999, 2000; Vatter 2004). While contributing to the understanding of individual federal systems, these pose problems for comparative research. To give one example, most cultural-historical accounts on IGR in Switzerland classify this polity as 'cooperative federalist' system in which power sharing in different arenas is mutually reinforcing (e.g. Wälti 1996; Armingeon 2000a). Such a classification rests on the *constitutional framework* and *informal structures and processes* as defining criteria which becomes problematic in any explanatory account of voluntarily created intergovernmental structures which presupposes a clear-cut distinction between the two. Intergovernmental structures are established *within* the framework of the given constitutional rules.[1] A definition of cooperative federalism which also refers to the informal processes circumvents the question of why these processes and structural patterns have been established in a constitutional context in the first place. In fact, it will later become clear that with regard to the formal legislative competence distribution between federal and cantonal levels, Switzerland is more accurately located on the dual federal side (Freiburghaus and Zehnder 2003; Bolleyer and Thorlakson 2008).

Most importantly, the lacking separation between the constitutional and the process levels very easily leads to circular reasoning in theoretical terms. More precisely, the distinction between particular 'incentive structures' from the resulting intergovernmental structures helps to avoid following type of reasoning: Some accounts of territorial politics in socially heterogeneous contexts are explicitly based on the axiom that IGR are necessarily conflicting and involve struggles over the distribution of power (Moreno 1999, 2000; Lecours 2004). Indeed, Lecours' approach can be applied to several cases. Due to its behavioural premise, it works well for Spain and Canada and accounts for rather weak IGAs in these two countries. However, it does not work for Switzerland which is also socially heterogeneous. The explanatory factor and the resulting intergovernmental patterns are not sufficiently separated. This is because the axiom does not allow for intergovernmental patterns to vary from competitive to cooperative, or to use the categories for modes of intergovernmental interaction just introduced, from unilateralism to supragovernmentalism.

This leads us back to the problem already touched upon before, that of implicitly or explicitly in-built behavioural assumptions which claim that there is either an orientation towards cooperation or competition in IGR. Already when discussing whether 'independence' should be used as criterion for federalism, it became evident that behavioural patterns need to be *accounted for* and that they are *part of the puzzle*. Consequently, behavioural predispositions may not be integrated ex ante in the theoretical frame or guide the specifications of the

---

[1] There is also the possibility that intergovernmental structures become 'constitutionalized'. This represents the strongest form of institutionalization. Accordingly, one needs to differentiate constitutional changes in the federal structure that do not qualify as constitutional context of IGR from those that are the latter's constitutional expression.

cases relevant for the analysis. This would easily amount to a selection bias reconfirming whatever an approach has predicted in the first place.

The resort to informal rules of appropriateness substantiating formal rules (March and Olsen 1984, 1989) leads into similar difficulties. March and Olsen assume norms to be central to the nature of institutions, but what if these institutions are not yet in place as in the case of voluntarily created IGAs? Peters distinguishes two partial answers to the problem of institutional building in March and Olsen's approach (Peters 1999: 31–3). The structure of meaning embedded in institutions, their inherent logic of appropriateness, derives from the society in which they are formed (March and Olsen 1989: 25–7). This is not greatly helpful in this context since this line of reasoning poses the same problems as when building our framework around behavioural premises. We easily 'explain' low institutionalization with a societal disposition towards competition which, to take Canada as an example, finds expression in the majoritarian dynamics within the interacting government units. Independent and dependent variables would be hardly separable. The second partial answer March and Olsen provide refers to the routines which appear to arise naturally already in a *proto*-institutional setting. These routines define the nature of the organization and the more established they become, the higher the degree of institutionalization within the given structure (1989: 21–5). Yet as Peters rightly points out, the core issue remains unaddressed:

> how do individuals decide to interact to create routines in the first instance?...the initial decision to institutionalize still seems to require a somewhat clearer treatment in the theory. In some ways the process of the institutionalization appears to be a two-step process. First, there must be some *conscious* decision to create an organization or institution for a specified purpose. The second stage appears to be then to fashion the institution over time, and to imbue it with certain values. (Peters 1999: 32–3; author's emphasis)

The fact that Peters points to a 'conscious' decision invites the adoption of a rationalist perspective implying that the absence of established routines of interaction makes a 'calculus approach' particularly fruitful. What intergovernmental actors know is which dynamics they (as well as their counterparts in other governments) will be subject to at home in the long run: the costs and benefits of intergovernmental cooperation imposed on them by intragovernmental dynamics which are fairly stable over time as empirically demonstrated later in this chapter.[2] This book argues that it is this knowledge which lies at the heart of the conscious decision in favour or against investing in strong cooperation structures in federal polities.

The insufficient separation of the explanans – agents' motives – and explanandum – structural choices – is all the more problematic if it goes hand in hand

---

[2] Lijphart (1999) indicates some moves of the 43 countries on his two-dimensional scheme of majoritarian versus consensus democracy over time. However, the basic character of each polity – especially when looking at the first dimension capturing the degree of executive–legislative power-sharing – showed considerable stability.

with a lacking micro-foundation and a failure to explicate the motives driving the agents in the first place. This tendency has already been observed above when discussing structure-oriented approaches on IGR which tend to describe structural configurations without disaggregating them. The reference to the central and regional political elites is thus crucial, but the reference to the 'actorness' of non-central governments (Hocking 1999) remains insufficient as long as the dynamics and pressures these actors are subject to are not systematically assessed. Regional institutions, once created, acquire a life of their own and become the central structuring forces of territorial politics. Their very creation leads the patterns of central–regional and inter-regional relationships (Lecours 2004: 86). But again, to assume that they necessarily become 'new arenas for power struggles' is misleading. The respective character of the internal dynamics generated within the lower level units differs considerably across federal countries. It is indeed correct that lower level governments tend to be concerned about their share of power and the loss thereof in face of central intervention. However, to maintain their influence, they might be interested in participating in collective decisions rather than individual autonomy implying zero-sum dynamics. As Chapman rightly emphasizes, patterns of IGR need not reflect in struggles for autonomy nor must they be competitive in character (1993: 75–6). In order to account for diverse patterns of institution building, it therefore is essential to allow for intergovernmental dynamics to vary and not to start out from either a cooperative or a competitive mode.

For all these reasons, the following approach relies on a rationalist micro-foundation. It assumes that actors pursue their individual goals and choose either cooperative or competitive pathways depending on whether the incentives generated in their home arenas favour it or not. Keeping these arguments in mind, the following sections explicate the hypotheses and measures of the respective lower level dynamics which generate incentives for or against intergovernmental competition or cooperation, in turn, finding expression in different levels of institutional development. The two core hypotheses will be developed based on a typology of power-limiting democracies which serves as a heuristic to classify federal systems. This macro-scheme will help to specify the mechanisms at work on the micro level by systematizing the presence or absence of different forms of power limitation in these polities which motivate different reactions on behalf of the intergovernmental actors.

LINKING MACRO AND MICRO LEVEL: INTERGOVERNMENTAL INSTITUTIONALIZATION IN POWER-LIMITING DEMOCRACIES

In order to obtain a systematic account of IGR in federal systems, it is crucial to understand the interactions between different types of power-limiting mechanisms in a political system. These mechanisms separate and link the constitutive units of a composite polity and most crucially structure lower level governments internally. A power-limiting democracy is characterized by institutional mechanisms and/or actor configurations, which prevent a simple majority from making collectively binding decisions without the participation or intervention of other actors. Subtypes of power-limiting democracy are characterized by different forms of power limitation. In this regard, the most crucial distinction is that between power sharing and power dispersion (Lijphart 1999). Power sharing denotes joint decision-making while power dispersion refers to the distribution of competences to distinct centres that cannot formally intervene in each other's jurisdictions. The most obvious example for power dispersion is dual federalism. Another institution corresponding to this logic are independent central banks established to steer monetary policy without the intervention of political actors.

In contrast to Lijphart (1999) who developed his type of 'consensus democracy' inductively, the following scheme is based on the analytical separation of power dispersion and power sharing as the two generic forms of power limitation. The concepts of *polycentric democracy* and of *power-sharing democracy* are characterized by power dispersion and power sharing, respectively.[3]

If a system is characterized by power dispersion, meaning that power is dispersed to different decision-making arenas which are internally dominated by majoritarian processes, it is called a polycentric democracy. It unites power-limiting structures between government units and majoritarian decision-making within these units.

If a system is characterized by power-sharing mechanisms and does not allow a simple majority or individual simple majorities to bring about decisions alone, it is called a power-sharing democracy.

This distinction helps us to systematize how the interplay of federal structures with other power-limiting or power-concentrating mechanisms leads to either power-sharing or power-dispersing dynamics in the intergovernmental arena. Further, it provides a useful heuristic device to select cases for a comparative design. Along the above-distinction, Canada as compared to Switzerland and the United States can be classified as 'most different' with regard to the degree of power sharing in their executive–legislative relations. While government units in Canada tend to be power-concentrating one-party majority cabinets, both Switzerland and the United States are composed of strongly power-sharing governments.

---

[3] This re-conceptualization has two advantages: First, the extreme type of consensus democracy which is always considered in relation to the majoritarian extreme is replaced by a distinct class of polities. Moreover, the constitutive criterion of the new type is less ambiguous and allows for a more clear-cut treatment of cases, in particular of those which Lijphart classified as majoritarian on the executive-party dimension and as consensual on the federal-unitary dimension. Second, a deductive strategy is useful since some indicators on the second dimension generate power sharing, while Lijphart denotes this dimension as largely power dispersing.

Having classified systems along these lines, however, the question remains still unanswered how power concentration and power sharing in lower level governments impact on the institutional development of IGAs. The core argument that majoritarian decision-making in lower level governments weakens the degree of IGAs' institutionalization draws on Lehmbruch's work on German federalism. In Germany, the tight coupling of arenas in which majoritarian processes interact with an interlocking system of horizontal and vertical intergovernmental cooperations causes considerable tensions. One crucial observation is that partisan competition delimits politicians' capacity to strike bargains in the federal arena (Lehmbruch 1978). For dual federal systems, systems in which lower level governments have considerable leeway to issue own legislation, this argument can be turned around. If federal systems do not provide ex ante strong constitutional predispositions to develop dense intergovernmental structures, it should follow that majoritarian processes within individual government arenas set incentives against the establishment of a strongly institutionalized system of IGR. This rationale underlies the following line of argument:

Hypothesis 1: Power-concentrating governments undermine the institutionalization of intergovernmental arrangements, while power-sharing governments support it.

Lehmbruch's work is crucial since it provides the main logic of how to account for different patterns of intergovernmental institutionalization in federal systems. His efforts to systematize processes on the meso and the macro level have been exemplary not only in his studies of German federalism but also of consociationalism in Western Europe (see Lehmbruch 1991, 1993). Yet, Lehmbruch's work does not link these tensions on the meso and macro level to motives on the micro level. This study, in contrast, attempts to specify the countervailing incentives actors face when being simultaneously engaged in processes in their home and in the intergovernmental arena (see also Benz 2004*a*, 2004*b*). This is crucial since Lehmbruch leaves open how exactly the 'systemic' tensions between majoritarianism *within* the individual governmental units and cooperation endeavours *between* these units show on the micro level where politicians and administrators interact across jurisdictional boundaries. To address this question, we need to specify the conditions – linked to the internal government dynamics at home – under which self-interested actors tend to set up strong IGAs or tend to refrain from it:

1. The first incentive refers to the *(in)stability of the interest configuration* among the constitutive arenas. Given mostly one-party majority cabinets in the constitutive government units, government turnover frequently alters the interest configurations among lower level governments. This raises the costs for them to maintain strong IGAs. Ad hoc coordination, by contrast, allows politicians to adapt to these changing configurations. They participate in a profitable agreement when interest convergence is given with a certain group of partners.

Where this is no longer the case, they resort to unilateralism. A strongly institutionalized context would delimit this flexibility. As soon as coalitions come into play, complete alternations are less likely and the interest configuration among lower level governments tends to change less frequently. Given mostly oversized coalitions, the interest configuration should be quite stable over time. Under these circumstances, ad hoc coordination has hardly advantages and this should find reflection in the strength of the IGAs established.

2. A second aspect that characterizes the interest configuration among lower level governments is its *ideological congruence* (Downs 1998; Thorlakson 2007). Instead of capturing the fluidity or changeability of the horizontal constellation of lower level governments, this characteristic aims to capture their internal ideological heterogeneity. If party systems are similar across the constitutive governments, congruence is most likely when oversized governments are formed. Then, parties of the same family are likely to participate in coalitions within different subunits and therefore lower level coalitions are likely to overlap in their partisan composition. By contrast, in federal systems with mainly one-party governments, the likelihood increases for ideologically non-overlapping governments to be in office.

3. In virtually any political system externalities complicate policy making. The misalignment of costs and benefits across multiple jurisdictional boundaries allows for destructive political maneouvring as politicians claim credit for benefits and shift blame onto other jurisdictions (Donahue and Pollack 2001: 78). At the same time, however, systems differ in the exent to which they invite such behaviour. Given a high likelihood of alternation, the immediate threat of electoral loss strongly motivates regional politicians to *shift blame* to the other governments. The competitive pressure is strongest in two-party systems which constitute a 'zero-sum game'. Therein, mutual distrust is fostered because each actor is aware of the pressure on others to focus on the short-term goal of electoral victory at the cost of the long-term goal of fruitful intergovernmental exchanges. In such a two-level game (Putnam 1988), the intergovernmental game is clearly subordinated (Cameron and Simeon 2002). The threat of government alternation and the resulting tendency to shift blame is comparatively weaker if coalitions need to be formed. Then, it is less likely that vote losses of a party lead to its loss of government participation.[4]

4. When engaging in intergovernmental interaction, *autonomy losses* are greater for parties which govern alone and are unrestricted by a second chamber than for parties which govern in a coalition and face a strong upper house. If power sharing is a part of daily decision-making in the home arena, the relative

---

[4] Based on this rationale, we can conclude that the less visible and the less relevant policies in the electoral arena, the denser cooperation in these policy fields will be. This is because the described counter-incentives linked to high electoral saliency are less pronounced. Still, it will show later that similar patterns show across different policy arenas.

autonomy losses when engaging in intergovernmental bodies are comparatively minor. Institutionally strong IGAs involve autonomy losses since they are constructed to induce governments to comply with collective decisions. This loss is most severe if agreements attempt to harmonize policy in areas of lower level legislation since the explicit goal is to restrict autonomous action in spheres of lower level authority. Still, irrespective of the type of IGA concerned, the more power concentration there is in lower level governments, the higher the costs of highly institutionalized IGAs in terms of autonomy losses.

Hypothesis 1 implies that these four mechanisms systematically vary along power-concentration or power-sharing dynamics within lower level governments. Corresponding to the resulting incentive profile, one would expect a higher institutionalization of IGAs in the two power-sharing democracies Switzerland and the United States than in polycentric Canada.

JUMPING TO THE SYSTEM LEVEL: TYPES OF POWER SHARING AND THE INTEGRATION OF INTERGOVERNMENTAL RELATIONS

The distinction between institutionalization and integration is essential because the two do not always go together. Strong institutionalization of individual IGAs does not necessarily lead to strong integration between IGAs. Therefore, we now need to hypothesize under which conditions different intergovernmental bodies are mutually supportive and under which they tend to conflict.[5]

In line with the first hypothesis, one factor that should affect the integration of a system is majoritarian dynamics in the subunits. With power-concentrating executives in office and the resulting high autonomy losses through intergovernmental interaction, bodies responsible for lower level exchanges are likely to be directed towards autonomy protection and against central encroachment. Simultaneously, lower level governments as the central government should be sensitive about mutual interference in general. Furthermore, the tendency towards blame shifting given governments operating under high electoral pressure should weaken integrative efforts. As majoritarianism is expected to complicate the institutionalization of IGAs, it should also complicate integration. The dynamics generated lead to the mutual suspicion that each government will readily exploit problems or weaknesses of other governments to improve its electoral fortunes which most likely feeds back into the linkages between IGAs representing different government configurations. As an extension of Hypothesis 1, majoritarianism

---

[5] If there is only one horizontal-multilateral IGA in place that is highly institutionalized, horizontal integration is necessarily high.

should affect the overall development of IGAs negatively – including both their institutionalization and integration.

The picture gets more complicated once we look at the group of power-sharing democracies since we do not only find one type of power sharing in them. Drawing on the literature on veto players which claims that different types of power sharing generate different effects (e.g. Birchfield and Crepaz 1998), we need to distinguish between two types of power-sharing democracy: *Constitutional power-sharing democracies* are dominated by constitutionally defined, hence, compulsory power-sharing, while *consensual power-sharing democracies* are dominated by voluntary power-sharing.

This distinction is substantiated by a frequent criticism of Tsebelis' very prominent veto player theory (1995) which explains systemic dynamics and decision-making outputs referring to the number of veto players in a political system. Various scholars argued that the approach needs refinement since not all types of power-sharing structures affect actor behaviour in the same way. Thus, they do not necessarily generate similar patterns of veto usage (Kaiser 1997; Birchfield and Crepaz 1998). In line with these arguments, it is hypothesized that a high level of integration is likely only if voluntary power-sharing is predominant as in consensual power-sharing democracies. By contrast, integration is undermined when governments are characterized by compulsory power-sharing constitutive for constitutional power-sharing democracies.

The mechanisms at work are the following: *compulsory power-sharing structures* (e.g. bicameralism and presidentialism) are constitutionally entrenched and can be considered as exogenous to the strategic choices of the actors which are embedded in them. By contrast, *voluntary power-sharing structures* (e.g. coalition governments and corporatism) are deliberatively established by the actors. They are endogenous and can only be maintained when they are sufficiently effective. For instance, if a coalition partner blocks intra-coalitional decisions too frequently, this behaviour brings down the coalition. In so doing, the partner risks losing its veto position. Consequently, in order to stabilize the decision-making structure, actors in voluntary structures are assumed to make a more restrictive use of their vetoes than actors in compulsory structures. Since externally imposed power-sharing is more difficult to overcome because vetoes are more likely to be invoked, compulsory power-sharing in the constitutive arenas of a federal state considerably complicates the aggregation of individual state positions. In such a context, the capacity of the constitutive governments to link IGAs is easily undermined because the constitutive government units are themselves internally fragmented. Since IGAs are institutional reflections of constitutive governments' investments, the intragovernmental fragmentation in a constitutional power-sharing democracy should also display itself in the patterns and structures of IGR. The capacity to achieve integration is limited because lower level governments are unable to represent one coherent interest in the intergovernmental area both individually and collectively.

This line of reasoning on the impact of compulsory as opposed to voluntary power-sharing structures directly contradicts what is often claimed with regard to constitutionally established veto structures, namely that because institutional actors know that they have to deal with each other in the long run, they are more cooperative (Axelrod 1984). Still, compared to voluntary structures, in a setting characterized by compulsory power-sharing, the short-term costs of non-cooperation and thereby non-decision for the actors are much lower. This is because actors do not place the decision-making structure itself at risk. Confronted with constitutional structures there are incentives to avoid continuous blockade. Yet, the scenario is one in which non-decisions have usually no immediate negative consequences. In coalition governments, internal non-decisions can have costs as heavy as a government's dissolution and new elections putting at risk government actors' present strength and positions. Following this rationale, we arrive at the second core hypothesis of this study:

Hypothesis 2: Compulsory power-sharing weakens integration between intergovernmental arrangements, while voluntary power-sharing supports it.

SELECTING CASES: CANADA, SWITZERLAND, AND THE UNITED STATES COMPARED

The former section has already provided some discussion of the rationale which leads to the selection of Canada, Switzerland, and the United States as comparative cases rooted in their variance on the side of the independent variables as specified by the hypotheses. The three cases constitute a most-different-cases design since we find power concentration in the Canadian lower level governments versus power sharing in the American and Swiss lower level governments (Hypothesis 1). Simultaneously, we find compulsory power-sharing in the United States versus voluntary power-sharing in Switzerland (Hypothesis 2). Since the variance on the side of the two explanatory factors is maximal, differences in the institutionalization and integration of IGR should display clearly. The distinction between power concentration in Canada and power sharing in Switzerland and in the United States is clear-cut. Yet before we can move on to competing explanations some words are necessary on the distinction between the United States as constitutional and Switzerland as consensual power-sharing democracy.

Hypothesis 2 pointed to the different impact of voluntary power-sharing on intergovernmental integration as compared to compulsory power-sharing. If a coalition partner – embedded in voluntary power-sharing arrangement – disagrees too frequently, the coalition can fall apart and he risks losing his veto position. Although the cantonal executives and parliaments are elected separately, such a cooperation-favouring logic is also at work in the Swiss referendum democracy.

It is the facultative referendum which leads to a situation in which executive actors have a strong interest in maintaining the effectiveness of non-compulsory decision-making arrangements. Both on the federal and the cantonal levels, we find a voluntarily maintained proportionality rule assuring the representation of the main parliamentary parties in the executives, which simultaneously ties executives and legislatures together. Scholars have convincingly argued that the threat of opposition parties to block government policy through a facultative referendum has been a major motivation to form these oversized, in the ideal case, all-inclusive government coalitions (Neidhart 1970).

Yet unlike parliamentary coalition governments, the terms of the members of the executive are fixed. Thus, they do not risk bringing down the government by destructive behaviour since they are independent from legislative or internal executive support. Given these circumstances, why should voluntary power-sharing structures in Switzerland induce more cooperative behaviour than the constitutional power-sharing in the United States? Don't we end up in circular reasoning? The answer is no since the party-proportional composition of Swiss governments would be ineffective if certain parties still dominated others in intra-executive decision-making. In this case, minor government parties would resort to referenda despite being part of the government to compensate for their weak internal position (which was the reason to include them in the first place). This is why, similar to parliamentary coalitions, the stronger government parties are reluctant to impose decisions on the weaker government partners in order to protect the government's decision-making monopoly. That is, they rather consider the interests of smaller partners to keep an avoidable veto player out of the decision-making arrangement, namely the people, who is less predictable and with whom negotiation is not possible. In this context, cooperation is not motivated by the threat of internal dissolution and early elections as in a parliamentary context, thus by the loss of the executives' decision-making power. It is motivated by the potential 'externalization' of decision-making power which, however, creates the same effect. It creates incentives to bridge the constitutional executive–legislative divide by voluntary power-sharing structures in the form of oversized coalitions.

The distinction between Switzerland as consensual power-sharing democracy and the United States as constitutional power-sharing democracy is further substantiated by the different levels of party organizational strength. Swiss parties – although from a European perspective rather weakly organized – steer political processes to a much greater extent than their American pendants. This is rooted in the core resource in which Swiss parties clearly resemble their European and differ from their American counterparts – the aspect that crucially constitutes parties' role as the core actors in political life: the control over candidate selection. The power of Swiss parties with regard to candidate selection becomes particularly obvious when looking at cantonal practices for the nomination of executive candidates. Until the 1970s open elections were exceptions, hence political competition for office was circumvented. In consolidated three- or four-party systems, usually not more candidates were nominated than positions available (Vatter 2002: 65). Nowadays, open elections have become more frequent since parties are pressed to be more transparent to the public (Vatter 2002: 67). Nevertheless, current practices still indicate how cantonal parties shape the power distribution in their political systems. The fact that legislative and executive candidates are selected by parties constitutes two organizational connections – one between party politician and party leadership and one between executive and legislative representatives of the same party. Although there is no automatism that executive proposals will pass the legislatures unaltered, most proposals pass. Accordingly, asking intergovernmental actors, they fear an intervention through referendum much more than through parliament. Factions might rebel against proposals supported by their own executive representative at times. However, there are regular party meetings at which members of the executives defend the compromises which deviate from individual party programmes but are necessary to avoid intra-executive blockades.

The core weakness of American parties is their inability to control candidate selection. Before running for state election, candidates have to succeed in a primary contest. Hence, candidates are selected by ordinary voters that enrol in an electoral register, not by a party leadership. Moreover, it is problematic to speak of those voters' 'party membership' in the first place; since parties exercise no control over registration, they cannot impose requirements or expel disloyal members. As Katz points out, the participation in the primary elections is open to any voter who meets minimal requirements – 'themselves set by state law rather than by the parties and in some cases allowing participation by people who need never make any pretence of party affinity or affiliation' (1994: 31). Accordingly, registrants pay no dues – a normal source of income for European parties. Furthermore, parties can neither name nor veto nominees. In some states, it is even prohibited by law to endorse particular candidates in the primaries (Katz 1994: 31).

This lack of party control has severe implications for a party's capacity to discipline its incumbent representatives and to link its office holders in the executive and legislative branches. This finds striking expression in the structure of the national parties which directly mirror the executive–legislative divide. The national committees of US parties that correspond to the national executives of the typical European party are only the national committees of the presidential parties. In addition, there are the two caucuses that are not only parliamentary wings but also autonomous organizations that perform most of the functions associated with parties: policy formulation, fund-raising, organizing campaigns, etc. The party platform adopted by the national presidential nominating convention is neither binding for the corresponding congressional parties nor for the individual members (Katz 1994: 28, 31). One consequence of this party organizational weakness is the considerable impact of the executive–legislative divide in the American states on the intergovernmental landscape, an impact which is much more crucial for intergovernmental dynamics than partisan differences. Institutional interests clearly coin the picture, a picture which is dominant in national and in state politics (Schlesinger 1965; Beyle and Dalton 1983; Beyle and Muchmore 1983).[6]

In a nutshell, the referendum threat generating the dominance of voluntary power-sharing in Switzerland backed up by stronger parties justifies its classification as consensual power-sharing democracy as opposed to the constitutional power-sharing democracy in the United States. As a consequence, their comparison allows for a systematic examination of Hypothesis 2 expecting different patterns of integration due to the respective type of power sharing dominant in the two systems.

COMPETING EXPLANATIONS

This section discusses the most important alternative explanations competing with the above hypotheses. It attempts to indicate why the given set of cases enables an adequate isolation of the link between intragovernmental incentives and patterns of intergovernmental institution-building. While the constitution of the most-different-cases design along the core explanatory variables is a major reason to analyse Canadian, Swiss, and American IGR, the control for alternative explanations for intergovernmental institution-building is equally crucial. Clearly, there is not one group of federal cases that shows the desired variance on the side of the independent variable and, simultaneously, controls for any possible alternative explanation. Nevertheless, the selection of the three systems outrules some of the most important alternative accounts.

One fundamental assumption underlying the approach on informal institution-building is that whatever infrastructure is chosen to channel IGR, it is chosen *voluntarily*. In principle, even if there are strong incentives to set up cooperation structures inherent in the constitution, the decision about how to react to these incentives remains with the political actors. The refusal of the Spanish regional governments to engage in formally established intergovernmental conferences (Morata 1991: 9; Graus I Creus 2000: 60) mentioned before is only one example. This implies that it is possible to examine the link between the dominant type of intragovernmental relations and the resulting patterns and structures of IGR in any federal or decentralized system. However, to test the given hypotheses comparatively, it is advantageous to look at federal constitutions that are as 'neutral' as possible with regard to intergovernmental cooperation. Such constitutional settings create only limited dependencies between governmental levels and individual

---

[6] For a comparative analysis of party organizational strength in seven federations, see Thorlakson (2009).

government units and thereby provide maximum leeway for intergovernmental actors to choose the type of IGAs they consider as most profitable. And, as laid out above, this profitability is expected to be defined by incentive structures in governments' home arenas.

Governmental choices to set up weak or strong IGAs are the least influenced in those systems in which each lower level government possesses considerable law-making authority and sufficient fiscal means to exert this authority, usually classified as dual federal systems. Under these conditions, a lower level government can withdraw from interaction and resort to unilateralism whenever it considers such a path to be more profitable than intergovernmental cooperation. Canada, Switzerland, and the United States are chosen as cases because they widely (albeit not perfectly) correspond to the dual federal model in constitutional terms. They can be expected to clearly display the assumed spillover from subunits' internal to their outside relations. Therefore the results will be less obscured by other incentive structures than would be the case when analysing cooperative federal systems such as Germany. In this sense, the study accounts for those forms of cross-boundary interaction and institution building which are not directly motivated by constitutional rules. Following Benz's terminology, the study focuses on modes of 'loose coupling' between lower level governments and the intergovernmental decision-making arenas. These are couplings in which – in contrast to tight coupling – the arenas considered are not formally linked and, consequently, unilateralism is a continuous possibility (2004a: 135). With a comparison of constitutionally dual federal systems, it is possible to demonstrate that intergovernmental processes vary from unilateralism, over ad hoc coordination and co-decision to supragovernmentalism as a function of the intragovernmental executive–legislative relations dominant in the respective polity.

The two core criteria to classify the three systems as formally dual federal are first, the way jurisdictions are allocated. The range of exclusive lower level competences provides leeway for autonomous action on behalf of individual lower level government. Concurrent competences are expected to set opposite incentives since decision-making power is assigned to both levels of government while usually federal legislation prevails in case of conflict. Second, the financial resources available to lower level governments influence whether they also have the financial means to realize their preferred policies. Both factors provide leeway for lower level governments' unilateral actions (whether they use this leeway is another matter).

A comparative assessment of the way jurisdictions are allocated in 10 federal democracies shows that when constructing indices of both concurrent and exclusive state jurisdictions, the three systems turn out to be similar (Bolleyer and Thorlakson 2008). The two indices capture the relative percentage of these types of jurisdictions over the total of all policy fields allocated in a constitution as classified by Watts (1999a). Values range from 0 to 1; higher values in each signify a greater amount of concurrent and exclusive state competences, respectively: The scope of concurrent areas amounts to 0.156 in the United States, 0.063 in Canada, and 0.136 in Switzerland. The values across the 10 systems studied range from 0.025 to 0.997, thus the three systems rank relatively low. The scope of exclusive state jurisdictions is even more similar with 0.178 in the United States, 0.146 in Canada, and 0.136 in Switzerland (with values ranging from 0 to 0.357).[7] In sum, while the range of concurrent competences is limited, lower level governments in all three systems possess a considerable amount of exclusive competences.

The fiscal power of lower level governments can be assessed by governments' revenue share[8] – a crucial measure for their capacity to act independently in their own spheres of competence. In 1995, the revenue share in all three countries was higher than in any other OECD country: 46.72 per cent in Switzerland, 41.65 per cent in the United States, and 52.21 per cent in Canada (Braun 2000: 39, 52–53; see also Thorlakson 2003). A more recent OECD study on fiscal relations reconfirms the special status of these three countries due to their lower level governments' exceptional taxing powers. Using the attribution of subnational tax revenue as percentage of the total tax revenue[9] in 2001 as a proxy, the three countries are again on top of the list – with 40.4 per cent in Switzerland, 31.7 per cent in the United States, and 44.1 per cent in Canada (Joumard and Kongsrud 2003: 164).

In this context, the role of federal grants deserves attention. They might create considerable dependence on the federal government and therefore favour intergovernmental institutionalization between the federal and the lower level governments. The share of grants (the sum of grants received by the local or regional level from the central government as percentage of the revenue of the local and regional level) as specified by Braun is as follows: Switzerland 46.72 per cent; Canada 61.9 per cent; and United States 58.9 per cent (2000: 52–3). This difference is unlikely to create a bias since the institutionalization of IGAs and their mutual integration are expected to be stronger in the Swiss than in the Canadian and the American case, yet Swiss cantons are comparatively less dependent on federal grants.

Conditional grants

One important element the above measure does not capture is the conditionality of federal grants. Whether the federal government attaches conditions to its grants or not is crucial because conditions delimit the recipients' leeway to decide upon policy based on their own preferences. Although the amount of federal money available to lower level governments might be roughly similar, whether strict conditions are attached to it or not makes a considerable difference with regard to

---

[7] For details on the construction of the measures see Bolleyer and Thorlakson (2008).
[8] The sum of revenues of the local and regional level as percentage of the total revenues.
[9] Including tax-sharing arrangements.

lower level autonomy. Recent comparative data on this particular issue is rare. Yet assuming that the basic cross-national variance has not drastically changed, Watts' (1999b: 57) research indicates that in the United States conditional grants make up to 29.6 per cent of the total lower level revenue, in Switzerland 12.3 per cent, and in Canada only 0.9 per cent. These figures imply that Canadian provinces are much less affected by substantial central influence in their decisions since the percentage of conditional grants is minimal, while in the United States it is one-third. In health and post-secondary education, Canada had already moved to a system of block funding in the late 1970s, and reformed its grant system again in the 1990, also moving to block grants in social assistance (Joumard and Kongsrud 2003: 213). In the United States, by contrast, the use of conditional grants and (even worse) unfunded mandates has intensified, clearly expressed in the concept of 'coercive federalism' introduced to describe this increasingly dominant constellation (Kincaid 1990). The problem is how to interpret these cross-national differences. We basically face a 'chicken and egg' problem since it is unclear whether the Canadian provinces are more autonomous because conditional grants do not play a big role or whether, the other way around, there are fewer conditions attached to federal funding because Canadian provinces defend their jurisdictional autonomy more aggressively.

Different pressures on lower level governments to accept federal money is no convincing argument to get out of this circle. In all three systems, lower level governments administer cost-intensive programmes in areas such as health and education, thus have to deliver cost-intensive services to their electorates. At the same time, electoral pressure is much higher in Canada than in Switzerland and the United States due to the majoritarian logic in its lower level governments which in turn allows for the easier assignation of responsibility for failure to provide certain services. The pressure on Canadian lower level governments to take federal money should be therefore higher rather than lower.

It is more convincing to argue that the different handling of federal grants originates in the stronger opposition against federal intrusion, an orientation rooted in intragovernmental incentive structures. In Canada, provincial actors are averse to any effort by the federal government to gain control over how funding is used. Looking at intergovernmental agreements, conditions for spending federal money are loose, and on top of this, the provinces refuse any federal checks into whether the money has been used as stipulated. In the two power-sharing systems, the situation looks strikingly different. The federal government checks how 'its money' is used which is accepted by the lower level governments. Formalized application procedures for the distribution of funding are in place as well as strict reporting requirements on the usage of federal funds. In both systems, the misuse of funds can be formally sanctioned. The orientation is opposite in Canada. Looking at the recent debate around fiscal imbalance, provincial actors deny the distribution of fiscal authority to be adequate in the first place. Since the provinces have too little taxing power in relation to the cost intensity of the services they have to deliver, they demand a reconfiguration of taxing authority to reduce their need for federal funds. This disposition to redefine policy conflicts as jurisdictional disputes is a recurring theme in Canadian federalism which is rooted in the cohesion of power-concentrating governments eager to protect their autonomy.

These are indications that the type of federal grants distributed – conditional or block grants – need to be considered as an outcome of the way lower level actors position themselves towards the federal government, rather than a cause for particular strategies. As Esman (1984) argues, one major source of the very different fiscal relations in Canada and the United States is the internal structure of the individual government. The cohesion of governments in the Canadian case effectively allowed them to push against federal strings. By contrast, the fragmentation of the American states weakened their incentive to unify and insist on their autonomy as political units. It led to vertically oriented intergovernmental structures evolving around individual federal programmes. In a nutshell, the relevance of conditional grants in a federal system can be traced back to the intensity of resistance of lower level governments against those conditions rather than being the reason for their limited resistance. Different levels of conditional grants in our three federal systems are therefore unlikely to bias the later analysis linking intragovernmental incentives with intergovernmental institution-building.

Constitutional courts

Moving on to another important factor, the influence of the judiciary demands consideration. Especially in the United States, pro-federal Supreme Court rulings are often referred to as one important source of state weakness. However, even in the United States, Supreme Court rulings cannot be considered as a major determinant for the states' general reluctance to insist on their own spheres of authority when confronted with Congressional intrusion, be it through federal grants or federal legislation more generally. Although the Supreme Court had supported centralization for several decades, rulings after the mid-1980s preserved state prerogatives 50 per cent of the time (Elazar 1990: 15). This is surprising since the 1985 case *Garcia v. San Antonio Metropolitan Transit Authority* revised earlier pro-state rulings in denying a clear distinction of 'traditional' as opposed to 'non-traditional' state functions leaving the protection of state rights to the political process and, with that, to Congressional grace (Gunlicks 1988: 147–8). Later in the 1990s, the Supreme Court adopted a much more protective position towards state sovereignty (Conlan 2000: 140). This trend led at the end of the 1990s to some Congress-curbing decisions which the court pulled back somewhat in 2003–4 (Dinan and Krane 2006: 328).

How did state governments respond to these shifts? Take the 1990s: the court narrowed federal power and bolstered state authority, thus one could observe a decentralizing push in terms of formal authority. The practical consequences in the intergovernmental arena were mixed. State discretion could be augmented in areas such as drinking-water safety and education. Yet at the same time, the federal government issued legislation in new areas such as voter registration, while criminal law was further 'federalized' (Donahue and Pollack 2001: 91). The reorientations of the court did not generate a more forceful or effective opposition of the states against federal encroachment. This is because only a small part of legal disputes reach the Court in the first place and state courts have – with reference to state constitutions – shown the willingness to extend the protection of states beyond the Supreme Court's interpretation (Hickok 1990: 84). Supreme Court rulings certainly facilitated centralization in the long run. Nonetheless, they do not account for the general reluctance of states to involve the judiciary in the first place or the limited willingness to defend state rights more generally, a tendency which has been observed long before the 1985 ruling as, for instance, Riker indicates in his seminal work on federalism (1964: 103–4). Usually, states only consider legal means when unable to extract sufficient concessions in exchange for central intervention. This disposition on behalf of the American states is reinforced by one major disadvantage of court decisions. Once taken, they cannot be negotiated anymore reducing the attractiveness of litigation, as many state actors interviewed pointed out. They prefer to negotiate solutions directly with the federal level, negotiations which are usually driven by executive actors more strongly interested in financing policies than protecting legislative powers. Here we arrive at the internal fragmentation of the states, in particular the separation between executive and legislative interests as generated by compulsory power-sharing in the states, an argument we return to in detail later on.

Bringing in a cross-national perspective, a judicial account looses further ground. In Switzerland, we do not find a constitutional court to protect the cantons from authority migration to the federal level in the first place. Accordingly, given enough political support for a national handling of an issue falling into cantonal jurisdiction from federal institutions, in particular the second house of parliament, the *Ständerat*,[10] there is – strictly speaking – no legal protection. Leaving the possibility of a popular vote aside, from a legal point of view, state rights are on comparatively safer grounds in the United States. Despite this difference, in both power-sharing democracies, intergovernmental actors reject the idea of passing decisions to an external, 'neutral' body which excludes any negotiation between the political actors concerned by a decision. A Swiss official put it the following way: 'This must not be – that a court makes the laws. It would disturb the negotiations between the different partners. There is a very sensitive balance...'.[11] Accordingly, during the recent federalism reform, the introduction of a constitutional court to resolve federal–cantonal conflicts over competences

---

[10] The *Ständerat* is composed of two directly elected representatives per canton (except of the half-cantons). Ständerat supports national legislation in areas of cantonal authority is not that unlikely since it does not represent cantonal governments but the cantonal populations (Linder 1999).

[11] Das könnte nicht sein, dass ein Gericht ersatzweise Gesetze macht. Das würde die Aushandlungen zwischen den verschiedenen Partnern aus der Balance bringen. Das ist sehr fein austariert...'. IGA CH XI, 28 March 2006: 2–3 (IGA CH indicates staff of Swiss IGA).

was debated but did not find sufficient political support. Given closely knit negotiation networks within and between the cantons and federal government, a strong constitutional court could easily bypass their negotiations.

Bringing in the Canadian case, an alternative line of argument could point at the much bigger interest of the cantons in inter-cantonal problem-solving to prevent federal intrusion than of the Canadian lower level governments which can call upon a constitutional court if necessary. Yet in Canada, Supreme Court rulings do not provide a sufficient protection of lower level autonomy either. While early judicial rulings favoured provincial autonomy, contemporary rulings swing the pendulum towards enhanced federal power (Baier 2002). This is also the perception of intergovernmental officials who are reluctant to pass an issue to the court because of its 'federal bias' and perceive any challenge of the status quo to result in a likely enhancement of federal power (Johns, O'Reilly, and Inwood 2006). Hence, it is not the case that individual provinces resort to unilateral strategies because they rely on favourable Supreme Court rulings whenever they get into conflicts over competences with the federal government and therefore do not need to strengthen their position through interprovincial collaboration. The Supreme Court's federalism jurisprudence tends to supplement rather than subvert political negotiations. It initiates negotiation processes whose outcome tends to be politically prescribed. The protection of federalism is not a court-centric process (Kelly and Murphy 2005: 221–2). In order to understand why the provinces wanted to and could protect their autonomy effectively, we have to look at them as political units and at the way they work internally. In sum, while constitutional courts are important actors when it comes to understanding the long-term evolution of federal systems, they do not give us a satisfying account of why and how lower level governments handle the competences assigned to them the way they do.

Size and complexity

When comparing Canada, Switzerland, and the United States, one natural question arising refers to the relevance of size. Roughly speaking, the sizes of lower level governments are similarly diverse across the three countries chosen. In all three systems, we find extreme discrepancies in territorial size and with it economic strength thinking of Ontario and Prince Edwards Island, Zurich and Uri, or Texas and Maryland. While these discrepancies can complicate the set-up of IGAs which presuppose the formal equality of each participating government, it goes for all three systems that stronger units try to get a special treatment. Thus, it is difficult to systematically link the differences in institutionalization and integration we find across the three systems systematically to this factor. Moreover, individual lower level governments might occasionally refuse to cooperate or even opt out because they can afford to go on their own (such as Québec in Canada, the bigger American states such as California and Texas, or Zurich in Switzerland). This, however, does not explain why in one country the medium-size and smaller lower level governments push for much stronger IGAs than in the other. They would profit from pooling power towards the federal government in each of the three contexts.

Nor can the differences in country size implying different levels of proximity deliver a convincing account. In contrast to the situation in the United States and Canada, the small size of the Swiss polity certainly creates additional pressure for cross-jurisdictional coordination due to scarcity of resources and spillover problems among the cantons. Yet simultaneously, 'smallness' leads to a scarcity of valuable resources and in turn motivates the cantons to insist on their territory, their political competences, their financial resources, and their independence (Neidhart 2002: 119–20).[12] Moreover, given the dense personal networks in Swiss federalism, it is puzzling that strong IGAs should be necessary at all. In sum, it remains unclear whether small size fosters cooperation or competition – investment in strong IGAs or reliance on direct interpersonal exchanges.

Nor do we solve the problem by using size as a proxy for social heterogeneity and linking large size to territorial and cultural diversity (thereby complicating cooperation), or assuming that small size implies homogeneity (in turn facilitating cooperation). Switzerland, characterized by a heterogeneous societal structure in a small-scale territory, cross-cuts this logic. Finally skipping size altogether and starting out from societal heterogeneity as explanatory factor, the latter implies a higher level of conflict than in homogeneous countries. Therefore, we should expect a lower institutionalization in the more segmented Swiss context than in the United States. The theoretical framework, however, expects institutionalization to be similar, while integration should be stronger in Switzerland. Since the empirics confirm the latter, heterogeneity is no strong rivalling factor.

Starting out from the number of lower level governments, one might argue that the lower the number of governments is, the lower are the transaction costs (Breton 1996: 211) that can be saved by IGAs. Vice versa, the higher this number is, the more valuable these bodies become. Again, this factor does not deliver an unambiguous account of differences in institution building. If the number of lower level governments was the major determinant of the strength of IGAs, arrangements including the same number of units (regional bodies in Switzerland and the United States as compared to Canadian national arrangements) should roughly show similar levels of institutionalization. The observation that regional and national IGAs are similarly weak or strong within one country, as the empirical chapters will show, indicates that one needs to look at a factor which has similar effects throughout a federal system - whether we look at regional or nationwide institutionalization processes. In contrast to the impact of intragovernmental dynamics, the relative number of lower level governments included in various IGAs does not fall into this category.

---

[12] Accordingly, the idea of permanently fusing several cantons to solve the problem of territorial entities perceived as too small has been repeatedly rejected, and the individual cantons still attempt to use their autonomy to considerable degrees (Freiburghaus and Zehnder 2003: 1).

Second chambers

In many works on federalism, the second chamber is considered the most crucial institution of 'intra-state federalism', meaning federal bargaining within national institutions (Simeon 1972). Does the nature of second chambers allow for any systematic conclusion about the patterns and structures of IGR in our three systems? Indeed, their second chambers differ considerably. The Canadian Senate is not an adequate channel for territorial demands. Although it can veto legislation, it is inferior to the first chamber in terms of representational make-up and legitimacy, hence, in practice, does not function as veto player. The Swiss and the American Senates, by contrast, are very strong second chambers which represent each lower level government equally through two directly elected senators. Both exert powerful vetoes (Lijphart 1999: 207–12). It has been widely questioned whether the directly elected Swiss and American Senates represent predominantly territorial interests. Yet even if territorial lines of conflict only occasionally shape their behaviour, they might nonetheless strengthen the positions of the 'constitutive parts' in their federations more than the appointed Canadian Senate does. Assuming now that strong interstate federalism – bargaining between central and lower level governments – can partially compensate for a weak second chamber,[13] the demand for strong IGAs should be stronger in Canada than in Switzerland and the United States. The theoretical framework just presented, however, expects the exact opposite, namely weaker intergovernmental structures in Canada than in the two power-sharing democracies. If this framework holds, the nature of second chambers cannot provide a convincing account.

SUMMARY

Since we find a rather small amount of concurrent legislation and considerable exclusive lower level competences as well as strong financial powers of lower level governments in all three systems, the different types of executive–legislative relations should display their impact on intergovernmental institution-building clearly. The conditionality of grants varies across three systems, which is more likely to be a consequence of different levels of collective resistance against federal intrusion than its root. Factors such as the size of the country or the nature of the second chamber doubtlessly have an impact on the working of the federal systems studied here. Still, they do not deliver a convincing account for the patterns of informal institution-building.

---

[13] This argument is ex ante problematic since it assumes some sort of trade-off between the participation of lower level governments in national law-making (through bicameralism) and IGR. The latter is usually concerned with either the coordination of lower level policies in spheres of subnational competence or the coordination of central and lower level activities in overlapping or shared areas of competence, thus clearly distinct from national decision-making, which bicameralism refers to.

THE ANALYSIS OF POLICY-SPECIFIC
INSTITUTIONALIZATION: SELECTING POLICY FIELDS

Up to this point we have been exclusively concerned with cross-national differences, factors that systematically vary across our three federal systems. This is in line with our theoretical framework which implies that such a factor, the nature of intragovernmental relations, drives institution-building processes in IGR. Quite naturally, this study takes a cross-country perspective: looking at a range of policy-specific intergovernmental bodies in each country. However, we cannot ignore that their institutional development might vary to a larger extent along policy characteristics – most notably along the mode of competence distribution in the particular policy field or the conflict potential inherent in the subject-matter dealt with. Simply put, looking at policy-specific IGAs, the variation across policy fields within the systems could be greater than the overall variation across systems. The theoretical arguments might indeed hold regarding the institutional development of generalist arrangements such as the Council of the Federation or the Conference of Cantonal Executives which deal with cross-sectoral issues. To show that intragovernmental incentives have an overall stronger impact than policy characteristics, however, we need to look at the differences between policy-specific bodies within the three countries in a systematic manner.

To do so, intergovernmental structures in eight policy fields are examined in each of the three federal systems. These policy fields capture core areas of subnational legislative competence. Due to their relevance for voters as well as their financial intensity, they rank high on government priority lists. Simultaneously, the types of conflict which dominate in the different policy fields differ considerably. As the policy literature emphasizes, each policy field embraces a variety of issues representing different interest constellations (Lowi 1964; Scharpf 1997).[14] Nonetheless, comparing a range of areas allows for a reasonable estimation of the relative conflict potential. For instance, in comparison to other areas, fiscal policy can, overall, be classified as a 'high conflict area' since those issues with redistributive implications can be assumed to be more numerous than, for instance, in environmental policy. If patterns of institution building in the eight policy fields (differing in their mode of competence distribution and conflict potential) are more similar within one systemic context than these patterns are in the same policy field across different contexts, we can be more confident about

---

[14] Accordingly, intergovernmental interaction patterns would be shaped by the interest configuration induced by the particular policy problem at hand (Lowi 1964; Scharpf 1997). This study, however, focuses on the organizational infrastructure created to frame all processes within one policy area, an infrastructure which therefore deals with a variety of different problem types. To check for policy-specific impacts on these overall infrastructures, it is therefore necessary to start out from the overall conflict potential based on an estimation which problem types are particularly characteristic for a policy field. Were the major aim to account for the substance of or the processes towards individual intergovernmental agreements, Scharpf's (1997) problem types would be the appropriate analytical starting-point.

the validity of the results. The areas considered are *fiscal policy, economic policy, transportation, justice and crime control, education, environmental policy, health, and social policy*. The presence of own (preferably legislative) competences is a crucial precondition because the analysis of intergovernmental structures in a policy area in which lower level governments do not have their own say will offer few insights. Incentives to institutionalize are usually weaker since lower level governments have no competences to handle or to protect.[15] If – based on this range of policy fields – a systemic pattern in the level of institutionalization across the sectors becomes visible, while policy-specific rationales do no not help to account for the given pattern, our cross-national approach most likely holds water.

Looking at IGR from a policy-specific perspective, one might however wonder why to focus on sector-wide structures in the first place, rather than issue-specific ones. Whole policy fields usually embrace a wide range of diverse issues. Coming from a legal background, one might further argue that in constitutional terms it is rare that whole sectors are assigned exclusively to one level of government. We indeed find IGAs that are responsible for only a particular sub-sector *instead of* or *coexisting with* an arrangement embracing a whole sector.[16] Nonetheless, the focus on whole sectors makes sense in light of the research question how lower level *governments* deal with cooperation demands and what kind of channels they set up to do so. Since within these governments, policy responsibility is usually assigned along sectoral lines to departments and ministries, it is reasonable to look at arrangements which reflect this internal distribution of policy-making power. In fact, the three systems analysed confirm that issues which are treated by different bureaucracies 'at home' are often considered by different interstate arrangements and vice versa – an insight also supported by research on international regimes (Keohane 1982: 341). While a focus on sector-wide structures simplifies the picture, it will still give us the insights we need to judge which factors shape IGR more strongly, policy-specific variables or intragovernmental dynamics.

---

[15] In most sectors, lower level governments have their own legislative competences in all three systems; in a few remaining areas, legislative subnational competences are present only in two systems. The policy areas which are not considered are agriculture, forestry, and immigration. This mode of selection deliberately excludes areas of exclusive federal competence. Although lower level governments can make joint efforts to influence areas such as foreign policy or international trade due to the impact which federal action in this area has on other subnational jurisdictions, these structures can be expected to be more fluid and less representative for the overall patterns of IGR. The motivation to invest in costly organizational structures is limited, since first, the subunits have no incentive to strengthen concertation in order to protect own powers collectively, and second, the chance that such endeavours pay off without having any formal say are low. Finally, areas which exist only in individual countries, such as Aboriginal issues in Canada, are not considered.

[16] For instance, in Switzerland, one finds a Conference of Health Directors and one responsible for the sub-area of sanitation.

EXAMINING STRUCTURAL PATTERNS AND THEIR MICRO-FOUNDATION: METHODS

In order to capture the incentives in lower level governments generated by power concentration or power sharing and the type of power sharing, I refer to election results, data on cabinet type, government composition, as well as on characteristics of the institutional setting. Institutionalization and integration as the two dependent variables are widely assessed on the basis of document analysis of IGA publications, secondary literature, and interview material. This mix of methods and material allows for the assessment of structural features as well as of the respective patterns of interaction underlying them.

To understand the *mechanisms* linking intragovernmental and intergovernmental features, and hence, the *motives* of the actors involved and their view on the driving forces of intergovernmental dynamics, 81 semi-structured interviews with intergovernmental actors of on average one hour have been conducted. These provide the basis for detailed process analysis (Silverman 1993; Bryman 2001). The three major groups of actors interviewed are federal and lower level officials as well as intergovernmental personnel employed in the respective IGAs. Furthermore, the interview material covers executive and legislative intergovernmental actors as well as personnel of IGAs representing different government branches. Finally, for the comparative assessment of policy-specific IGAs, I included officials and staff active in the range of policy fields. Since these groups pursue different interests, triangulation of their viewpoints helps to strengthen the validity of the findings. Since not all lower level governments, totalling 89, and not all IGAs on the national and regional level could be covered through interviews, officials have been consciously selected according to the varying size, territorial location, and language of their lower level governments to assure a maximal variation of opinions and avoid a regionally biased perspective. Interviewees are primarily non-elected officials and IGA staff, while politically elected officials (executive or legislative) have been interviewed in smaller number. All three groups have equally detailed insights on the daily processes of intergovernmental management and the typical dynamics. However, the risk that the group of elected officials depicts the process dynamics in a biased manner is higher than in the case of non-elected officials, especially if cooperation failure results from a prioritization of short-term political interests over long-term benefits.[17]

---

[17] To assure anonymity, the following abbreviations are used when interviewees have been cited directly: IGA – staff of intergovernmental arrangement; Fed – federal government; POfficial – provincial official; SOfficial – state official; and COfficial – cantonal official.

THE INTERNAL LIFE OF LOWER LEVEL GOVERNMENTS IN CANADA, SWITZERLAND, AND THE UNITED STATES

The following section introduces measurements for the four mechanisms resulting from lower-level power-concentration or power-sharing: the stability of the interest configuration, the competitive pressure, the degree of government congruence, and the autonomy losses involved in IGR.

Among the four mechanisms springing from the intragovernmental dynamics generated by power concentration and power sharing, the measurement of the relative *autonomy loss* of lower level governments when engaging in IGR is the most straightforward. To capture this feature, I refer to the average number of one-party cabinets with and without a majority in the constitutive governments. Both cabinet types reject sharing power already in the inside which can be expected to spill over to the outside. Minority cabinets can be expected to generate similar dynamics as one-party majority governments, since they are often located in the centre and have a bilateral opposition. Under these conditions, assuring legislative majority support for own legislative proposals should be fairly unproblematic (Green-Pedersen 2001; Tsebelis 2002). Finally, we need to question what configuration corresponds to a one-party cabinet in U.S. presidentialism. Here, the average number of united government configurations is considered as an analogous proxy for the relative autonomy loss. In Switzerland too, executive and legislative elections are separate but in contrast to the United States divided government configurations are unusual.[18] Consequently, as in the Canadian case, the measure will be based on the executive configuration.

In order to measure the internally generated 'competitive pressure' which affects the *stability of the interest configuration* and the tendency towards *blame shifting*, the average *alternation rate* is used as indicator. With regard to government turnover, a distinction can be made between partial and complete alternations. A partial alternation is given when some government parties are replaced while others stay in office (Strøm 1990). Complete alternations are most likely given one-party cabinets. They become less likely the more fragmented a party system is and the more parties participate in coalitions. Evidently, complete alternations generate more competitive pressure than partial ones. Since it is crucial to capture the electoral pressure in particular, I count only those governments that have been formed after an election without considering alternations during the term. Thus, the alternation rate will be assessed in relation to the absolute number of elections. Regarding the presidential systems characterizing the American states, I qualify a shift from one unified government configuration[19]

---

[18] For a detailed analysis of cantonal executives see Vatter 2002: ch. 2.

[19] Unified government is defined as the configuration when the majorities of both chambers and the executive belong to the same party.

dominated by Democrats to one unified configuration dominated by Republicans and vice versa as complete alternation.[20] Again, in the Swiss case, the alternation rate will be assessed based on the number of executive turnover only as in the Canadian case. Using the rate of complete alternations as main indicator, the number of partial alternations is considered in addition to get a more detailed picture.

To capture the substantial make-up of the *interest configuration*, we must specify the average ideological *congruence* between the governments in office. A measure of congruence does not primarily tell us how frequently actors have to adapt to changes such as the alternation rate. Instead, it qualifies the ideological complexity of the respective configurations. Congruence is assumed if parties in different governments belong to the same party family even if the party system is decentralized since, all in all, the conflict potential between these parties should be lower than between completely different ones.[21]

To capture government congruence in the three systems, a measure of non-overlapping governments is introduced based on the Laasko–Taagepera index. It captures the weight of dominant party configurations on the horizontal level.[22] Generally speaking, one has to assess the degree to which the same type of parties tend to be in office across the different Power level governments. As proposed in the literature, the congruence between the two levels of government is assessed by the average percentage of lower level governments that deviate in their composition from the national government in office (Downs 1998: 138–9; Thorlakson 2007). The *congruence on the horizontal level* crucial for this study can be measured similarly.

The proposed measure captures ideological discrepancies between individual governments and the weight of different government constellations on the horizontal level. The operationalization proceeds in two steps. The more the different governments overlap, the more moderately the governments tend to behave towards each other. Accordingly, one proxy for the conflict potential is the percentages of non-overlapping governments. Where this percentage is low, also the conflict potential tends to be low. Where it is higher, intra-horizontal

---

[20] It could be argued that this is more demanding than the measure for parliamentary systems since three different elections need to favour one party to lead to unified government. This, however, is difficult to avoid. A similar problem occurs, for instance, when comparing a two-party system with a multiparty system. Usually, given two-party systems complete turnover is much easier than in multiparty systems.

[21] When using means one has to pay attention to the changes over time. In the cases analysed in this study, they have been moderate.

[22] Note that it ignores the strength of the individual parties composing coalition cabinets and is not based on a positioning of cabinets on the left-right scale (see, for an alternative measure, Bolleyer and Bytzek 2009).

conflict becomes more likely.[23] I count one-party cabinets plus all configurations which are composed of different sets of parties as non-overlapping governments.

In a second step, the relative weight of non-overlapping governments will be assessed according to the Laasko–Taagepera index on the effective number parties (Laakso and Taagepera 1979). Based on this index, the formula for the effective number of non-overlapping governments is $N = 1/\Sigma s_i^2$ in which s_i is the proportion of subunits governed by the ith party configuration. The higher the figure which indicates the number of distinct configurations (5.0 instead of 2.0), the more complex agreement becomes. The more even the distribution of the party configurations' representation in the subunits at a given point (indicated by 2.0 or 3.0 instead of 2.4 or 3.6), the greater the conflict potential that exists because the ideological profiles are represented with about equal strength. Taken together, an average of 5 in one country as compared to 3.5 in another indicates that in the first country five equally represented configurations have to find agreement compared to four non-equally distributed in the second. In the latter configuration, the conflict potential is lower.

Note that the percentage of overlapping governments and the effective number of non-overlapping governments need to be considered together. For instance, an average 95 per cent one-party cabinet indicates a high potential for conflict. However, if all governments are formed by the same party, the effective number of non-overlapping governments is 1 and indicates that in fact the opposite is the case, that the horizontal level is ideologically very homogenous. Moreover, the greater the overlap, the less relevant the relative weight of the non-overlapping governments. If the overlapping governments form over 80 per cent, the effective number of non-overlapping governments is of limited interest and will not be analysed. Although this measure is rather simple, it captures the weight of dominant party configurations on the horizontal level of a federal system and the degree to which lower level governments are likely to be unified or divided quite adequately.

The range of measures is used to assess the intragovernmental dynamics in Canada, Switzerland, and the United States. The comparison of the figures in Table 2.1 allows specifying an incentive profile of each country whose impacts on institutionalization and integration are analysed in the following chapter. The data used covers the governments formed after the regional elections of 1980 to 2005. The time frame of the analysis is limited, but the case study literature indicates a considerable continuity with regard to the overall working of executive–legislative relations already before this period. Therefore, the results of the analysis should

---

[23] The relative size of parties which participate in different subnational coalitions also makes a difference. Yet even if only a small coalition partners 'links' one lower level government with the other, a moderating effect can be expected.

A Rationalist Account of Intergovernmental Institution-Building 57

TABLE 2.1. *Characteristics of lower level governments in three federal systems*

Federal System	One-Party Governments (%)	Complete Alternations (%)	Non-Overlapping Governments (%)	Average Effective Number of Non-Overlapping Governments
Canada	100	28.7[a]	100	2.735
United States	43[b]	0	43	1.651
Switzerland	3	0	3.5	—[c]

Note: Results based on Dyck (1986) supplemented by own data, data provided by the Swiss Office for Statistics and by the National Conference of State Legislatures.

[a] Range 0 per cent Alberta to 50 per cent Québec.
[b] Range 37–49 per cent.
[c] The percentage of non-overlapping governments is only 4 per cent, the effective number of non-overlapping governments need not be assessed since it cannot tell something substantial about the nature of the configuration.

paint a broader picture since the period under examination shows typical features for the working of these systems, thus reflects long-lasting tendencies.

As Table 2.1 indicates, Canada has the highest percentage of one-party governments, the highest rate of complete alterations, the lowest average number of decision makers, and the lowest rate of overlapping governments. Starting with the dominant cabinet type, all lower level governments since 1980 were formed by one party alone and virtually all of them had a majority of seats. Autonomy losses generated by intergovernmental interaction are therefore high and should weaken the provincial actors' willingness to invest in IGAs. In addition, the number of complete alternations indicates a comparatively high competitive pressure within the provinces, which favours blame shifting and thereby undermines cross-boundary exchanges. Moreover, the interest configuration is likely to change rapidly, which makes flexible ad hoc coordination profitable. Since there is only one decision maker per province,[24] the transaction costs caused by ad hoc coordination are low and with these the incentive to invest in bodies, which could lower these costs even further. This effect is enhanced by the average ideological incongruence of horizontal interest configurations. There are no government coalitions; none of the ideological configurations have overlapped compared to an average of 43 per cent non-overlapping governments in the United States and an average of 3.5 per cent in Switzerland. An average effective number of non-overlapping governments of 2.735 indicates that there has been no dominant government type which could have unified the horizontal level ideologically. Instead, two to three configurations have been continuously competing for influence.[25]

---

[24] The territories have improved their position within the federation over time. However, they are not independent from the central government, hence are in a weaker position than the provinces.

[25] This is supported by the bifurcated party system (Rentzsch 2001: 2–3), which increases the likelihood of ideologically hostile governments being in office. This is particularly true since the collapse of the Progressive Conservatives in 1993 and the rise of regional parties like the Reform Party and the Bloc Québécois considerably weakened the potential for inter-regional brokerage between federal and regional parties (Meekison, Telford, and Lazar 2002: 11).

Overall, intra-provincial and with it intra-horizontal dynamics in Canada should clearly render the institutionalization of IGAs and their mutual integration difficult.

The American case takes a middle position between Canadian and Swiss lower level dynamics. The effective number of non-overlapping governments (1.651) shows that one party has usually ruled in most of the states. Hence, the conflict potential between the states due to ideological incongruence has been fairly moderate. The percentage of non-overlapping governments is on average only 43 per cent, meaning that in a majority of states each party occupies at least one branch of government, which also moderates conflict in interstate relations since parties tend to be represented in core government institutions in most of the states. At the same time, it complicates intra-state relations. The separation of branches as a constitutional power-sharing structure characterizes the internal political process to a wider extent than party dynamics. This brings us back to the organizational weakness of parties in the United States (Katz 1994) and the dominance of constitutional structures which necessarily has implications for the interpretation of the effective number of non-overlapping governments as laid out in Table 2.1. Although there has been an overweight of unified state governments over the years, this indicates a limited conflict potential rather than a unifying effect on the horizontal level. The complexity of the configuration remains high due to compulsory power-sharing in each state. Moreover, since there have been no complete alternations, the competitive pressure is limited, which reduces incentives for blame shifting. In sum, the rather low competitive pressure and the low autonomy losses involved in horizontal cooperation from the perspective of individual states imply that states should willingly invest in institutionalized IGAs able to facilitate interstate interaction. The party-based measures have reinforced the claim that constitutionally defined compulsory power-sharing exerts a stronger impact on both intra- and interstate processes than programmatic differences between political parties. Correspondingly, constitutional fragmentation – hence voluntary power-sharing – within the states is expected to weaken IGAs' mutual integration.

In Switzerland, intra-cantonal dynamics set very favourable incentives for the institutionalization of IGAs and their mutual integration. The competitive pressure is very low since there have been no complete alternations. By contrast, the number of partial alternations in Switzerland (29 per cent) is quite high. However, one needs to be careful when interpreting this figure. With on average four to five effective parties, the Swiss party system is considerably more fragmented on the subnational level than the Canadian one (Fagagnini 1978; Ladner 2001: 127). Logically, partial alternations are much more likely, where the respective executive constellations are more complex. In fact, the impact on partial alternations on the overall interest configuration is limited. As Vatter's analysis of changes in the partisan compositions of cantonal executives (1945–95) shows: most partial alternations are minor since they change less than half of the executives' composition (2002: 69).[26] Consequently, despite 29 per cent of partial alternations, the stability of the interest configuration remains high. This favours the investment into and the maintenance of strong intergovernmental bodies.

Moreover, only 3 per cent of the cantonal executives have been one-party governments and the number of non-overlapping governments is only 3.5 per cent. Hence, autonomy losses for the individual governments are low and the conflict potential between governments is limited. Ideological conflict is neutralized intragovernmentally since most political parties are in office across the range of lower level governments (Vatter 2002). Again, the conditions to set up strong IGAs are favourable. Moreover, there is little incentive for blame-shifting strategies since electoral pressure is low, as indicated by the absence of complete alternations. Simultaneously, due to the high number of oversized governments, a party easily blames executives in which own partisan pendants participate. Finally, in contrast to the United States, Swiss parties are organizationally sufficiently strong to bridge the constitutional executive–legislative divide. They allow the cantonal executives to monopolize IGR and represent one cantonal position in the intergovernmental arena which should facilitate intergovernmental integration.

Based on the theoretical framework and the incentive profiles specified above, we end up with the following expectations: in Canada, due to power concentration in the range of lower level governments, neither the institutionalization of individual IGAs nor their mutual integration should be high. In the United States, the institutionalization of IGAs should be considerable since power sharing within the states sets favourable incentives. The mutual integration of these IGAs, however, is likely to be negatively affected by the constitutional fragmentation resulting from the compulsory nature of power sharing in them. In Switzerland, due to voluntary power-sharing in the cantons, the internally generated incentives favour both institutionalization and integration. In order to examine these claims empirically, the following chapters will assess the institutionalization and integration of generalist and policy-specific IGAs in Canada, Switzerland, and the United States.

---

[26] Only once were four executive mandates changed after an election. The same is true regarding changes of three mandates.

3
Intergovernmental Institutionalization in Canada

Before we move into the individual case studies, the first section of this chapter provides an overview of the patterns of IGR in the three countries as they are presented in the literature. It shows that each 'country literature' rests on certain assumptions about the nature of the system it deals with. These assumptions are uncontested and taken as self-evident, which is problematic. It means that due to the lack of a comparative framework of analysis, each country's literature has systematically generated its own biases with regard to the working of intergovernmental patterns and structures. When adopting a comparative point of view, it becomes evident in the literature that certain questions have been systematically sidestepped and, as a consequence, remained unanswered. Unresolved questions are the following: why should the Canadian provinces behave as competitively towards each other as towards the federal government if the provincial level as a whole could strengthen its position through collectively coordinated action? Why should one expect that intra-cantonal power-sharing leads to power sharing in the intergovernmental arena as well? Why does the literature on American federalism treat the American states' limited resistance against central intrusion as a premise rather than a puzzle?

The introductory section also addresses the implication of a central restriction of the analysis, the question of long-term changes of IGR in our three countries. Neither the theoretical framework nor the empirical study accounts for long-term developments since they do not identify triggers which motivate changes in intergovernmental patterns and structures. However, they do specify 'corridors of adaptation' and, hence, constraints on institution building resulting from intragovernmental dynamics which remained quite similar over time as demonstrated above. To substantiate this claim, it is crucial to show that the case study literature has identified enduring features, an 'overall logic' characterizing federal dynamics in each country, irrespective of changes on the micro level of intergovernmental management which occurred over time. Following these general sections, the chapter moves on to the analysis of intergovernmental institutionalization in Canadian federalism.

INTERGOVERNMENTAL RELATIONS IN THREE COUNTRY LITERATURES: BLUEPRINTS, PREMISES, AND UNRESOLVED PUZZLES

The Canadian blueprint

In the already considerable literature on Canadian IGR, the existing institutional structures have been usually described as weak and processes as ad hoc and predominantly bilateral. At the same time, however, scholars point to changes in intergovernmental interaction over time. It has been argued that after a period of central dominance via funding after the Second World War (when establishing the welfare state) and a very competitive period from the 1960s onwards, the present climate is one of 'collaborative' (i.e. cooperative) federalism. The core of this mode is the principle of codetermination of broad national policies through a partnership of two equal, autonomous but interdependent orders of government whose aim is to exercise power 'in a coordinated manner' (Simeon 2001: 55–7; Cameron and Simeon 2002: 49, 63). From a comparative viewpoint, the term 'collaborative' federalism is somewhat misleading. This is especially the case when comparing the Canadian situation to Swiss federalism, where actors strongly engage in co-decision processes across jurisdictional boundaries framed by highly developed IGAs. More importantly, the basic interaction patterns have not changed as much as the appraisal of the recent 'collaborative style' indicates. Multilateral agreements struck during the last decades have been interpreted as the most evident expression of this move towards collaborative federalism. In this period, several multilateral agreements such as the Agreement of Internal Trade in 1992, the 1998 Canada-Wide Accord on Environmental Harmonization, and the Social Union Framework Agreement in 1999 have been signed by provincial governments. Some scholars have interpreted these agreements as a major turn in Canadian IGR, in particular as steps towards a more reliable and more inclusive mode of intergovernmental interaction. In terms of their capacity to settle intergovernmental conflict and achieve cross-jurisdictional policy-harmonization, however, the results have been rather mixed (Kennett 1998; Lazar and McIntosh 1998; Skogstad 2000; Winfield 2002; Simmons 2004).

Indeed, as far as the mere signing of these agreements expresses the participating governments' endeavour to stabilize IGR, they can already be read as a success. Yet changes in the basic character of Canadian IGR have still been minor. Most fundamentally, the institutional machinery established by the Agreement of Internal Trade, for instance, is not considered capable of inducing governments to agree on the host of outstanding issues. Comparing the Agreement of Internal Trade with the European Treaties, observers noted that governments avoided precisely those aspects of the European Treaties to be implemented in Canada that have been most successful in removing internal barriers in Europe. Accordingly, instead of establishing an external body able to propose regulation transcending individual government interests, the function of the secretariat created through the agreement is purely administrative. It also lacks the resources to draft proposals. In fact, the Agreement of Internal Trade is run on the administrative level while ministers do not meet for periods of several years. There is no qualified majority voting, hence the removal of any sectoral barrier still requires unanimity. Furthermore, there is no way to enforce compliance. Although retaliatory action is possible to punish non-compliance, it is often costly to impose. The rather pessimistic conclusion to be drawn is that the agreement fails to create confidence in the ability of intergovernmental negotiations to fashion effective arrangements for collective action (Kennett 1998: 30).

The Social Union Framework Agreement points to a second typical problem in Canadian IGR: the low precision of agreements. The agreement refers to a series of substantial yet very general principles. These principles are difficult to reconcile which allows each participant to weight and implement them in a very different way. According to experts, this agreement is not mainly about the content of policy. Instead, it intends to strengthen the commitment related to mobility and public health care as well as the coherence of policy making through joint planning (Lazar 2000: 101, 107), which leads us to the core dynamic in the Canadian intergovernmental arena, which easily undermines efforts of such joint planning. While the federal government makes considerable efforts to steer provincial policy-making through financial incentives, the lower level governments' willingness to 'exit' and to act unilaterally is very pronounced. This is a general disposition rooted in intragovernmental incentive structures, as will be shown later. The relevance of this pattern for the Canadian federation can hardly be overestimated since formal competence redistribution through constitutional reform has proven unfeasible. Hence, intergovernmental negotiations have become all the more important as a functional equivalent to renew the federation (Lazar and McLean 2000: 166).

Quite naturally, depending on the type of policy, intergovernmental exchanges vary, as assessed in greater detail below. Yet despite these cross-sectoral differences, the inclination to avoid power sharing in the intergovernmental arena can be identified as an overall pattern. It is immediately reflected in the institutional make-up of IGAs and is clearly distinguishable from dynamics prevalent in other federal systems. The disinclination towards power sharing, while facing growing coordination demands, has produced the somewhat paradoxical result in that Canadian federalism has become more disentangled (Lazar and McLean 2000: 166). This observation indicates that growing coordination pressure does not imply more cooperation. In the opposite, depending on the governments' orientation, they might try to reduce the overlap of competences instead.

Irrespective of the growing density of exchanges, structural adaptation can be easily prevented by intragovernmental dynamics. The impacts of the latter become visible in agreements such as the Agreement of Internal Trade. Intergovernmental actors try to separate spheres of competences more clearly in order to protect their spheres of autonomy instead of strengthening IGAs. At the same time, growing interdependence intensifies interaction and multiplies situations in which conflict can arise (Meekison, Telford, and Lazar 2002: 22). Since intergovernmental structures are not well equipped to moderate conflict, intense interaction leads to a vicious circle in which high conflict intensity systematically undermines the creation of IGAs able to moderate conflict in the first place.

Certainly, it is bold to claim that over the last decades Canadian IGR have not changed. Yet, it is far less bold to argue that the basic patterns – nourished by rather stable political dynamics that drive the intergovernmental game – show a remarkable resilience and continuity and forcefully feed back into the micro-dynamics of intergovernmental management. As Simeon characterizes the provinces' behaviour in 2005 when assessing the changes in Canadian IGR since the publication of his path-breaking book on 'Federal-Provincial Diplomacy' in the 1960s:

> Today's story seems much the same: yes, greater funding to assure Ottawa's place in leading areas, such as child care; but no, you have no right to tell us what to do, because you no longer have the political and fiscal levers to make it so. If we are to have national standards, they cannot be dictated; they can only emerge from intergovernmental consensus. This was also the message of the 60s. (2005: 12)

Recent studies of IGR across different policy fields support this portrait. When looking at the basic institutional structure and operations typical for Canadian IGR on the macro level also Johns, O'Reilly, and Inwood (2006) find no noteworthy changes over the last ten years. Patterns remain similar because the driving forces defining the nature of the system remained similar as well.

Surprisingly enough, the competitive nature of Canadian IGR has not been made subject to a comparative and theoretically informed analysis. In particular, competitive relations between provinces demand explanation, since horizontal cooperation would allow them to push for subnational interests much more effectively. To account for the restrictions imposed upon the institutional development of Canadian IGR systematically, the following argument is made: In Canada, institutionalization and integration processes are constantly undermined by internal majoritarian dynamics prevalent in the individual governments. The micro-incentives generated by the given intragovernmental relations create a barrier towards the development of strongly institutionalized IGAs. In terms of the dominant macro-dynamics, majoritarianism in the constituent government units prevents the constitutionally prescribed logic of power dispersion inherent in dual federalism from being undermined in favour of power sharing – irrespective of growing coordination pressure. Compared to Switzerland and the United States, where informal power-sharing structures were set up, in Canada the corridor for institutional adaptation remains small.

The Swiss blueprint

With Switzerland we deal with a federal system that has usually been labelled as 'cooperative federalist' (e.g. Braun 2000; Vatter 2002). Furthermore, as a regime type, the system is regularly classified as the prototype of a consensus democracy (Lijphart 1999). Research on consociational and consensus democracy has extensively analysed polities whose basic logic is most fundamentally characterized by power sharing and dispersion. This logic is thought to apply to executive–legislative relations, corporatist structures, and IGR alike. Following Armingeon:

> cooperative behaviour [in the federalist arena] is stabilized by the surrounding fora of decision-making. Conflictual strategies in the federalist arena would be in sharp contrast to the style of decision-making in the remaining arenas. (2000a: 124)

Whilst intuitively convincing, this claim needs to be specified. Most fundamentally, it remains implicit which mechanisms drive a positive spillover of internal power-sharing processes within cantonal governments – often labelled as 'consociationalism' – into the intergovernmental arena. In fact, the idea that different forms of power sharing should reinforce each other is not self-evident, neither theoretically nor empirically (Czada 2000, 2003). While we faced an immense conceptual and empirical literature on power-sharing democracies and decision-making styles (e.g. Benz, Scharpf, and Zintl 1992; Armingeon 2000b, 2000a; Benz 2000, 2003; Czada 2000, 2003), the impact of voluntary power-sharing within cantonal executives on institution building in the Swiss intergovernmental arena has so far remained under-explored. The Swiss system has often been treated as 'most likely case' for intergovernmental cooperation, but the grounds for such a judgement have not been properly specified. There is hardly dispute about the dominant interaction mode in the Swiss case, a dispute one can observe in the literature on American IGR for instance. In fact, there is so little disagreement over the basic interaction prevalent in the Swiss polity that it seems odd to inquire about the motives that drive cooperation in the different arenas in the first place.

Yet as soon as we distinguish between the developments on the process level and the federal constitution, it becomes clear that, constitutionally speaking, in the phase of policy formulation power dispersion dominates over power sharing. The constitution assigns considerable exclusive powers to the cantons, among these health, energy, regional construction and planning, education, and higher education (Armingeon 2000a: 118; Fleiner 2006). And unlike the United States, the central government in Switzerland could extend its competences to an only limited degree. 'Implied powers' do not exist in the constitution and the definition of the respective responsibilities is rather precise. Another aspect that supports the power-dispersing character of Swiss federalism is the principle of non-centrality that requires considerable freedom of action for the cantons and the acceptance of their respective characteristics as independent political entities (Braun 2003: 64). Moreover, the financial autonomy of the cantons is considerable. Cantons levy their own personal and corporate income tax, inheritance tax, and wealth tax; and different tax burdens across cantons indicate that cantons actively use their autonomy (Adamovich and Hosp 2003: 9–10; Hueglin and Fenna 2006: 170).

The federal constitution also shows 'non-dualist' elements which, however, cannot account for the institutional choices in the intergovernmental arena. First, whenever legislation is proposed on a certain matter, all groups and institutions affected by it must be consulted in advance. The so-called *Vernehmlassungsverfahren* is a consultation procedure preceding the legislative decision-making process. This 'voice mechanism' does invite power sharing but not in the decision-making stage since the cantons do not have a formal veto (Armingeon 2000*a*: 111, 121–2). Further, the consultation procedure affects horizontal coordination only to a very limited degree. Each canton can issue a position individually and it is by no means 'natural' that cantons try to use this channel collectively. As a second 'non-dual' element, most federal laws are implemented by the cantonal administration which favours dense interaction between the federal government and the individual cantons (Bächtiger and Hitz 2006). This brings up the question whether the Swiss case is – despite the considerable legislative competences of the cantons – not really one of 'functional federalism'. Whilst this concerns the implementation phase, policy formulation as the major focus of this study is less affected. Similarly, the bureaucrats who deal with policy implementation are different from those actors involved in legislative decision-making and cross-jurisdictional policy-coordination in the formulation stage. Therefore, the centre's dependency on cantonal administrative capacities is of limited relevance for horizontal processes in Swiss federalism. All in all, the strong investments of the cantons in IGAs still await explanation.

The American blueprint

The evaluations of American federalism in the literature are extremely diverse and, paradoxically, at the same time very uniform. While the model of dual federalism is by now considered as inadequate to describe processes of federal interaction, it is less clear what could reasonably substitute this approach. Scholars like Elazar (1990, 1991) argue that 'cooperative federalism' is the framework which provides for the best account of the existing pattern of intense interaction;[1] others have observed a shift towards more 'coercive cooperation' due to the growing dominance of central funding and federal pre-emption (Kincaid 1990, 2003; Derthick 2001; Gerlak 2006: 233). Since there is a wide agreement that

---

[1] Note that Elazar's conception of 'cooperative federalism' is based on the strong tendency among intergovernmental actors in the United States to cooperate and negotiate as opposed to exerting hierarchical control. Thus, it refers to behavioural elements, not to formal–legal aspects used to distinguish cooperative from dual federalism in Chapter 2.

due to its heavy constitutional fragmentation American IGR is an inherently difficult phenomenon to study, debates circle around the specification of periods characterized by particular (predominantly vertical) interaction patterns instead of identifying enduring features of American federalism per se.

Ironically, the perceived diversity and variability of IGR led to a remarkably narrow range of areas of study. Political science studies of American IGR tend to focus overwhelmingly on federal grants and the implications of conditions attached to them (Trench 2006: 228; see, for instance, Nathan and Lago 1990; Tannenwald and Cowan 1997). The latter are one important component of the vertical dimension of American federalism, but still are only one component. The same patterns appear in more specific analyses of state lobbying in the federal arena which distinguish phases of intergovernmental lobbying according to the dominant interplay between states' fiscal dependency and federal activism (Haider 1974; Camissa 1995: 117). If the horizontal dimension is studied at all, works on interstate relations tend to be descriptive and seldom link up to the overall working of IGR (Zimmerman 2001, 2002; for an exception see Bowman 2004*a*, 2004*b*). Systematic cross-national comparisons of American IGR with IGR in other federal systems are similarly rare.

In an attempt to remedy some of these shortcomings, this study tries to pinpoint some basic yet enduring features of American IGR. The observed variability of vertical federal–state relations over time implies a particular vulnerability of the state level towards power shifts. These shifts are primarily initiated by federal activism or passivity to which states respond in an uncoordinated manner. They lack an efficient institutional back-up which would stabilize the 'state level' as a collective actor towards the federal government. Correspondingly, Trench's (2006: 228) observation that the academic production in American federal research is restricted to a narrow focus on vertical relations mirrors the empirical weakness and the fragmentation of interstate relations. This weakness is usually taken as a premise in research on American IGR rather than a puzzle requiring exploration which is problematic. The complex and somehow chaotic cross-jurisdictional 'network' of American IGR, which has been metaphorically described as a 'marble cake' of shared activities within a formal three-layer structure (Grodzins 1966), has not be transferred into a 'system' of IGR; 'system' meaning an institutional framework composed of mutually interrelated units able to efficiently coordinate state demands towards the centre and, as a consequence, to prevent the federal government from dominating the state level.

Similar to the situation in the other two country literatures, also here we find a blind spot: Overall, the observation of a 'state level' characterized by fragmentation due to a multitude of highly developed yet mutually competitive IGAs is treated as a premise rather than a puzzle. Camissa, for instance, examined the influence of American IGAs such as the National Governors' Association on federal legislation. An opening statement asserts that the implementation function of the states has led to the second function of state governments as constituents for federal programs. This implies that such a development was a matter of course and thereby self-explanatory. As a consequence, Camissa argues, the federal system has become circular: Federal programs are implemented by state and local governments, while they simultaneously lobby federal legislation (1995: 1).[2] While the indication of circularity might capture dominant federal–state dynamics, taking a comparative perspective, lower level governments in many other federal countries have major – or nearly exclusive – responsibilities for policy implementation. Nonetheless, in these countries, IGAs have not developed along similar lines into interest groups as in the United States as Camissa's study on 'Governments as Interest Groups' implies.

Following Sbragia (2006), we need to consider lower level governments in their dual role as independent decision-makers and as implementors. We need to ask why lower level governments in the United States have set up – at least from a comparative viewpoint – IGAs with a very specific functional orientation and cannot consider the latter as 'natural' side-effect of the states' implementation responsibilities. This study addresses this puzzle and claims that one important factor at the heart of the states' weakness – states which, according to Riker, never acted as one unit against the centre (1964: 103–4) – lies a coordination problem. This coordination problem roots in intra-state divisions. Elazar identifies the diversity between state interests as a major reason for the incapacity of the states to 'develop a common front on a wide variety of issues' and the weak monetary and career incentives to develop the will for leadership on the state level. More fundamentally, it is argued here that there is simply not one coherent state will or interest to represent in the first place.[3] Compulsory power-sharing in each state leads to the creation of IGAs representing either legislatures, governors, or other state officials. It multiplies the actors speaking on behalf of one state and thereby undermines any effort towards collective coordination.

NATIONAL AND REGIONAL INTERGOVERNMENTAL ARRANGEMENTS IN THREE COUNTRIES: AN OVERVIEW

Before addressing the puzzle of institution building with the help of the theoretical framework introduced above on a country-by-country basis, it is useful to categorize IGAs along their basic characteristics. The relevant criteria are the number

---

[2] See also Krause and Bowman who start their analysis of the impact of partisan politics in U.S. federalism from the claim that a hierarchical perspective on policy making in U.S. federalism is rooted in the constitution. Therefore, an examination of the balance of intergovernmental policy-making power can be made looking at vertical relations only and exclusively be based on the analysis of national level decisions (2005: 364).

[3] Elazar cited in Crihfield and Reeves (1974: 106–7). For Kincaid (2003) too, the diversity of the country is one major force shaping the particular make-up of American IGR.

TABLE 3.1. *Classifying intergovernmental arrangements*

Scope of Interaction	Participating Units
Horizontal–regional	Two or few lower level governments
Horizontal–multilateral/national	More than half or all lower level governments
Vertical–regional	The federal government with few lower level governments
Vertical–multilateral/national	The federal government with more than half or all of the lower level governments

of participants who take part in IGAs and the location of the respective participants (McRoberts 1985). Thus, it is crucial whether interaction is bilateral or multilateral. For reasons of simplicity, if more than half of the constitutive governments take part, structures are '*multilateral*' (or '*national*' if they include all subunits), while those with fewer members are '*regional*'. Further, we distinguish *horizontal* from *vertical IGAs*. While the former include lower level governments only, the latter include the federal government as well. We end up with four categories displayed by Table 3.1.

Table 3.2 gives an overview of the range of Canadian, Swiss, and American IGAs along these categories. It shows that particular forms are set up with different frequency across the systems, which is already quite telling. It indicates that the degree of complexity is far higher in the two power-sharing democracies than in polycentric Canada. That the number of regional IGAs is lower in Canada is certainly an expression of the lower number of government units which has nothing to do with the type of democracy per se. Yet in Canada and Switzerland, IGAs are dominated by executives which represent provincial and cantonal interests, respectively. Only in the United States, the executives and the legislatures are organized separately both on the national and on the regional level. Moreover, policy-specific IGAs in Canada and Switzerland obviously reflect government departments and their respective area of responsibility, while in the United States structures tend to follow a functional or issue-specific pattern. As Chapter 5 will demonstrate, both features of American IGR can be traced to the fragmentation of the states.

Referring to the distinction between majoritarian and power-sharing democracy, Canada shows hardly any regional bodies for policy-specific, interprovincial coordination[4] indicating the weaker development of Canadian IGR. Many exchanges occur through direct interdepartmental, weakly institutionalized, channels. It also indicates a tendency to maintain governments as coherent units of action on which power is concentrated resisting the creation of strong IGAs outside the individual government unit. On the other side of the coin,

---

[4] The Council of Maritime Premiers is an exception as a regional conference which runs several agencies in the area of education (Dennison 2005: 6).

TABLE 3.2. *Intergovernmental arrangements in Canada, Switzerland, and the United States*

Type of IGA	Canada	Switzerland	United States
Multilateral/national (generalist)	First Ministers' Conference (vertical) Council of the Federation (horizontal)	Conference of Cantonal Executives (horizontal)	National Governors' Association National Conference of State Legislatures Council of State Governments National Association of Attorneys General
Multilateral/national (policy-specific)	Ministerial councils (vertical or horizontal)	Conferences of Directors (horizontal)	Interstate commissions (e.g. Education Commission of the States) (vertical or horizontal)
Regional (generalist)	Western Premiers' Conference (horizontal) Conference of Atlantic Premiers (horizontal)	Conference of Northwestern Switzerland (horizontal) Conference of Central Switzerland (horizontal) Conference of Eastern Switzerland (horizontal) Conférence des Gouvernements de Suisse Occidentale (horizontal)	Regional branches of National Governors' Association (Western Governors' Associations, the Midwest Governors' Conference, New England's Governors' Conference, Border Governors' Conference, Coalition of Northeastern Governors, Council of Great Lakes Governors, and Southern Governors' Association)[a] (horizontal) Regional branches of the National Conference of State Legislatures (Midwestern Region, Southern Region, Western Region, and Eastern Region) (horizontal) Regional branches of Council of State Governments (CSG-Midwest, CSG-South, CSG-East, and CSG-West)[b] (horizontal)
Regional (policy-specific)		Regional conferences in various policy fields (vertical or horizontal)	Interstate commissions in various policy fields (vertical or horizontal)

[a] http://www.nga.org/cda/files/RegGovOrgs.PDF
[b] http://www.statesnews.org/CSG/Regional+Offices/default.htm

the coexistence of two generalist bodies – the First Ministers' Conference including the federal government and the purely horizontal Council of the Federation – reflects the stronger competition between the two government levels than in the two power-sharing systems. Finally, in contrast to the power-sharing systems, vertical IGAs including the federal government are much more common. Yet, due to the structural weakness of these bodies, the inclusion of the federal government may not be equated with intense cooperation on the vertical axis as explicated below.

INTERGOVERNMENTAL INSTITUTIONALIZATION IN CANADA

The major national bodies in Canadian IGR are the exclusively horizontal Council of the Federation (the former Annual Premiers' Conference), the vertical-national First Ministers' Conferences (FMCs) in which the federal Prime Minister and the Premiers meet, and a variety of nationwide ministerial conferences and councils (of which some include the federal government, some do not). On the regional level, we find the Western Premiers' Conference and the Council of Atlantic Premiers. Finally, there are bilateral agreements such as the British Columbia-Alberta Cooperation Agreement as well as Manitoba-New Brunswick Memorandum of Understanding, arrangements in which the various provinces and territories engage with different frequency. Since bilateral agreements tend to address particular issues and are directly negotiated between the respective partners, the following analysis will focus on multilateral and regional IGAs. Overall, these IGAs tend to be institutionalized on a weak-to-medium level and remain weakly integrated.

The vertical dimension of Canadian federalism

The FMC, in which the provinces, territories, and the central government participate, has long been the pinnacle of the intergovernmental system linking the horizontal with the vertical dimension of the Canadian federal system. It resolves conflicts on the highest level and gives direction to the network of lower level meetings. The FMC comprises meetings of the federal prime ministers and the premiers. Frequently, it has been suggested that these meetings be held annually. It has even been suggested that they be given constitutional status. Neither measure could be realized (Cameron and Simeon 2002: 62). The reason for this is simple. Actors do not want to be constrained too much by (or even to be obliged to enter into) intergovernmental cooperation. This is particularly true for the federal government since the convening of an FMC is the prerogative of the Prime Minister.

Typically, federal officials claim that these conferences are used by provinces simply to attack federal policies. They are said to be employed for electoral purposes rather than to seriously confront the challenges facing Canadian society (McRoberts 1985: 95). The strategy of blame shifting is clearly visible in the Canadian context and the actors are very aware of this tactic. Actors use it very consciously to advance their electoral goals and strengthen their position at home. Correspondingly, despite being almost a hundred years old, the FMC has remained an ad hoc event and although regularity has been demanded it was never achieved (Meekison, Telford, and Lazar 2002: 16). A constitutional status of IGR is even less feasible since the non-binding character of agreements would be affected; even if not formally, then in terms of legitimacy. They could delimit actors' freedom for action when it comes to translating agreements into provincial legislation, a constraint which is clearly opposed. Given this constellation, the success of interprovincialism is fairly limited. Collective agreements are as good as the good will of the participating governments (Lazar and McLean 2000: 168). Their meetings serve mainly as a forum for consultation and information exchange. Anything beyond that would interfere too much with the autonomy of the governments involved.

Recent developments have similar implications. Despite having been the core of IGR for many years, few FMCs have been called since the Liberal federal government was elected in 1993. This is particularly crucial since the mid-1990s when the central government started to pursue a policy of deficit reduction. The ensuing reduction of federal transfers weakened Ottawa's capacity to act through its spending power alone (Cameron and Simeon 2002: 54, 62). The Liberal government under Martin applied a more pro-federal rhetoric. However, this was, at least in part, related to the cabinet's minority status. It made the federal government particularly vulnerable to political pressure from the provinces, a fact of which the latter were well aware. In such a context, IGR could be seen as an instrument to compensate for a process of central decline. From a provincial perspective, however, it is more profitable to use IGAs to speed up this process and to exploit federal weaknesses.

This orientation found expression in a recent strengthening of purely horizontal coordination, in particular the restructuring of the Annual Premiers' Conference into the Council of the Federation. Up until this point, the Council has been used to unify the provinces more efficiently within bargaining processes for federal funding but not for horizontal policy-harmonization. Simultaneously, the Martin government made bilateral deals with individual provinces such as the Northwest Territories and distributed additional funds, a move fiercely criticized by other provinces. The 2006 election installed a Conservative minority government and is unlikely to change these conflict-prone dynamics. Premier Howard promised to address the problem of fiscal imbalance during his campaign, thereby creating strong frictions between the two orders of government. Finally, as one additional indication for the dominant pattern of intergovernmental instability, the Howard government refused to recognize the Kelowna Accord struck by Prime Minister Martin with the Premiers and the Aboriginal leaders right before the election in November 2005.

To return to the general rationale, the centre is not interested in a fully fledged system of IGR that institutionally links a well-coordinated provincial level to the federal government. One reason for this is that horizontal arrangements primarily serve the facilitation of provincial position-taking. Furthermore, a more institutionalized system to facilitate nationwide policy-harmonization could threaten the centre's privileged status: An institutionalized system of IGR is likely to generate greater equality among the participants. Given the strong tendency towards autonomy protection, each participant will insist on a veto. Only a shift to some kind of majority rule would make such arrangements more attractive for the centre. Yet, such a step is highly unlikely. Instead, up to now, there has been no formal decision-rule in IGR which secures a maximum of flexibility for each participant and represents a 'sine qua non' mirrored in the institutional set-up of IGAs in general, and more specifically in the weak institutionalization of the FMC.

Meetings are organized by the Canadian Intergovernmental Conference Secretariat which was established in 1973. It has its own personnel and own resources contributed by the different governments. It is responsible for organizing meetings not only of the heads of governments, but also at the ministerial level. Further, it organizes regional conferences such as Western Premiers' meetings. Due to this multitude of services, the secretariat does not function as the 'arm' of one particular configuration of actors characterized by a particular interest profile as the secretariat of the Council of the Federation does. That is, 'institutional boundedness' is only present in formal terms since substantially, there is no 'institutionally bounded' configuration of actors which the secretariat could attempt to stand for and whose interests it could actively pursue. This becomes even clearer if we consider the interaction between the FMC and the regional conferences. The regional conferences try to unify their members before FMC conferences to assure the inclusion of regional issues in the national agenda. Hence, despite the presence of a secretariat with own resources which deals with IGAs on the national and regional levels, institutionalization (and integration) remain weak.

While there is a general tendency of the provincial governments to maximize their freedom of action and to minimize external constraints, as in other federal systems, the fiscally weaker jurisdictions in particular are ready to trade-off some autonomy in return for financial assistance (Cameron and Simeon 2002: 65). In the context of weak multilateral IGAs, there is considerable room for manoeuvre to strike bilateral arrangements between the centre and individual provinces. For the federal government, this is desirable. It cannot expect to form a stable multilateral alliance at equally low costs once strong provinces are included in negotiations likely to push for more concessions. For the centre, the freedom to form bilateral agreements in which it is in the stronger force is more beneficial than a multilateral frame, in which the provinces have better means to form a front against federal plans. Accordingly, the federal government made regular efforts to divide the provinces within negotiation processes. Due to some provinces' stronger need for federal funding, this strategy has been quite successful. All in all, the perception of a federal–provincial antagonism that boils down to a distributional conflict over money and autonomy substantially shapes the tactics of governments on both levels. The centre's rejection of any limitation of its freedom to act unilaterally has become evident in its handling of grant programs during the last decades. It repeatedly altered their structure and reduced transfers to the provinces unilaterally. The provincial government tried to achieve more influence over the federal government's use of its spending power through negotiated agreements like the Social Union Framework (Lazar 2000: 103). In the end, however, the provinces were still unhappy with the Social Union Framework because they were under strong pressure to accept federal money in order to deliver services at home, pressure which considerably delimited their capacity to extract concessions.

In order to strengthen their bargaining position, provincial ministers are increasingly mandated by their cabinet or by their Intergovernmental Affairs Office. The latter define before the actual negotiations which offers are acceptable and which are not. As a consequence, communication has little substantial impact. It prolongs the process to give all people bound to a mandate the possibility to call home and get the permission to make a particular deal, yet hardly establishes common ground to find a 'collective' solution transcending the smallest common denominator. Although agreement is achieved regularly since politicians are under pressure to present an acceptable result to the media after several days of session, such 'ex ante mandating' complicates the formulation of a compromise considerably. This is accompanied by the strategic positioning in the media before or after meetings which some provincial governments exploit very skilfully. In sum, the interaction mode within FMC meetings does not transcend hard bargaining on the basis of predefined preferences.

This is supported by an institutional environment much too feeble to support any processes transcending mere ad hoc coordination. The approach chosen by the actors – multilateralism or bilateralism – heavily depends on the governments' calculations as to which strategy helps to secure maximal benefits – either in terms of impact on a given policy sector or credit among its citizens. Although shared authority in a policy field affects the behaviour of the two orders of government, they may nevertheless decide that the price of collaboration in terms of control over policy making and implementation is too high and prefer contradictions and duplications in policy delivery (McRoberts 1985: 74). Again it becomes clear that shared competences do not necessarily generate more cooperation. Correspondingly, during the 1980s, the competitive relations between the two levels motivated the federal government to strengthen its immediate link to the citizens via the direct delivery of benefits. This again expressed the endeavour to maximize federal autonomy from the provincial level. It circumvented the provinces, hence central–provincial collaboration, to make citizens more aware of the federal contribution to the services delivered. On the one hand, the centre circumvented the provinces from interposing themselves between the federal government and the individual citizen. On the other hand, it tried to win citizens over to the federal position in its struggles with the provincial governments. A study of federal advertising activities showed that these campaigns were the most important factors in explaining the sharp increase in federal advertising expenditure (McRoberts 1985: 95–6, 106–7) indicating the high relevance of federal–provincial conflict in the Canadian context.

As mentioned before, the weakness of multilateralism is not exclusively a product of the federal government's resistance against it. Of course, if the centre expects the provinces to form a common front against its plans, it prefers to deal with them one at a time. Alternatively, if provincial positions are quite diverse, instead of trying to obtain unanimous agreement, it is more advantageous for the federal government to enter separate but equal agreements with those of the provinces which are willing to accept the centre's conditions. This pattern became visible in the multilateral agreements of the 1990s mentioned before. Although they represent valuable achievements in themselves, these agreements preceded bilateral federal–provincial agreements pinning down the specifics since the overall framework remained too vague to assure implementation (Cameron and Simeon 2002). Hence, most vertical interaction takes place outside multilateral frameworks. Often also individual provinces prefer bilateral bargaining in order to pursue very particular interests or as a result of interprovincial competition (McRoberts 1985: 87). Looking at the formally established joint committees on the vertical level, the number of federal–provincial liaison bodies illustrates the relevance of bilateral interaction. Of 482 federal–provincial bodies in the year 1972, far more than half are bilateral (McRoberts 1985: 78–9). What is more, these numbers do not capture the relevance of vertical bilateral consultation and bargaining on a less formal level. Whenever the federal government wants to impose new controls and expects provincial resistance, it avoids multilateral bargaining (McRoberts 1985: 79). Vice versa, as one member of staff of a ministerial council put it, it cannot be presupposed that individual provinces gain more when being part of a collective. Depending on the issue at stake, individual provinces might get more from the federal government by 'going alone' and given the lack of strong intergovernmental institutions, there is little reason not to go for it. Quite naturally, such an opportunity occurs more frequently for larger, economically strong provinces, a pattern that shows across all three federal systems analysed in this book. In Canada, however, the tendency to exploit such situations is particularly pronounced.

The horizontal dimension of Canadian federalism

Moving on the horizontal dimension of Canadian federalism, after the relative decline of the First Ministers' Conference, the Annual Premiers' Conference has become increasingly important. As an exclusively provincial body, it was long considered as less relevant. Yet, since the core IGA, the FMC, has been used less often, the Annual Premiers' Conference gained strength. Before 2003, this association of provinces has been held every August under a rotating chairmanship and supported by provincial civil servants (Cameron and Simeon 2002: 62). In July 2003, however, the Annual Premiers' Conference accepted the proposal issued by the Québec Liberal Party to create a Council of the Federation in order to strengthen provincial–territorial cooperation. At this point, the Annual Premiers' Conference had already been more institutionalized than the FMC since it met regularly. Its successor, the Council of the Federation, meets at least twice a year (i.e. more often and more regularly than the FMC). It is supported by a steering committee of deputy ministers and a secretariat, and hence has clear institutional boundaries and is internally differentiated. The steering committee of deputy ministers prepares the Council meetings. Moreover, ministerial committees can be called on an ad hoc basis. According to the founding agreement, the Premiers' Council of Health Awareness is under the responsibility of the Council of the Federation as well as the Secretariat for Information and Cooperation on Fiscal Imbalance. However, up until now the Council of Health Awareness is not longer active after government priorities have changed which emphasizes the fluidity of the Council's internal structures which corresponds to the overall picture of Canadian IGR. In terms of resources, the secretariat started with two and now has three employers. Hence, looking at resources only, it is considerably weaker than the Canadian Conference Secretariat with thirty-one employees.

In terms of institutional developments, it is clearly an achievement in the Canadian context that the Council of the Federation rests on a codified founding agreement and has a mandate to exchange information and develop shared positions among the provinces. Priorities of premiers are identified through unanimity. Although there was initial discussion about an alternative decision-making procedure, provincial representatives did not consider this realistic and these plans soon evaporated. In sum, the Council is institutionalized on a medium level, while its potential to institutionalize further is likely to be limited. Although the Council tried to engage actively in policy areas such as health policy, the arrangement is restricted to identifying already existing common priorities which tend to focus on the provinces' interest in more federal funds. It has neither the resources nor the mission to actively bridge interprovincial conflict. Problematic issues are excluded from the shared agenda ex ante. So far, the Council has served one prior goal, to form a stable provincial front to extract the maximal amount of money in negotiations over federal funding. Provincial officials consider the

IGA as a vehicle to prevent the federal government from disuniting provincial office-holders in FMC and ministerial meetings. Such an outcome was prevented during the negotiations of the latest health negotiations in which the Council was actively involved. The provinces managed to stick to a shared position for several days – a comparatively long period in contrast to former negotiations. In the end, they achieved considerable concessions from the federal government and widely prevented substantial influence on the part of federal government as regards health policy in the individual provinces. As a consequence of this initial success, the Council of the Federation might be involved in further negotiations in areas such as education. In such an early stage of development, however, the risks of a stronger involvement are as considerable as its potential benefits. Failure can easily paralyse the Council in the long run by questioning its status in the intergovernmental arena, a status which is not yet fully consolidated, as Council staff pointed out.

The dominant line of conflict in Canadian federalism evolves along the vertical axis between federal and provincial governments. Nonetheless, one may not overlook that when it comes to the intrusion in provincial spheres of competence, provinces are equally averse against such intrusion by a fellow province as by the federal government. The federal government is simply the bigger threat. As an unfavourable side-effect, the strong endeavour to protect autonomy easily undermines cooperation between the provinces. This failure to solve cross-jurisdictional problems through purely interprovincial agreements strengthens the federal government which can justify national interference much more easily by referring to cooperation failure on the side of the provinces. The weakness of horizontal policy coordination becomes evident in the functional profile of the Council of the Federation which is directed towards position taking and federal–provincial negotiation.

The creation of this purely horizontal IGA did not require the agreement of the federal government, although federal participation was originally proposed by the electoral platform of the Liberal Party of Québec in 2001 which pushed for the creation of a Council of the Federation after its electoral victory. In the end, federal involvement was opposed by other provinces, which is an interesting observation. It implies a general disposition towards forming an arrangement that facilitates collective opposition against the federal government on the part of the provinces, rather than being result of a 'Québec factor' which is often referred to a source of the conflicting nature of Canadian IGR. As a further expression of this general disposition, Council staff have so far not made efforts to establish linkages with the federal government. In the long run, this is problematic since more far-fetching goals such as annual First Ministers' meetings or the establishment of federal–provincial–territorial protocols of conduct are not feasible without federal involvement (Meekison, Telford, and Lazar 2002: 18). It is nonetheless doubtful that cooperation between the Council and the federal government will develop in the future. As one federal official put it: '... otherwise it would not be a forum for the provinces and territories'.[5] Federal actors perceive the Council as a provincial–territorial instrument. Reflecting such mutual distrust, the postwar period has seen both the provinces and the federal government intrude into areas which are designated exclusively to the other level. In the mid-1980s, unilateral action even occurred in areas which had been marked by rather well-established procedures of federal–provincial interaction (McRoberts 1985: 94). Intergovernmental collaboration has remained unstable. It stands and falls with the interests and the attitudes of the actors presently involved as does the Council of the Federation which remains highly dependent on the particular constellation of premiers. Especially the chair of the Council who rotates yearly has a heavy impact on whether the body is run mainly by bureaucrats or directly shaped by the premiers. The turnover of political personnel caused by government alternation has a heavy impact on the character of the processes and IGAs do not provide a structural counterweight.

This dominance of personality over structure clearly indicates that the Canadian system of IGR has not developed a 'life of its own'. It clearly lacks the capacity to steer actor behaviour substantially and is unable to shape the ways actors pursue their interests. A further expression of this tendency is the limited role of Council staff. They do not take over any representative function towards the federal government. It is solely the chair who initiates communication with the federal government after a common position has been released and he meets the federal government on behalf of the Council. This prevents the Council as an institution from getting involved in 'political business'. Equally, staff cannot pool resources by accessing provincial officials as bureaucratic back-up to prepare collective positions on a lower administrative level. They have no contact to line departments which tend to be policy oriented and deal with intergovernmental issues from a more problem-oriented viewpoint than the premiers. Instead, their contacts in the individual provinces are the Premiers' offices and the Departments for Intergovernmental Affairs. These tend to be politicized and keen to guard provincial autonomy rather than assuring effective interprovincial decision-making.

In sum, the transformation of the Annual Premiers' Conference into the more institutionalized Council of the Federation indicates that the endeavour to achieve a stronger position towards the federal government was a good enough reason to invest more resources into an IGA strengthening interprovincial relations. Still, the protection of autonomy against any external intrusion, high electoral competition within the provinces, blame shifting among them, and a rapidly changing configuration of government parties clearly restrict the potential to set up IGAs that are sufficiently institutionalized to support regular co-decision processes. As in the FMCs, ad hoc coordination is the dominant interaction mode. Effective policy-coordination between the provinces is rarely achieved as agreements issued by the Council indicate. This weakness is reinforced by the limited role of Council staff who are hardly able to go beyond the provision of basic bureaucratic support and the mere highlighting of issues to the outside already agreed upon by the ministers.

[5] Fed Can III, 5 April 2006, p. 3.

Regional intergovernmental arrangements

Like the Council of the Federation (and its predecessor the Annual Premiers' Conference), also the horizontal-regional IGAs are more institutionalized than the First Ministers' Conference – all of them meet regularly – which again emphasizes the greater willingness of the Canadian provinces to coordinate horizontally than to engage in more reliable interaction with the federal government. At the same time, they are institutionalized to very different degrees. The Council of Atlantic Premiers[6] meets twice annually, the Western Premiers' Conference[7] once. Both strive for common positions on national issues. More concretely, the Council of Atlantic Premiers' mandate is to forge a common Atlantic Canadian position for the Council of the Federation and the FMCs. Analogously, the Western Premiers' Conference meets shortly before the Council each year to agree upon shared issues. Regional positions are therefore often integrated in the wider provincial–territorial outcome (Meekison, Telford, and Lazar 2002: 17). Quite naturally, it is easier for provinces and territories to define shared interests on a regional basis than would be the case on a nation wide basis, since the diversity of interests is lower. The stronger capacity for regional cooperation finds also expression in boundary-crossing international arrangements such as the annual meeting of the Western Premiers with the Western Governors' Association as well as the annual meeting between the Eastern Canadian Premiers and the New England Governors (Meekison, Telford, and Lazar 2002: 23–4).

While the Western Premiers meet regularly, they do not have their own secretariat, thus the arrangement is only weakly institutionalized. This contrasts strikingly with its Eastern pendant, the Council of Atlantic Premiers. The latter is the most consistent and enduring premier level arrangement in Canada. In 2000, it replaced the Council of Maritime Premiers which until then included only Nova Scotia, New Brunswick, and Prince Edwards Island. In 2000, Newfoundland and Labrador joined as a fourth member. While it is an important regional platform for position taking, its principle focus is collective action on matters of provincial responsibility which is unusual in the Canadian context. Experts attribute its record of endurance to its strong institutional base, which scores higher than the other generalist arrangements discussed so far. Compared to the Council of the Federation which started with two and now has three positions, the Atlantic Premiers run a secretariat with a total of 28 employers serving the Council and its agencies. Currently, there are four agencies at work of which three are dedicated to education and attempt to handle shared policy problems collectively[8] and hence engage in substantive policy coordination (Dennison

---

[6] Members are Nova Scotia, New Brunswick, Prince Edwards Island, and Newfoundland and Labrador.

[7] Members are British Columbia, Alberta, Saskatchewan, Yukon, Northwest Territories, Nunavut, and Manitoba.

[8] For example, the Maritime Provinces Higher Education Commission, the Council of Atlantic Ministers of Education and Training, and the Atlantic Provinces Special Education Authority; see for

2005: 6). To give two examples, the Council of Atlantic Ministers of Education and Training is composed of the Atlantic ministers of education and training. It is therefore a regionally restricted, policy-specific IGA directly associated with the Atlantic Premiers. It was established in April 2004 replacing the Atlantic Provinces Education Foundation set up in 1994. The purpose of the Council is to provide the framework for joint undertakings of the four provinces in the needs of public and post-secondary education. Over the past ten years, projects have focused on joint development of curricula, procurement of school buses, and the development of learning resources.[9] The Atlantic Provinces Special Education Authority as a second example was set up in 1975. It is based on a shared-cost arrangement and is authorized to provide educational services, programs, and opportunities for persons from birth to 21 years of age with low incidence sensory impairments. This agreement is the only one of its kind in Canada.[10] The institutional development of the Council of Atlantic Premiers, its focus on policy coordination, and its linkage to policy-specific IGAs in the education sector are clearly exceptional.

Nevertheless, it still substantiates two general points about Canadian IGR. First, the major weight of coordination is clearly at the lower levels. The more inclusive IGAs are, the less likely it is that they pick up issues since interest convergence is a precondition for an issue to travel to a higher level. As we have seen, due to frequent government alternations, such convergence tends to be short-lived. Second, only to a very limited degree do governments allow for the disaggregation of government interests and, with it, the development of strong intergovernmental structures along policy or departmental lines. The observation that such strong policy-specific structures only exist on a small territorial scale in Atlantic Canada and that these structures are closely tied to the Council of Atlantic Premiers (instead of being a separate parallel-structure as set up in the two power-sharing democracies) is telling. It shows that the potential to decouple policy-specific, ministerial councils from the political calculus of the core executives is limited.

POLICY-SPECIFIC INSTITUTIONALIZATION: INTERGOVERNMENTAL POLITICS AND MANAGEMENT

So far we have only looked at intergovernmental peak arrangements which tend to channel the major political exchanges cross-cutting a variety of policy areas. Inter-governmental administrative relations, sometimes labelled as 'intergovernmental

---

a full list of associated and independent regional organizations, http://www.cap-cpma.ca/default.asp?mn = 1.62.8

[9] http://camet-camef.ca/default.asp?mn = 1.2   [10] http://www.apsea.ca/about.htm

management', by contrast, structure the day-to-day working of the Canadian federation. Over the last decades, meetings of ministers and of officials on levels below them, which can take either a federal–provincial or an inter-provincial form, have gained importance and point to considerably more collaboration than visible in the political peak institutions. There is a wide range of committees of ministers and officials that are now held increasingly regularly and partially carry out mandates assigned to them by the first ministers. Particularly in the second half of the 1990s, provincial–territorial activities have increased. Moreover, since the late 1980s, there is the general trend of decentralization of intergovernmental policy and management to line departments (Johns, O'Reilly, and Inwood 2007), a trend that sheds light on the importance of policy-specific, inter-administrative cooperation. Despite these developments reflecting an increasing need to cooperate across provincial borders, the frequency and the regularity of meetings still vary considerably across policy fields from several meetings per year to one every three years (Cameron and Simeon 2002: 62; Meekison, Telford, and Lazar 2002: 22).

A comparative study of nineteen intergovernmental programs and policies has shown that half of the relationships were characterized by independence and half by interdependence. While the independent pattern reflects governments' endeavour to protect their spheres of autonomy, in the group of interdependent relationships, the number of hierarchical relations dominated by the federal government was only three which indicates a rather strong position of the participating provinces. Furthermore, note that interdependence does not preclude competition or even conflict of ideas and interests. Despite the partially considerable frequency of interaction, experts indicate that the informal character of the councils weakens their capacity to achieve relations that transcends the exchange of opinions (Meekison, Telford, and Lazar 2002: 21–2).

It is plausible to expect that the cooperation-harming effects of majoritarianism on IGR are comparatively weaker the less salient, the less visible, and the more technical a policy is. On the whole, a more private setting is likely to be rather conducive to fruitful intergovernmental interaction. For instance, research has shown that, in contrast to health care, the area of disability policy is characterized by a history of low conflict and dense bargaining networks (Prince 2001: 817). Such policies can be more easily handled because they are of little relevance for most parts of the electorate and are difficult to exploit in the political arena. Yet, this is only part of the picture since policy areas are usually not isolated from each other. Again, this is a result of the coherent character of power-concentrating governments and the dynamics generated by them. Conflict between governments spills over from one policy area to the other – usually from electorally more into less salient areas. Although the differences across policy areas are visible, these spill-over effects explain why the set-up of strong IGAs fails regularly, also in low-conflict areas.

Staying with the overall patterns of IGR for the remainder of this section, senior officials place a stronger priority on overseeing the development of intergovernmental strategies where sharp disagreement between federal government and provinces prevails. 'Hot political issues' are more subject to political control. This linkage between political and administrative level is clearly visible: first, the more politicized an issue is the more likely the Office for Intergovernmental Affairs or the Strategic Office in a province will take over. Only if politically salient issues are very complex and demand a lot of expertise and resources do they remain in the responsible ministry. This is important because senior intergovernmental officials, at the executive rank in particular, are more politicized than their counterparts in other departments (Johns, O'Reilly, and Inwood 2007). Second, although in most of the provinces, as well as on the federal level, the bureaucracy is professionalized, officials closely attached to the former government tend to be replaced. At the same time, recent research indicates that continuity of personnel in intergovernmental offices has decreased and increasingly complicates exchanges on the administrative level (O'Reilly, Inwood, and Johns 2006; Johns, O'Reilly, and Inwood 2007). The capacity within the intergovernmental system is not ensured by the warmth between officials. Ultimately, they must answer to their political leader and this is where political pressures feed into intergovernmental processes on the working level.

The underlying tendency to compete and pursue one's own advantage in a competitive manner is not only present on the vertical dimensions – hence an immediate expression of federal–provincial conflict. To the same degree, it complicates interprovincial relations. To give an illustration of the lack of trust among the lower level governments themselves: in an interview, a financial official stated that 'every time a document is circulated among the provinces, it somehow ends up in the fed's hand' (Johns, O'Reilly, and Inwood 2007). Obviously, even within administrative relations that are comparatively denser, actors behave unreliably which weakens the capacity for horizontal cooperation. Also in this less politicized context, co-decision is not feasible. An official notes that ' ... we talk and talk. This is inefficient and frustrating. It is a process of purely political dynamics' (Johns, O'Reilly, and Inwood 2007). Despite their lower visibility, IGR on the working level show similar patterns as negotiations on the highest political level.

Having already alluded to potential differences in the interaction patterns and institution-building strategies occurring in different policy fields, this concluding section has a closer look at policy-specific institutionalization. To check whether the link between intra- and intergovernmental processes cross-cuts the variety of policy fields, we look at the ministerial councils established in eight policy fields in greater detail. Education, environment, and transportation show a medium institutionalization. The remaining five policy fields (economic and trade, fiscal and economic policy, health, social policy, and justice and crime control) are only weakly institutionalized. Overall, this picture corresponds with the expectation on federal systems composed of power-concentrating units inviting weak institutionalization.

As Table 3.3 indicates there is no clear pattern between the mode of competence distribution[11] and the level of institutionalization. Since it is often claimed that shared competences invite more cooperation, it is rather surprising that areas of exclusive subnational competence are more often institutionalized on a medium level than shared areas. While we find a medium institutionalization in environmental policy as a shared competence, the same effect cannot be observed in social policy which is shared as well. Arguing in the opposite direction that exclusive competences give lower level governments more to protect and therefore make the investment in a stronger infrastructure more worthwhile is not convincing either. Medium institutionalization does not presuppose provincial exclusivity given shared areas on a medium developmental level. Neither does exclusivity consistently generate medium institutionalization.

While the mode of competence distribution could be classified ex ante, it is much more difficult to assign conflict potential to the different policy fields in a deductive manner. As the policy literature emphasizes, each policy field embraces a variety of issues representing different interest constellations (Lowi 1964; Scharpf 1997). Despite this complication, we still can orient ourselves along 'extreme cases' which can be roughly classified relative to other policy areas – in the case of fiscal policy, for instance, as highly conflicting due to its strong redistributive implications. Table 3.3 displays some policy-specific variance which corresponds to policy-based expectations. Particularly sensitive areas such as fiscal policy and trade are indeed weakly developed, lower than environment, for instance. Looking at the three medium institutionalized areas, two of them – environment and transportation – have a strong spatial dimension which might provide a further rationale to build a stronger infrastructure for cross-jurisdictional cooperation. While it makes a lot of sense that policy-specific factors should play a role, the problem is that once we look at the patterns of policy-specific institutionalization in Switzerland and the United States, these factors do not work in a similar fashion, thus do not provide a coherent alternative account of institution building, an issue I will return to later.

Whatever mainly underlies the given policy-specific variance, institutionalization remains within the expected corridor of adaptation. In no area we find

---

[11] In operational terms, the mode of competence distribution is assessed based on Watts' classification (1999a) of the core areas in federal constitutions backed up by more recent analyses of the three federal constitutions. Areas are classified along the following three categories: They are denoted as *exclusive* when *whole* sub-areas or the whole area are either an exclusively subnational *or* federal competence, as *concurrent* when federal and lower level governments can legislate in the *same* sub-areas on the same issues, or as *shared* when federal and subnational units have *different* competences within the *same* sub-area. Note that this classification does not imply that authority is shared this way in practice. A purely formal classification is nevertheless insightful since contrasting it with the structures set up in individual areas allows us to draw conclusions about how substates deal with their constitutional authority in practice.

TABLE 3.3. *Intergovernmental institutionalization in Canada in eight policy fields*

Policy Fields	Degree of Institutionalization Mode of Competence Distribution
Economic and trade policy	Low institutionalization Exclusive
Education	Medium institutionalization Exclusive
Environment	Medium institutionalization Shared
Fiscal and tax policy	Low institutionalization Shared
Health policy	Low institutionalization Exclusive
Justice and crime control	Low institutionalization Shared
Social policy	Low institutionalization Shared (one sub-area concurrent)[a]
Transportation	Medium institutionalization[b] Exclusive
Overall distribution	Five low/three medium institutionalization

[a] The federal government is responsible for pensions and unemployment insurance, while since the mid-1990s the provinces are responsible for labour market training and social services (Watts 1999: 126–30; Simeon and Papillon 2006: 99–103). Note that in this case concurrency is coupled with provincial supremacy, which is very unusual from a comparative point of view.
[b] http://www.comt.ca/default.htm

high institutionalization. While policy-specific variables seem to have some influence, this influence seems less pronounced than intragovernmental dynamics. Accordingly, intergovernmental actors in a variety of policy fields coherently identify intragovernmental dynamics rather than the conflicting nature of their policy field as a core factor complicating cooperation. Taking these findings together, both types of factors might be complementary. Intragovernmental incentives drive intergovernmental interaction patterns and constrain institutionalization across the range of policy fields and thereby constitute a system-specific corridor of adaptation. Policy-specific features, by contrast, seem to account for where exactly policy-specific institutions are located relative to each other within this corridor. Overall, the following detailed analysis of policy-specific institutionalization in the eight policy fields substantiates the claim that intragovernmental dynamics play the relatively more important role for informal institution-building.

Based on the two levels of institutionalization found in the Canadian context, two types of institutional structures can be distinguished which channel intergovernmental processes. In policy fields which are institutionalized on a medium level, secretariats with own staff have been established outside the individual member governments to organize the exchanges between them. Although they can be quite strong in terms of resources, decisions are still made by consensus and council staff emphasize the freedom of each member to deviate from agreements or collective positions issued by the council whenever the priorities of individual governments change. In principle, these IGAs engage in both position taking and policy coordination. Yet, especially the nature of coordination agreements reflects their fundamental weakness. Agreements often remain on the level of general principles and provide considerable leeway for interpretation and adaptations to the needs of individual governments. Non-compliance is hard to detect. IGR in Canada are governed by press releases which are often not even signed. These so-called communiqués are often package deals in which provinces agree to some aspects, in which they have little interest, in order to achieve another province's agreement. Naturally, governments tend to be less eager to comply with such provisions later on. Finally, if agreements manage the distribution of federal funds, the provinces refuse all federal checks on whether they really use these federal funding for the purposes collectively agreed upon. Equally, they refuse the intrusion of any other lower level government.

IGAs cannot provide a counterweight to these general tendencies, even when institutionalized on a medium level and equipped with considerable resources. In a certain sense, they are 'built around' these constraints. In practice, their main focus is the provision of expertise and information exchange rather than intergovernmental negotiations with the federal government or cross-jurisdictional policy-coordination and policy-harmonization. Accordingly, like the Council of the Federation staff, council staff do not play a proactive role in fostering intergovernmental cooperation. Instead, they function as 'non-political' service-providers and bureaucratic back-up. If member governments do not raise an issue, it remains untouched – irrespective of whether cooperation could be useful or not. Thus, council staff cannot use their expertise to become neutral problem-oriented advisors in order to compensate institutionally for cooperation-undermining political dynamics. Finally, only a small subset of intergovernmental issues are channelled through these arrangements. Most exchanges are bilateral and are handled less visibly, which points to the limited capacity of ministerial councils – and Canadian IGAs in general – to carve out their own sphere of responsibility within the intergovernmental arena.

Accordingly, Table 3.3 indicates, in most policy areas, no secretariats are installed in the first place. Institutionalization is low and IGR are handled directly by the respective line departments or, if issues become politically sensitive, by the respective 'Department of Intergovernmental Affairs'. In larger departments such as health, which is a crucial provincial jurisdiction, every department of health on the subnational level has a special intergovernmental affairs unit headed by a director of intergovernmental affairs. The health sector is an important example given its cost intensiveness and its electoral saliency. Teleconferences on the official level take place once a week. Ministers and deputy ministers meet about once a year. Despite the much more frequent exchanges on the working level, the link between working and political level is nonetheless tight. As one health official put it:

> these individuals [intergovernmental officials] are well aware of their respective department's or government's positions through constant liaison with other program staff within their department as well as their respective ministers, deputy ministers, and Department of Intergovernmental Affairs officials. They also develop official positions by recommending them to their respective deputy minister who will then usually approve the recommended position or strategy thereby making them official.[12] [insertion by author]

The fact that exchanges are handled by the individual line departments strongly reduces the capacity to develop collective standpoints which transcend the sum of individual positions. Alternation and the resulting discontinuity in personnel and rapidly changing government priorities easily offset past achievements. Since intergovernmental agreements are purely political, it also means that as soon as a new party enters government, it might withdraw from major agreements entered by its predecessor. A federal official working in social policy reports:

> Every time there is a change in membership, a minister is replaced, one has to start the working relationship all over again. The worst you can get is that in one jurisdiction is a lot of change down to the official level. But usually there is some continuity on the lower level. There is a cycle of 4–5 years where the people are fully replaced, every six months there is someone new at the table.[13]

On the whole, the chance to overcome cross-jurisdictional differences is considered to be greater on levels below ministerial councils since alternation is less frequent. More insulated arenas dominated by experts provide a better context for conflict settlement, yet in the end decisions still need political approval. The higher one moves up, the more difficult this becomes since, before entering negotiations, ministers are often mandated by their intergovernmental offices or directly by the cabinet. The potential to develop a problem-oriented outlook and to move away from hard individualist bargaining is low – a restriction visible across the range of policy fields.

As observed with generalist IGAs, policy-specific arrangements suffer from majoritarian dynamics implying high competitive pressure, a strong orientation towards individual autonomy protection, and a rapidly changing interest constellation due to frequent government alternation. Even in 'low key' areas, there is little reliability and continuity. The impact of intra-executive patterns on federal dynamics becomes structurally visible in the internal working of the lower level governments. A province's 'Department of Intergovernmental Affairs' takes over issues from the respective line departments when they become too 'political'. This

---

[12] POfficial V, 20 July 2005: 1.   [13] Can Fed Gov II, 13 December 2005.

means that any specific policy issue might be transferred from a more policy-driven arena into a political arena which is fully subject to the strategic calculus of politicized officials being directly responsible to their core executives. As Johns, O'Reilly, and Inwood put it, intergovernmental offices tend to be 'process-oriented', while line departments are rather 'problem-oriented'. While line officials assert politicians' right to make policy decisions, they express frustration about policy files being made subject to political rather than policy considerations. Due to these political dynamics that may take over at any moment, the capacity for policy and institutional innovation remains restricted (O'Reilly, Inwood, and Johns 2006; Johns, O'Reilly, and Inwood 2007). Issues are freely shifted from the officials' to the ministers' level, from ministerial councils to the premiers. This pattern reflects intra-executive hierarchies which prevent the establishment of stabilizing institutional boundaries between intergovernmental arenas and the maintenance of policy-specific IGAs' continuous ownership over a particular set of issues. It comes as no surprise that despite the considerable frequency of interaction in some of the policy areas, the informal character of IGAs weakens their capacity to achieve relations beyond the exchange of opinions (Meekison, Telford, and Lazar 2002: 21–2). The active bridging of conflict hardly occurs, a tendency which also shows in less visible areas. Moreover, when conflict occurs it tends to be resolved either on the political level or outside of IGAs altogether between the governments directly concerned.

That intergovernmental institutionalization does not reach a high level and, moreover, is mostly weak, confirms the expectation of the framework underlying this study. This framework, while making us expect a narrow corridor of adaptation, makes no predictions about the factors leading to a medium institutionalization in one area, and to a weak one in another. Table 3.3 implied that policy-specific conflict potential might be one factor keeping institutionalization lower in one policy area than in the other, while a strong spatial dimension might support institutionalization. While fiscal and economic policies were indeed identified as particularly sensitive by intergovernmental actors, the problem is that policy-specific accounts do not travel across countries as laid out in the following chapters (e.g. in Switzerland fiscal policy is a highly institutionalized area). They enrich our perspective rather than providing an alternative to the framework presented.

Interestingly, when being asked why in Canada politicians set up a secretariat in one area and not in another, intergovernmental officials or experts on IGR uniformly point at the contingency of decisions. Steps towards a stronger institutionalization, they argue, were chosen because the actors involved believed that in the given circumstances a secretariat is necessary. The explicit emphasis that there is no consistent pattern underlying such choices reflects the fluidity and unpredictability of intergovernmental processes. Rejecting any severe restrictions possibly imposed by IGAs, individual governments decide according to the preferences they hold in a specific moment which can weaken (yet not offset) negative intragovernmental incentives. To systematically capture the underlying mechanisms for distinct institutional choices falling within the systemic corridor of adaptation, it would be necessary to look at the individual choice situations. This is beyond the scope of this study and of the approach it puts forward. On an abstract level, however, the interviews pointing to decisions' contingency reveal an important aspect: Leaps of institutionalization from a weak to a medium level are – necessarily – to a wider extent affected by situational factors than leaps from a medium to a high level. This is simply because in the first constellation there is no external infrastructure that pre-structures the choice situation and increases the reliability of processes. This is why a perception of contingency is much more common among Canadian actors than in the more pre-structured Swiss arena.[14]

Recent developments in Canadian federalism reconfirm this interpretation emphasizing systemic restrictions on institutional developments rather than policy variables. Instead of strengthening 'externalized' IGAs institutionally, there is a trend that policy-specific exchanges are concentrated and intensified intragovernmentally. As mentioned above, since the late 1980s, there has been a general trend of decentralizing intergovernmental management to line departments (Johns, O'Reilly, and Inwood 2007) which tends to decrease processes' visibility. The trend towards strengthening intra-ministerial bodies corresponds with the logic of this composite polity since it protects and maintains the boundaries of the governments involved. Intra-ministerial units conflict much less with the dominant logic of competition between governments than 'externalized' IGAs would. Canadian ministers hardly develop a problem-oriented perspective and remain first of all part of their particular government. Provincial governments resist any outside intrusion to maintain the coherence of their own planning, which is backed up by political and senior officials eager to maintain their own sphere of influence (Esman 1984: 29). It is not what ministers want, but what governments want that drives intergovernmental processes in Canada which is felt in generalist and policy-specific arrangements alike. Correspondingly, the cabinet decides whether, for instance, environmental priorities fit into the particular picture of government policies. The internal power-concentration and the intra-executive hierarchy are impressively projected onto the provinces' outside relations.

SUMMARY

Framed in terms of a conflict of goals, Canadian IGR is structured by the incentives resulting from power-concentrating dynamics in lower level governments

[14] On the whole, in the Swiss context, actors consistently refer to more limited competences to explain why areas are less developed than others.

on the one hand and the desirability for more reliable IGR on the other. In this conflict, the former are the stronger force. Autonomy protection as a response to power concentration in the units, blame shifting as a response to high electoral pressure, a rapidly changing interest configuration – in terms of priorities and in terms of personnel – favouring ad hoc coordination and ideological differences could be identified as factors complicating intergovernmental processes. Overall, due to the weak linkages between federal and regional party systems, partisan divides have been considered as the weakest source of conflict among the four mechanisms. However, all of the four mechanisms played their part and are closely tied to the presence of power-concentrating one-party governments and the constellation of lower level governments resulting from it. Throughout the interviews with Canadian intergovernmental officials and IGA staff discontinuity of processes, the heavy impact of alternation and electoral pressure have been repeatedly identified as problematic and have been traced back to the nature of the governments in the system.

Facing such incentive structures, intergovernmental actors try to maintain maximal flexibility in order to react to momentary internal demands preventing the set-up of strong IGAs diminishing this flexibility. Parallel policy developments are often more the result of responding to similar pressures or emulating each other's strategies than the result of explicit discussion and agreement (Cameron and Simeon 2002: 69). Horizontal coordination through unilateral adaptation assures the protection of spheres of autonomy and, moreover, clarifies responsibility. Evidently, lacking explicit cooperation, this pattern easily invites inefficiencies through policy duplication and contradictory policy measures on different levels or by different units. Furthermore, it is important to note that such 'non-interactive' coordination does not necessarily indicate intergovernmental harmony. They can mean the opposite, policies can also be explicitly designed on one level of government to offset the impact of a policy on the other level (McRoberts 1993: 158). In practical terms, power concentration within the subunits facilitates such free-floating adaptation processes because, at home, strong executives can implement their preferences due to the absence of internal opposition comparatively easily. Parliamentary parties are disciplined and 'institutionally based opposition' on the side of the legislatures is neutralized by the adversarial relations between government majority and opposition.

Breton has argued that citizens are best served in terms of policy outcomes when governments compete for their loyalty (Breton 1985) and, thereby, implicitly questions the relevance of intergovernmental structures. Indeed, coordination does not necessarily generate superior outcomes. However, whenever the cross-jurisdictional coordination of policy is held to be useful, in Canada intergovernmental competition tends to generate unstable outcomes since only incomplete and self-enforcing contracts between the governments are possible. There is no 'third party' to enforce agreements (Breton 1996: 215). Strong IGAs are not functionally equivalent to these enforcement mechanisms. Yet, they increase the reliability of exchanges, facilitate monitoring and provide the expertise to set up more specific agreements that strengthen mutual commitments, and make non-compliance more transparent as the analysis of intergovernmental agreements in Chapter 7 will show. Hence, while competition can favour the selection of superior policy outputs within the individual government units, it complicates the agreement and implementation of common solutions across units because it weakens IGAs which support voluntary self-enforcement.

Compared to other federal countries, IGR in Canada remains highly fluid and ad hoc. The process has no constitutional or legislative basis and little backup from bureaucrats (Forget 2001: 133; Cameron and Simeon 2002: 64). It has no formal decision-rules and no capacity for authoritative decision-making. Most importantly, the scope and extent of IGR is heavily dependent on whether the first ministers, in particular the prime minister, find it advantageous or not (Cameron and Simeon 2002: 64; Lazar and McLean 2000: 166; Smiley and Watts 1985). On the whole, informal intergovernmental institutions are much too weak to steer the handling of boundary-crossing problems from a competitive to a more cooperative mode. Bilateralism as the least demanding form of coordination remains the dominant form of interaction. It is based on smallest common denominator solutions between the respective partners, hence demands the least substantial concessions. Consequently, we find a considerable divergence in policy implementation across the different provinces (McRoberts 1993: 157). This is also the case when intergovernmental agreements are in place since provinces refuse any checks on how federal money is used within their jurisdiction.[15] Multilateral collaboration only gains ground on the level of general frameworks that are non-binding, while on the level of program design provincial governments act independently (Lazar and McLean 2000: 168). Horizontal coordination remains on the level of consultation and ad hoc coordination which often serves strategic position-taking instead of cross-jurisdictional harmonization. Also here regular co-decision processes are absent since due to the high competitive pressure within each government unit interprovincialism is characterized by jealousy and competition.

In sum, power-dispersion inherent in the dual-federal constitution of polycentric Canada is preserved by internal majoritarian decision-making in its constitutive governments. The fundamental logic of the polity is self-reinforcing. It is nourished by the internal dynamics of governments which shape the strategies intergovernmental actors choose when responding to cross-jurisdictional

---

[15] For instance in social policy, even if the centre finances everything, the federal government cannot impose harmonization because it has no effective means to hold provincial government accountable for their use of federal funds (Forget 2009: 128–9, 133).

coordination pressure. While federalism research indicates that the density of intergovernmental exchanges has been increasing over time, the leeway for institutional adaptation of Canadian IGR has been restricted, as is visible in an overall low level of institutionalization. Although the impact of intragovernmental dynamics is most pronounced on the highest political level, the dynamics exacerbating informal institution-building are clearly felt on the administrative level and cross-cut the variety of policy fields.

4

Intergovernmental Institutionalization in Switzerland

This chapter analyses the institutionalization of the various Swiss IGAs in detail. Due to the incentives flowing from voluntary power-sharing, institutionalization in Swiss IGR should be high. In this system the policy-specific channels are older, with generalist channels having gained relevance only recently. In contrast to the other two case studies, we therefore look at the policy-specific IGAs in a first step, followed by the generalist ones. This historical succession of policy-specific preceding generalist IGAs' foundation is already quite telling since it reflects the internal nature of cantonal governments characterized by multiparty government and departmentalism which mutually complement each other. It also implies a greater engagement in policy coordination usually handled within policy-specific rather than generalist arrangements. Both features contrast with the Canadian findings where intragovernmental dynamics set opposite incentives.

POLICY-SPECIFIC ARRANGEMENTS: THE CONFERENCES OF DIRECTORS

The Conferences of Cantonal Directors (*Direktorenkonferenzen*)[1] are responsible for the exchanges in major areas of cantonal competence. Currently, 16 of them exist. Quite a few have a considerable history, the oldest, the Conference of Education Directors, dates back to 1897 (Bochsler et al. 2004: 99–100). The Conferences of Cantonal Directors are, overall, highly institutionalized and are responsible for joint decision-making and inter-cantonal harmonization (Frenkel 1986; Bochsler et al. 2004; Bochsler 2006). Even in areas where the cantons widely lost their competences over the last decades, such as in defence, the policy-specific structures showed a considerable capacity to survive organizationally.[2] Most of these conferences have a permanent secretariat with their own staff or

---

[1] Director is a synonym for cantonal minister.
[2] To give one example, formerly the cantons had their own armies which made a conference in the area of military a useful tool. The army reform did not lead to the abolishment of this conference.

a mandated professional who represents the respective conference in committees and working groups on the cantonal and national levels during the year. As a crucial vertical linkage, quite often a delegate of the respective federal ministry is invited to take part in the executive meeting or the plenary sessions of the conferences. However, in contrast to many ministerial councils in Canada, Conferences of Cantonal Directors are horizontal arrangements in which the 'federal guest' has no formal say. In few cases, organizational responsibility and representation are – as the case in public transportation or planning, construction, and environment – transferred to a layer's office. A third solution is the provision of the infrastructure by the respective conference president which rotates from one canton to the other. This last model as the least institutionalized one is mainly used in areas which are dominated by federal legislation such as economic policy. In most areas (education, health, financial and tax policy, social policy, and justice and crime control) secretariats have been established to defend cantonal positions which provide the context for efficient cross-jurisdictional information-exchange and coordination.

Applying the criteria to assess institutionalization (regularity of meetings, internal and external institutional differentiation, the decision-making rule, the formal status, and the precision of agreements) Conferences of Cantonal Directors tend to be institutionalized on a high or at least on a medium level as Table 4.1 indicates. In contrast to the Canadian case, the conflict potential inherent in a policy is not a crucial factor to explain the relative institutionalization of policy fields in Switzerland. Otherwise one would clearly expect a lower development in fiscal than in environmental policy, for instance. A similar problem occurs looking at the two policy fields characterized by a strong spatial dimension. Both transportation and environment are only institutionalized on a medium level. They are located below the Swiss average while belonging to the most developed areas in the Canadian context. Neither does the nature of competence distribution convincingly account for the existing pattern. IGAs in both concurrent and exclusive areas are highly institutionalized. As laid out in detail in the following, incentives resulting from the executive–legislative relations in the cantons exert a favourable impact on institution building across the range of policy fields visible in an at least medium institutionalization, even in areas in which the cantons hardly exert own legislative competences.

Looking at these conferences' internal structures, besides the plenum which embraces the cantonal directors responsible for the respective area, each conference has an executive which runs the respective arrangement.[3] Both the

---

[3] Partially they are further subdivided in commissions consisting of policy experts out of the cantonal administrations dealing with more specific policy problems.

TABLE 4.1. *Intergovernmental institutionalization in Switzerland in eight policy fields*

Policy Field	Level of Institutionalization Mode of Competence Distribution[a]
Economic and trade policy	Medium institutionalization Exclusive (federal)
Education	High institutionalization Exclusive[b] (cantonal)
Environment	Medium institutionalization Exclusive (federal) (Implementation cantonal)
Financial and tax policy	High institutionalization Exclusive[c] (cantonal)
Health policy	High institutionalization Exclusive (cantonal)[d]/concurrent
Justice and crime control	High institutionalization Exclusive (cantonal)
Social policy	High institutionalization Concurrent
Transportation	Medium institutionalization Exclusive (federal) (Implementation cantonal)

[a] Classification based on Watts (1999) and Fleiner (2006).
[b] The legislative competences of the federal government in the area of education and universities are restricted to federal grants. Professional education, research, and statistics are shared. The educational needs of adults and young people, culture, and language are cantonal matters (Fleiner 2006: 289).
[c] In the areas of personal and income tax and corporate capital tax, the Confederation and the cantons have concurrent powers. However, the federal government is very much the junior partner. The Constitution explicitly limits the federal government's power to raise income tax to 11 per cent of the income of individuals (Art. 128) and the value-added tax to 6.5 per cent (Art. 130). The federal power to levy direct taxes and the value-added tax expires in 2006 (Arts. 13 and 14 Transitory Provisions). Due to these constitutional limitations, there is a relatively low level of centralization. Cantons can decide upon the taxes they levy, the tax base, the tax rate, and exemption. Direct taxes, including the federal ones, are collected by the cantons (Fleiner 2006: 284–6, 288).
[d] Hospitals are an exclusively cantonal matter.

executive and plenum meet several times a year, the executives more often than the plenum. The decision-making rule varies across conferences from majority rule to unanimity. Again, those bodies responsible for major policy fields are more strongly institutionalized and most of them have adopted majority rule to make collective decisions. The major Conferences of Cantonal Directors run working groups dealing with particular policy issues or particular projects. Beyond their own institutional infrastructure, the conferences maintain close networks to the respective cantonal departments and to conferences on the working level linking different groups of officials active in the respective area. Conferences of Cantonal Directors are active in position taking and policy coordination, while, in contrast to the Canadian situation, in most conferences the latter is the dominant function. Regarding position taking, they can issue recommendations as well as collective positions on drafts of federal legislation (*Vernehmlassungen*). In principle, each canton is free to issue individual positions next to a collective one (as regional IGAs can issue regional positions next to national ones) since agreements are voluntary and non-binding. After the conference members agreed upon a position on a piece of federal legislation (in between sessions drafts are circulated to get the directors' confirmation), each canton receives the agreement in written form. Then, if necessary, it can add particular issues or demands before it is sent to the federal government. Evidently, staff of a directorial conference cannot control what individual cantons do with these collectively issued positions in the end. Still there is a constant flow of information to the individual conference whether cantons stick with agreements or not. Overall, both conference staff and cantonal officials confirm that if agreement can be found in Conferences of Cantonal Directors, cantons do not tend to deviate since, by doing so, they weaken the cantonal level (and themselves) towards the federal government, thus easily violate their own interest.

Regarding the more central function of policy coordination, meetings can result in guidelines, benchmarks, or inter-cantonal treaties, so-called concordats. The concordat is the most formal instrument and considered as binding 'inter-cantonal law' (Abderhalden 1999).[4] Concordats aim at regulating concrete policy matters and are therefore highly precise (Bochsler et al. 2004; Bochsler 2006). There is no complete register of these treaties, yet the most extensive database includes 733 of them. About three-fourth of them are bilateral and only a few include all cantons. Most concordats are struck in the areas of financial policy (23 per cent), education and cultural policy (22 per cent) (Bochsler et al. 2004; Bochsler 2006), mainly those areas in which cantons have considerable competences and in which they are most concerned about their autonomy. Most agreements drafted in IGAs, however, have a non-binding character. Nevertheless, experts argue that these provisions become cantonal law (Armingeon 2000*a*: 115). Intergovernmental officials confirm this picture although sometimes guidelines are considered as unsuitable by some of the cantons due to cantonal specificities, hence are not realized 'at home'. Nevertheless, cantons tend to comply also with non-binding recommendations which are usually passed to the department in charge where they provide the basis for cantonal legislation.

Although policy emulation is quite common in Switzerland, the endeavour to find common solutions across cantonal boundaries transcending mere unilateral adaptation is by far more pronounced than in Canada. Efforts to protect

---

[4] With regard to inter-cantonal treaties, the procedures highly differ from canton to canton of how involved the legislature and/or the cantonal peoples are when it comes to ratifications. As an illustration, fifteen of the cantons either allow for a facultative referendum or apply the normal legislative procedure. Executive and administrative agreements can also be struck without demanding ratification by the legislatures (Freiburghaus and Zehnder 2003: 6–7).

cantonal autonomy are primarily directed towards the federal level and intra-cantonal power-sharing lowers the autonomy losses of individual cantons when engaging in horizontal cooperation considerably. There is no reason not to follow collective guidelines if they are useful. In contrast to Canada, they are considered much less as a threat for individual cantonal autonomy.

While the number of staff of the individual IGAs varies considerably from one secretary to over thirty full-time positions, the nature of the institutional set-ups and their functional orientation already support cross-jurisdictional cooperation. Interviewees pointed out that Conferences of Cantonal Directors do not only facilitate information exchange but also issue own initiatives, hence play a proactive role and provide a forum for discussion in which opinions can be changed and conflict overcome. Even when anticipating conflict, conferences might get involved if a collective solution is considered crucial by some members. This again contrasts with the Canadian situation, where IGAs are structurally weak and explicitly not considered as instruments to deal with conflicting issues which tend to be excluded from the agenda beforehand.

Processes in these conferences are widely insulated from political dynamics and have rarely electoral implications. Due to the oversized coalition format, Swiss actors are much less sensitive to these dynamics since (although the directors are directly elected) elections do not have the character of a zero-sum game. Alternation is much less frequent in the first place and, if it occurs, it does not introduce a rupture within cantonal governments comparable to the Canadian situation. A new director is expected to adapt to the group of more experienced colleagues and the internal dynamics in the individual conference have much more of an impact on cantonal representatives than in the Canadian context.

Although cantons might prefer horizontal harmonization of a regional over horizontal harmonization of a national scope (depending on their size and their geographical location[5]), they consider effective cross-jurisdictional coordination as necessary for two reasons that are intertwined: Facing a growing demand for harmonization, successful cross-cantonal coordination is considered necessary as a functional response. Simultaneously, it is considered to be the only way to prevent authority migration to the centre in the long run since continuously unresolved inter-cantonal problems provoke national initiatives justified by the failure of the cantons to deal with problems on the subnational level. In the United States, by contrast, failure of interstate coordination due to compulsory power-sharing often justifies extensive national regulation as laid out later because the lower level governments neither reject federal intrusion as forcefully as in Canada, nor do they solve cross-jurisdictional problems themselves as the cantons.

---

[5] Officials from big, economically strong and central cantons tend to be more open towards nationwide solutions as long as the cantons remain in charge, while smaller, weaker, and more peripheral cantons tend to insist on regional solutions.

The most explicit step to avoid authority migration by assuring a more efficient horizontal coordination can be seen in certain provisions of the NFA (*Neuer Finanzausgleich*), the most recent federalism reform passed in 2004. It originated in a fiscal reform of the federal equalization scheme initiated by the Conference of Finance Directors[6] which in the end had a much broader scope than fiscal concerns only. Some parts of the reform disentangle federal and cantonal competences along the lines 'who decides also pays',[7] which moves the Swiss system further towards the 'dual end' of the federal continuum. Other parts – which is very telling with regard to cantonal coordination strategies – establish 'new instruments of cantonal cooperation' applicable in nine areas of cantonal jurisdiction.[8] The core of these instruments is an enforcement mechanism that can be used to impose an inter-cantonal agreement favoured by a majority of cantons on an opposing cantonal minority. More concretely, a supermajority of cantons can ask the national parliament – who plays the role of a neutral arbiter – to make an agreement obligatory for the deviating minority. Cantonal officials clearly perceive the paradoxical character of this solution. In order to protect own spheres of autonomy from central intrusion, the federal parliament receives the authority to impose inter-cantonal agreements on a minority of cantons. However, they perceive this 'shadow of the hierarchy' (Scharpf 1997: 144) as a necessary means to prevent free-riding on behalf of individual cantons which undermines successful horizontal coordination (Sciarini 2005). For instance, small cantons tend to profit from facilities provided by neighbouring cantons such as the small canton Zug and can afford low tax rates while being unwilling to enter a formal compensation scheme. Another example one finds in the area of hospitals. Here Zurich, the biggest canton, opposes an inter-cantonal solution which would introduce a decentralized coordination of hospitals, while Zurich prefers their centralized coordination within its own boundaries. It is a recurring experience of cantonal officials that cross-jurisdictional problems with financial, especially redistributive implications are hard to solve by self-coordination.

These new mechanisms of inter-cantonal cooperation are thought to strengthen cantonal actors' capacity for intra-horizontal self-coordination. In abstract terms, the NFA provisions illustrate that cantons are ready to trade a part of their 'individual autonomy' against the better protection of the 'collective autonomy' of the cantons as a level of government. 'Without this rule, cantonal competences become federal competences' [translation by author] – as one IGA representative put it. Indeed, some cantonal representatives speculate that this 'shadow of the hierarchy' established through the new instruments remains only a shadow in the literary sense. They expect that the mere existence of the rule will have a

---

[6] For a discussion of the fiscal dimension of the reform see Wälti (2003).

[7] IGA CH V, 28 June 2005. See also http://www.nfa.ch

[8] Among them competences regarding cantonal universities, hospitals, cultural facilities of overregional relevance, and crime control (http://www.nfa.ch/de/dokumente/faktenblaetter/fb11.pdf).

disciplining effect on inter-cantonal negotiations making its actual application unnecessary. Still, it is remarkable that despite some critical voices, the inter-cantonal mechanisms have not been one of the very difficult issues during the reform negotiations. Similar moves are hard to imagine in federal systems such as Canada where individual autonomy protection regularly undermines joint action not to mention institutionalization processes. This is the case even if, overall, such moves weaken the provincial level of government in favour of the centre.

Mechanisms of inter-departmental coordination

The impact of inter-party cooperation – voluntary power-sharing – in the cantons is twofold and at first glance seems somehow contradictory. It opens up space for problem-oriented interaction within each Conference of Directors as separate intergovernmental arena. Simultaneously, it creates reliable ties of each director to his or her executive which assures the cross-departmental coordination of policy-specific, intergovernmental decision-making. Executives are internally less cohesive in Switzerland than in Canada. Simply speaking, intra-party linkages in Canada create stronger government cohesion than inter-party linkages in Switzerland which opens up leeway for departmental autonomy. In practice, this leads to a 'policy of mutual non-interference' between the directors holding different portfolios with regard to minor decisions. Regarding major decisions, and here we arrive at the integrative impact of inter-party cooperation within cantonal executives, the colleagues at home need to agree, a situation which is absent in the United States where party linkages are much weaker. Asked for cooperation-facilitating factors, IGA staff as well as officials pointed to the linkage between intra-cantonal and intergovernmental power-sharing as one core mechanism accounting for the nature of IGR. This statement of the secretary of the Conference of Education Directors describing the dynamics at work is representative for a range of statements made in different areas:

> The political composition of the plenary session of the conference cannot be controlled, it is determined by the cantonal level. It is a reflection of politics in Switzerland. According to me, party politics does not play a big role. Through the involvement into executive processes politicians become less ideological, more moderate. The integration through the principle of collegiality which overall holds prevents that political questions are determined by partisan interests.... The Swiss system of government is certainly the main reason. There are nearly always grand coalitions in the cantons, usually there is a conservative majority, yet also a strong left. It is a broad range of parties, three to four on average.[9] (Translation by author)

IGAs are therefore considered as useful instruments by cantonal and federal actors alike – and the broader the competences (irrespective of how they are

[9] IGA CH IV, 28 June 2005: 1–2.

allocated to the levels), the more reasonable to set up strong IGAs. It fits the picture that compared to Canadian ministers members of directorial conferences are usually not mandated. Hence, there is leeway to deviate from 'hard bargaining' in favour of a problem-oriented mode of interaction. Although partisan conflict can enter the discussion, it is mostly considered as a minor factor. If it does, it tends to complicate the interaction between different conferences. For instance, the conference responsible for social policy tends to represent rather the left, the finance directors rather the right side of the partisan spectrum. Although they try to avoid weakening each other mutually as we will see in Chapter 6, they sometimes put forward different opinions.

Overall, the systemic environment in the Swiss federal polity favours IGAs' institutionalization. Conferences of Cantonal Directors are strong enough to create an environment in which a 'departmental' rationale becomes relevant without directors being disconnected from their multiparty cabinets. Cantonal executives form a collegial body and are tied together by voluntary party-cooperation. Through this linkage, favourable political dynamics impact upon the different policy fields in a similar way and mutually reinforce each other. The nature of intra-executive power-sharing does neither disaggregate the executive branch nor the canton as a whole. Otherwise it could generate intergovernmental patterns affected much more by policy- and issue-specific features as observed in the United States. The following citation of conference staff underlines this point:

> Usually the directors are not mandated. A director has a sensor how it [an issue] will be received by his government, by the population, by the exponents of a position in parliament. He realizes immediately, there is resistance and says 'at home there is no majority'. Immediately he says 'hold on, this cannot be realized'. It is always a forth and back. One needs to assure oneself at home, in order not to get lost.[10] (Translation and insertion by author)

Intergovernmental patterns and informal institutions remain executive-centred and maintain a coherent representation of the cantons across the range of policy-specific arrangements. Further, Swiss intergovernmental actors have tried to link policy-specific IGAs themselves through regular secretarial meetings. They also drafted a framework agreement as a mechanism to avoid and to settle conflict between Conferences of Cantonal Directors. Finally, the linkages between sector-wide and issue-specific IGAs, which exist in all major policy fields, are much tighter and much more stable in Switzerland than in Canada where mandates to expert commissions are assigned on a need basis. These more specific bodies include conferences of senior officials, conferences of professional groups in the administrations, and conferences dedicated to policy issues important in the respective policy field.[11] Their number in each field nicely corresponds to

[10] IGA CH XI, 28 March 2006: 5.
[11] Konferenz der Kantonsregierungen: Liste der bestehenden fachtechnischen Konferenzen nach Direktorenkonferenzen (Stand 2005).

the degree of institutionalization of the directorial conference in this area and the latter's relative strength in resources. In the education sector, fourteen sub-conferences are in place followed by health and justice and crime control with seven sub-conferences, respectively.[12] We will return to the linkages between IGAs in detail in Chapter 6 comparing intergovernmental integration across our three systems. Ironically, in Canada, where conflict spills over from one area to the other and integrative efforts would be more necessary to stabilize processes, such a response is – due to the dominant political dynamics – not feasible. In Switzerland, the level of conflict is lower, while intergovernmental actors nonetheless invest in structures to handle cross-cutting issues more efficiently. Due to favourable intragovernmental incentives, the corridor of adaptation is wide.

SUMMARY

The high policy-specific institutionalization in Swiss IGR can be traced back to intragovernmental incentive structures generated by voluntary power-sharing in the cantons. Regular co-decision directed towards policy coordination is the dominant interaction mode. Voluntary power-sharing links the different departments within their cantonal executives – despite considerable departmental leeway to engage in inter governmental problem-solving. This link reinforces cooperation processes across different policy fields and thereby accounts for the considerable convergence of institution building.

GENERALIST CANTONAL COOPERATION: THE CONFERENCE OF CANTONAL EXECUTIVES

While policy-specific institutionalization has a long tradition, the creation of generalist IGAs is fairly recent. Beginning of the 1990s, the cantons were less and less satisfied with the general representation of cantonal interests on the federal level. Although the *Ständerat*, the Swiss Senate, can veto legislation and each canton is equally represented by two directly elected Senators, the chamber is more strongly dominated by party politics than by regional and territorial interests (Linder 1999). Thus, the Swiss Senate was less and less considered as an effective vehicle for territorial representation. In 1993, this critical attitude found its expression in the set-up of the horizontal Conference of Cantonal Executives (*Konferenz der*

---

[12] Depending on the policy field, contact is either established on a demand basis as in education. Alternatively regular meetings are set up, or protocols exchanged as in transportation, in fiscal policy, or in health.

Kantonsregierungen). Its initial purpose was the defence of cantonal interests in the bargaining processes with the EU which functioned as a major trigger for its foundation since the cantons feared to loose out in these negotiations otherwise. Yet the Conference of Cantonal Executives ended up filling a broader gap in the Swiss system of intergovernmental cooperation. Although it started as a policy-specific conference for foreign relations corresponding to the so far dominant departmental patterns of Swiss IGR, up to now the Conference of Cantonal Executives developed into an IGA with a cross-sectoral outlook which channels general inter-cantonal and inter-institutional transactions. To give a concrete example, together with the Conference of Finance Directors, it was a major cantonal player during the NFA reform negotiations, the most recent federalism reform.

The institutional structure of the Conference of Cantonal Executives is very similar to the Conferences of Cantonal Directors. Its plenum, consisting of representatives sent by the cantonal executives, meets four times a year. In these sessions, political decisions are made, which largely boil down to 'common positions' on issues or plans of the central government that concerns cantonal authority in general. Decisions are taken by majority rule (18 of 26 cantons). The plenary session is accompanied by four meetings of a smaller executive committee which is composed of nine members selected through a distributive scheme based on regional affiliation (interestingly, party affiliation was not taken up as a criterion). The executive committee makes strategic decisions and prepares the plenary sessions. While in ordinary meetings one representative per canton participates, once a year in January the Conference of Cantonal Executives invites the whole governments to a session which is widely attended and settles basic questions which guide the operations of the conference throughout the year.

In order to cope with the diversity of topics it needs to handle simultaneously, the conference has established a number of committees and working groups on issues of particular cantonal interest such as redistributive policy (Jahresbericht CH Stiftung 2000: 21). Both the majority rule applied for plenary decisions and the composition of the executive indicate that the participating cantons do neither insist in equal representation nor in equal veto positions since cantons do not consider agreement as feasible otherwise. In principle, each canton can issue an own position to emphasize aspects specific to the canton, but if the quorum of 18 is reached, the resolution counts as the overall cantonal position.

This does not mean that cantonal governments are not eager to defend their interests: In contrast to members in directorial conferences, cantonal representatives in the Conference of Cantonal Executives are mandated by their governments, which emphasizes these meetings' higher political profile. This can complicate the formulation of common positions considerably since cantonal executives reduce the potential of discussion dynamics to generate outcomes they do not unambiguously support and delimit the impact that the institutional context can play in altering representatives' positions. This contrasts with the problem-oriented discussions within the Conferences of Cantonal Directors where representatives can be more open. Moreover, the Conference of Cantonal

Executives only allows elected representatives to participate in their meetings without any official staff present. Again, the stronger political character of the conference becomes visible in a greater focus on position taking on sensitive questions concerning cantonal powers than typical for policy-specific directorial conferences. This also means that cantons are more critical towards trading individual autonomy against collective strength in the Conference of Cantonal Executives since positions formulated in this context have broader implications and receive more public attention than directorial recommendations. The critical distance expressed by some cantonal officials towards the strengthening of the conference in the last couple of years points in similar directions. In particular, small and peripheral cantons fear the conference – now having an own operational structure and an established position in the intergovernmental arena – to develop a life of its own and to get increasingly detached from 'real' cantonal interests. As cantonal officials pointed out:

> We need to be careful that no hegemonic, centralist structure will grow that says: 'We are the cantons'.[13]

> Since then [its foundation] the Conference of Cantonal Executives has tried to introduce an additional level next to the cantonal chamber into the power game between *Bundesrat* and national parliament, to become a linchpin which tries to gain own strength towards the *Ständerat*, without constitutional legitimation.... This created an additional level of power without a popular mandate.[14] [insertion by author]

What becomes very clear is that the cantons do not simply interpret the growing strength of the Conference of Cantonal Executives as a power increase for themselves. Instead, they perceive it as an independent entity whose loyalty to cantonal interest needs to be actively assured. The stronger the conference gets, not only in terms of mere resources but also in terms of 'standing' within the intergovernmental system, the more the cantons are inclined to consider their relations with the Conference of Cantonal Executives as a principal-agent constellation. The potential cheating on cantonal preferences of an agent who also pursues its institutional self-interest (in this case the conference) gets increasingly problematic the more power the agent accumulates. Accordingly, even for those cantons very actively using the conference to pursue own goals, the latter's development remains a double-edged sword. Simultaneously, the French-speaking cantons perceive the conference as a vehicle of the German-speaking cantons pointing to a cultural divide. The German-speaking cantons used the conference much more actively right from the beginning, while the French-speaking cantons remained distanced and paid little attention. With the increasing presence of the Conference of Cantonal Executives in Swiss IGR, however, also French-speaking executives get more aware of this platform for cantonal interest representation and

---

[13] COfficial X, 28 September: 6.   [14] COfficial IV, 8 August: 3–4.

intergovernmental officials on the bureaucratic level try to motivate executive representatives to get more actively involved.

All in all, cantonal support still outweighs existing criticism, in particular since the Conference of Cantonal Executives delivers important expertise that many cantons cannot provide on their own. Moreover, the conference had some considerable successes, for instance in coordinating the cantons during the NFA negotiations or the successful cantonal referendum in 2004 to which I will come back later on. However, one needs to be aware of the tension between individual cantonal interests to increase their weight in the system through the Conference of Cantonal Executives and the fear of this vehicle's alienation from its members in the course of its institutional strengthening. Thus, the flipside of an IGA's growing capacity to bridge cross-jurisdictional conflict due to increasing institutionalization is the simultaneous development of an institutional self-interest. Signs that this interest is too actively pursued can be easily evaluated critically by lower level governments and other IGAs and, as a consequence, complicate inter-institutional relations as Chapter 6 on integration will demonstrate.

REGIONAL INTERGOVERNMENTAL ARRANGEMENTS

Finally, since the Swiss federal system is a system characterized by considerable social heterogeneity, a look at regional IGAs is necessary to complete the picture. The major goal of this section is to contrast the Swiss with the Canadian situation. The latter is characterized by a 'bottom–up logic' driven by power-concentrating governments which tend towards solutions of the smallest common denominator of only limited scope (in terms of concessions and territory). As we will see below, the Swiss situation points towards a balance between the two levels of government nourished by voluntary power-sharing in the cantons. Again, we will look at the policy-specific IGAs in a first step and at the generalist ones afterwards.

Reflecting the nationwide pattern, in the major policy fields the Swiss regions are organized in policy-specific IGAs. Although policy-specific IGAs are not always set up in all of the regions, in areas such as fiscal policy; education; health; social policy; justice and crime control; and construction, planning, and environment, we usually find them. All in all, over thirty of these conferences exist. In contrast to the three regions Western Switzerland, Eastern Switzerland, and Central Switzerland which have regional conferences in all major areas of cantonal responsibility,[15] only Northwest Switzerland lacks regional Conferences of Cantonal Directors in some of the major areas such as

---

[15] Some even in areas in which cantons widely lack any responsibility such as the conference of the military departments in Western Switzerland (Trees 2005b: 20).

fiscal policy and justice and crime control (Trees 2005*b*: 19–23). Depending on the respective policy fields, these regional conferences are institutionalized on different levels. On the whole, the policy-specific IGAs are more weakly organized on the regional than on the national level and have been set up later than their national pendants. In education as a major cantonal responsibility, most regions run their own secretariats which are in part institutionalized on a high level.[16] Again, areas which are either of comparatively minor importance or in which federal regulation is dominant, structures tend to be weakly institutionalized. As Chapter 6 on integration will show, one finds a similar diversity of linkages between the two levels.

As a shared feature, it is important to note that these regional bodies are institutionally independent from their national counterparts, they are no subunits of the national branch. Thus, there is no clear hierarchy between the levels. Regional IGAs decide on which topics they want to take a collective position and quite regularly both levels take positions on the same type of issues. How much cooperation occurs again depends on the degree of inter-institutional integration in the respective field. The policy-specific structures on the regional level indicate that cantonal governments willingly invest in structures to stabilize intergovernmental processes. This is noticeable since the national Conferences of Cantonal Directors are already considerably institutionalized and the overall defence of cantonal authority is strongest when cantons cooperate on a national scope, thus when no parallel regional positions are issued. Nevertheless, cantonal governments obviously consider an additional regional layer of intergovernmental structures targeting issues from a regional viewpoint as desirable.

Since the Conference of Cantonal Executives was founded in the 1990s only, one would expect that generalist IGAs with regional scope have been quite strong, in particular since regional interests tend to be more homogenous than national ones. However, due to the strong institutionalization of Swiss IGR along policy lines, there has not been much pressure to invest in the overall representation of cantonal governments pursuing goals through a generalist lens. Until the 1990s, regional IGAs have been of rather limited relevance (Trees 2005*a*: 4). Up until now, there are four regional IGAs in place. The Conference of Northwest Switzerland was founded already in 1964, followed by the Conference of Central Switzerland in 1966. The Conference of Northwest Switzerland was set up in 1972, while the Conférence des Gouvernements de Suisse Occidentale only followed in 1993. Some cantons such as Berne and Zurich participate in several conferences, while usually having access to full membership and voting rights only in one (Trees 2005*a*: 2–6). The Conference of Eastern Switzerland and the Conference of Central Switzerland are strongly institutionalized, while

---

[16] Bildungsdirektoren-Konferenz Zentralschweiz, Statut, 21 September 2001 (http://www.ciip.ch/ciip/pages/navigation_entetes/som_quisommes.htm).

the other two are structurally weaker but still institutionalized on a medium level.

It seems surprising that regional IGAs are weaker than national ones since they have to deal with less heterogeneous preferences. However, there are good reasons to invest more resources in a national IGA with a generalist outlook than in several regional ones. One has to do with the generalist IGAs' major function of position taking on national issues. In order to influence the federal government most effectively an overregional coalition is necessary. Such a coalition is easily undermined by strong regional bodies reinforcing inter-regional divides if not closely linked to the national arrangement. Moreover, the differences in institutional development are partially rooted in the respective functions of the IGAs. While the national IGAs have traditionally focused on the phase of policy formulation in those policy fields in which cantons are traditionally strong, regional Conferences of Cantonal Directors deal much more with implementation issues. Horizontal coordination in the implementation phase is a newer phenomenon than coordination in the phase of policy formulation. Finally and most importantly, in the major policy areas, one does not only find the national Conferences of Cantonal Directors but also regional pendants which sufficiently assure the representation of regional interests in major areas of cantonal interest. Given this institutional context, it is rather surprising that the cantons nevertheless were willing to invest and strengthen regional IGAs with a generalist profile.

The growing awareness of the cantons to strengthen collective interest representation was triggered by the increasingly difficult financial situation, the transferral of tasks and burdens from the federal to the cantonal level, as well as the NFA reform negotiations. This trend has become equally visible in the set-up of the Conference of Cantonal Executives as in the efforts of regional arrangements to reform their internal structures to facilitate the flow of information and increase decision-making efficiency (Trees 2005*a*: 1). At the same time, one can also read the strengthening of regional directorial conferences as a response to the stronger representation of a national cantonal profile through the Conference of Cantonal Executives in order to maintain a balance between national and regional interest representations – a need the cantons might have felt with the increasing strengthening of the nationwide conference. The Conference of Eastern Switzerland underwent reforms and established a professional secretariat in 1996 and the Conference of Central Switzerland established a secretariat in 2001. The Conférence des Gouvernements de Suisse Occidentale was only founded in 1993 at the same time as the Conference of Cantonal Executives. The Conférence des Gouvernements de Suisse Occidentale and the Conference of Northwest Switzerland try to keep up with the other regions which initiated reforms first, attempting to actively maintain an inter-regional balance (Trees 2005*a*: 1, 7), which might be upset by a one-sided strengthening of regional representation. Similar 'chain reactions' did not occur in the Canadian case due to the individualist lens of governments. The increasingly strong back-up of the Conference of Atlantic

Premiers has not triggered any reactions on the side of the Western Premiers. An opposite 'chain reaction' towards fragmentation rooted in intragovernmental incentives occurred in the second power-sharing democracy, the United States, as highlighted in the following chapter.

SUMMARY

The highly institutionalized IGAs facilitating generalist position-taking and policy harmonization indicate that regular co-decision is the dominant interaction pattern in Swiss federalism. Although one finds some variance in the make-up and resources of the individual IGAs, most of them are institutionalized on a high level. This is the case for the older policy-specific as for the more recently established generalist IGAs. Patterns are similar on the regional level, which is – on the whole – not as developed (contradicting 'transaction cost arguments' that institutionalization is higher, the less complex the government configuration concerned). From a cross-national perspective, the number and the institutionalization of IGAs in the Swiss context is remarkable.

The in-depth analysis revealed that all mechanisms linked to intra-cantonal incentives identified by the theoretical approach support informal institution-building. One major claim was that the absence of competition within the Swiss cantons weakens tendencies for blame shifting and provides the leeway to adapt to demands for cross-boundary cooperation rather easily. In fact, 'blaming' was – if at all – only mentioned as a force in favour of cooperation, namely referring to the cantonal populations which blame their governments for having failed to comply with inter-cantonal standards when it comes to the coherent delivery of services. It has not been mentioned as a destructive impact on intergovernmental cooperation as in Canada. Most importantly, since oversized coalitions are the most frequent cabinet type, the actors are considerably protected from electoral punishment. Responsibility for individual policies is hard to assign to particular parties or politicians. Accordingly, electoral pressure does not constitute a harming impact on intergovernmental interaction and institution building. Furthermore, the ideologically moderating effect of oversized party executives in the cantons has been clearly identified as a reason why IGR in Switzerland can progress rather smoothly. In fact, several effects have been mentioned that result from the internal decision-making mode, which have the same cooperation-favouring impact. First, the necessity to compromise across partisan differences within oversized coalitions forces any executive members to move away from extreme positions. This heavily reduces the potential for ideologically based conflict also between cantonal executives in the intergovernmental arena. Second, when engaging in IGAs, each representative knows that the position he or she takes, needs to be also acceptable at home – at least if it is a question of some political relevance and not purely technical. Positions need to be moderate enough to avoid resistance within one's cabinet or the cantonal legislature if the latter's approval is necessary. Cantonal parliaments have been increasingly critical towards IGR where executives strike agreements in areas of cantonal authority, while, in the end, the parliaments face a 'take it or leave it decision'. As a response, cantonal executives have made efforts to involve their parliaments already in the negotiation stage in order to satisfy the parliamentary demands for a stronger involvement. Overall, however, the representatives of Conferences of Cantonal Directors consider a potential parliamentary veto as the minor problem compared to a potential popular veto which can also be initiated by small coalition partners ignored too often within the executive. Therefore, executive coalitions (as well as legislative support) tend to be broad. Simultaneously, party linkages between members of the executive and the legislature belonging to the same party are sufficiently strong to bridge the institutional divide between the branches which are – as in the United States – elected separately. Finally, the perceived autonomy losses are limited due to power sharing in the cantons which facilitates power sharing in the intergovernmental arena.

Note, however, that this does not mean that cantonal actors are automatically willing to share autonomy with the federal government as well. They clearly oppose centralization. The moderating impact of oversized coalitions due to lowering the perceived autonomy losses works strongest on the horizontal level, where individual cantonal autonomy is traded against the stronger protection or strengthening of the collective autonomy of the cantonal level towards the federal government. And also these costs of horizontal collaboration are clearly perceived – in particular by smaller cantons that tend to view even the Conference of Cantonal Executives suspiciously as an expression of hegemonic tendencies. While the incentives generated by voluntary power-sharing within the cantons favour intergovernmental institutionalization, each government is still aware of the share of power it is willing to invest or, alternatively, eager to defend.

Swiss intergovernmental actors are not per se more cooperative than actors in power-concentrating contexts such as Canada. Relative autonomy losses are estimated strategically against the benefits of cooperation and in the Swiss context they are low enough. Consequently, a reduction of individual autonomy in exchange for the protection of collective cantonal power is acceptable. Autonomy protection is regularly mentioned as the major driving force behind the cantonal endeavour to engage in and strengthen horizontal IGAs, while cantons know that this reduces their individual power. Limited autonomy losses also facilitate federal–cantonal relations, for instance visible in the invitations of federal representatives to the meetings of Conferences of Cantonal Directors. However, the effect is weaker since the federal government constitutes a bigger threat. Vice versa, the potential costs of cooperation are higher since the federal government is more likely to dominate the relationship. Finally, the interest configuration is comparatively stable, visible in the high number of overlapping governments. IGR are characterized by continuity and, as interviewees pointed out, the alternation of cantonal directors – when it occurs – has only a very weak impact on intergovernmental processes. Overall, we end up with the complete opposite of the Canadian situation: due to favourable intragovernmental incentives in the Swiss cantons, intergovernmental institutions tend to be highly developed across governmental levels and policy fields.

5

Intergovernmental Institutionalization in the United States

This chapter analyses the impact of compulsory power-sharing on informal institution-building in the American intergovernmental arena. One distinct feature of American IGR which differs from the executive-dominated pattern in both Canada and Switzerland is the coexistence of IGAs that represent the interests of the different governmental branches in the states. The core state arrangements are the National Governors' Association, the National Conference of State Legislatures, and the Council of State Governments. While they are highly institutionalized and indicate the cooperation-favouring impact of intragovernmental power-sharing, they simultaneously reflect the divisive nature of the type of power sharing prevalent in the American states.

To give a short overview of the intergovernmental landscape, the Council of State Governments was founded in 1937. It is the mother institution of the Governors' Association and the National Conference of State Legislatures which split from the Council in order to lobby for their particular institutional interests (Haider 1974; Arnold and Plant 1994). This process of institutional dissociation along constitutional lines is characteristic for the American intergovernmental arena. The executive–legislative divide coins patterns of institution building on the national and the regional levels.[1] The coexistence of three generalist state IGAs already points to a major side-effect of the compulsory nature of power sharing which needs to be kept in mind – its fragmenting impact on the states as political units. Unable to represent the states as coherent actors, IGAs focus on lobbying for the interests of their particular members, members perceived predominantly as professionals, not as representatives of a political system with a particular interest profile.

Inter-institutional division becomes visible not only in the coexistence of IGAs reflecting the interests of individual branches, but also in IGAs reflecting

---

[1] While diverging interest profiles created the necessity for a separate representation platform for each branch, there were also practical reasons for the split. In order to maintain a tax-exemption status, the Council of State Governments can only spend a restricted amount of money on lobbying. The Governors' Association and the Conference of Legislatures overcame this restriction by becoming independent in order to maximize their potential to push for their members' interests.

splits within branches. The Governors' Association and the Conference of State Legislatures are in principle bipartisan. As one structural indication the presidency of the latter rotates between the parties. Nonetheless, the perception of the Conference of Legislatures as too liberal led to the foundation of the conservative American Legislative Exchange Council. Yet while partisan divides are important, the members of the Legislative Exchange Council are still members of the more inclusive Conference of State Legislatures. In recent years, also the Governors' Association had to cope with situations on the executive committee level in which Republican governors criticized proposals as being too hard on the current federal administration, political interferences which the IGA staff rejected. In particular during the last decade, partisan influences are increasingly felt, especially in the federal arena. State governments, by contrast, have been less affected by these processes of politicization and tend to be more pragmatic and problem-oriented (Dinan and Krane 2005). All in all, instead of constituting a stand-alone rationale along which intergovernmental processes evolve, partisan divides complement the complex picture of immensly fragmented IGR.

Fragmentation is reinforced by numerous 'lower level' arrangements competing with state IGAs. Some of them – such as the United States Conference of Mayors – are very powerful (Haider 1974; Cigler 1995). As a consequence, states are often depicted as being downgraded to a 'middle tier' with little responsibility unfettered by formal national constraints or potent local pressure (Wright 1982: 238; Reeves 1990: 85). It comes as no surprise that the third branch, the judiciary, is also represented in the intergovernmental game. The National Association of Attorneys General sheds light on an additional divide that reflects the internal nature of the state executives in particular: In 43 states the state attorney is directly elected, has considerable independence from the governor, and is often ambitious to obtain higher political office (Provost 2003: 37). The National Association of Attorneys General, which was founded 1907, attempts to facilitate interstate cooperation on legal and law enforcement issues, conducts policy research, and provides a communication channel between the chief legal officers of the states.[2] Hence, even actors belonging to the judiciary pursue their interests separately and sometimes do so against the explicit will of their governors (Derthick 2001; Provost 2003: 37).

In contrast to the chaotic patterns of informal institutions, the Advisory Commission on IGR was a formal–legal attempt to bridge inter-branch and federal–state divides in American federalism, which had, however, little success. It was created in 1959 and abolished by the Clinton administration in 1996 in response to the commission's handling of the unfunded mandates issue. In contrast to other IGAs, the Advisory Commission was based on federal law

---

[2] http://www.naag.org/naag/about_naag.php

as a bipartisan body for the examination of the federal–state relationship and in charge of recommending improvements. It was composed of three members of each house of Congress, four governors, four mayors, three state legislators, three elected county officials, three members of the president's cabinet, and three private citizens (McDowell 1997: 111–12). Despite the achievements of the Advisory Commission on IGR in the generation of expertise, federal institutions were clearly overrepresented. The composition precluded ex ante that this commission would be able to speak on behalf of the federal government and the states since most of the latter were not even represented. In this sense, the Advisory Commission was a valuable infrastructure for exchanges but its functions were restricted to information gathering and advice, a pattern which reoccurs in the analysis of horizontal IGAs in U.S. federalism. Guiding policy coordination or generating politically binding commitments through informal agreement are rarely part of these arrangements' functional repertoires. The abolition of the commission followed its involvement in a highly politicized debate over unfunded mandates for which the federal government is still nowadays frequently criticized (which is also a core issue for a number of IGAs). Reflecting its high sensitivity, during this debate the commission lost most of its federal support. Furthermore, in the course of the conflict three members of the executive branch (not of whole government units) withdrew from its meetings, while legislators stayed (McDowell 1997: 116). This division within the commission as a formally established body re-emphasizes the pervasiveness of inter-branch differences. It points to a dynamic in American IGR shaped by functional roles rather than divides between lower level governments as we have observed in Canada and Switzerland.

To understand the patterns of informal institution-building in U.S. federalism, the implications of the constitutional structure of the states is central. Focusing on the position of state governors who are often considered as very powerful actors, the following citation depicts the consequences of the states' internal structures:

> Whatever approach or posture a governor adopts, it seems certain that a governor cannot escape from entanglement in a web of (...) political, policy, and administrative relationships. (Wright 1982: 271)

Beyond the impact of inter-branch divides as one expression of compulsory power-sharing, governors' deficient steering capacity is reinforced by compulsory power-sharing inside the executive branch. A U.S. governor has by far less control over the executive branch in his or her state than a Canadian premier. Department heads might be appointed by the governor. Other departments, however, are run by directly elected officials or by independent board. In both cases, gubernatorial control over the administrative apparatus is diminished (Dye 1985). Governors' offices are organized separately from the bulk of the executive branch. They have been professionalized over the years and tried to increase their capacities for steering the state administration (Muchmore 1983: 183). Facing tremendous structural barriers and increasing managerial demands, however, governors remain nonetheless unable to achieve an overall integration of their states as political units, a feature reflecting the internal nature of the states essential to understand American IGR.

GENERALIST ARRANGEMENTS: INSTITUTIONALIZATION AND FRAGMENTATION

As in Canada and Switzerland, also in the United States, we find that informal institution-building corresponds to the incentive structures in its lower level governments. Given power sharing within the states, overall, generalist IGAs on the national and regional levels are highly institutionalized. Starting with the nationwide institutions, the National Governors' Association, the Council of State Governments, and the National Conference of State Legislatures as the three major state arrangements meet regularly and are run by an executive committee supported by a permanent secretariat. Internal decisions are taken by majority rule; the Conference of Legislatures, for instance, decides with a three-fourth majority. As mentioned above, the Governors' Association and the Conference of Legislatures are lobbying groups, while the Council of State Governments is a service association functioning as a loose umbrella of the two (Arnold and Plant 1994: 102). Exceptional in the U.S. context, the Council is predominantly directed towards facilitating exchanges between the states and is not a lobbying organization in formal terms. Although it responded to the general trend towards lobbying by running a smaller office in Washington D.C. which focuses on federal activities, its headquarters are still located in Lexington indicating the arrangement's stronger focus on state politics.

IGAs in American federalism have two main functions: (1) lobbying; and (2) the provision of services to their members as professionals. This double orientation as political and professional body is clearly visible in these arrangements' infrastructures. The Conference of Legislatures is governed by an executive committee of sixty members of which forty are legislators – representatives – and twenty legislative staff – professionals without any political function. Correspondingly, the Governors' Association is divided in two arms, the 'core NGA' which represents the governors politically and the Center for Best Practices which consults the individual states on concrete policy problems.[3] The political activities of the 'core NGA' are entirely vertically oriented. Like private interest groups, American IGAs, usually classified as 'public interest groups' (Arnold and Plant 1994; Cigler 1995), try to

---

[3] Note that the political arm is funded by the states and the Center for Best Practices by foundation money.

ensure that their members' views are channelled into federal policy-making. They issue detailed policy resolutions which articulate the members' shared positions, positions which are annually updated. Staff and members regularly testify on behalf of the arrangement in Congressional committee hearings where crucial legislation is discussed. IGA staff pursues regular contacts with highly specialized federal officials presupposing a high degree of expertise which reflects in their internal differentiation along policy lines. The Governors' Association runs several standing committees on core policy areas such as health and legal affairs. Correspondingly, the Conference of State Legislatures has fifteen standing committees which mirror the areas state legislatures deal with. Horizontal policy-coordination does not constitute a major task.

In substantial terms, the financial implications of federal regulation and, more particularly, unfunded mandates issued by the federal government are a central problem for both IGAs simply because their members are compelled to prevent cost-shifting to the states. Yet, while they share a resistance against federal cost-shifting, they have different sensitivities about how willingly legislative state autonomy is traded against federal funding in those cases in which the centre is willing to pay for it. The Conference of State Legislatures focuses on the prevention of federal pre-emption, hence federal encroachment upon state authority in general. If mandates are unfunded or federal tax legislation restricts state revenues, this makes things only worse. The governors' position on federal mandates is much less dogmatic and less oriented towards the protection of legislative authority per se. This is unsurprising. Due to the separation of powers, legislative authority is a major concern of state legislatures for which the executives feel less responsible:

> The NGA [National Governor's Association] has a permanent policy against federal encroachment. However, we also recognized the changing relationship in the international market place. States become smaller political units as the market expands. States' relevance shrinks. This is a challenge for the governors to carve out the role of the states in the international market. Economics drive centralization rather than politics as in the EU. In some cases federal mandates are the best way to handle problems, unfortunately.[4] [insertion by author]

Interviews with state officials underline this division. The governors are interested in obtaining as much leeway as possible in the implementation phase in order 'to get things done'. As long as the federal government gives funding with limited restrictions on state action, the intrusion into spheres of state authority is not of overriding importance from an executive point of view. And although executive IGAs complain about unfunded mandates, their opposition is less pronounced since they apply the same strategy of cost-shifting with regard to the local level. The differences in the preferences of legislative and executive actors regarding

---

[4] IGA US II, 4 April 2005: 2.

the protection of state authority highlights why the separate representation of governors' and legislatures' interests has become necessary. It also explains why these bodies often end up competing for influence while, in principle, both are thought to pursue 'state interests'.

Compared to legislative arrangements, executive IGAs tend to have a stronger presence in Washington, D.C., and better access to the federal government. From the federal officials' point of view, executive IGAs can deliver expertise with regard to policy implementation, a resource to which legislators have no access. As a state official explained: 'It comes from the nature of government. The executive has two roles. It does the implementation and administrates programs'.[5] Therefore, federal agencies and Congressional members tend to be more receptive towards executive influence. Preventing a mutual weakening of state executive interests, we find a distribution of labour between the state offices representing individual governors and the Governors' Association, both of which are located in the Hall of the States. While the former deal with state-specific issues, the latter takes over when broader interests are shared by several states. As a consequence, the Governors' Association and the state offices are much more closely linked than the governors and the Conference of State Legislatures. Both factors weaken IGAs strongly oriented towards the protection of legislative state autonomy. To a certain degree, the National Conference of State Legislatures profits from the institutional linkage between Congressional members (often former state legislators) and the resulting personal ties to state legislatures. On the whole, however, this does not compensate for the executives' better access to federal officials. While, from the governors' point of view, cooperation with the legislatures thus becomes less profitable, it simultaneously implies that neither of the two can effectively speak on behalf of 'their states'. Whenever the legislatures and the governors issue different testimonies on federal legislation, the likely influence of both is reduced.

The coexistence of multiple, highly institutionalized IGAs present in the American system can be attributed to the striking inability to pool power within the individual state as well as the inability to speak with one voice for the states as a level of goverment. This has proven particularly detrimental to any cooperation efforts between the states (Smiley and Watts 1985: 40–2; Cigler 1995: 150). Of course, the size and internal diversity of the country (Kincaid 2003) exacerbates coordination between the states beyond a certain regional scope. However, the next section will demonstrate that the same divides can be observed on the regional level where diversity is less pronounced. The main barrier against effective inter-state cooperation is structural and originates in intragovernmental incentive structures. In contrast to parliamentary systems, the state executives face strong legislatures eager to protect their power. Since parties are weak, they cannot bridge the differences between the branches either. Thus, if

---

[5] SOfficial III, 13 July 2005.

a formal resolution of the Governors' Association is achieved, that is, if divergent views between governors are overcome, they cannot be sure that whatever they approve will find support at home. Intense legislative–executive battles, particularly concerning federal funds, are not unusual (Wright 1982: 295). Facing state legislatures' strong control activity, it seems hardly worthwhile to invest energy in policy coordination presupposing legislative agreement. Certainly, whether a governor can pursue any policy leadership internally also depends on the particular state, since both the formal resources of the executives and legislative professionalism vary across the states (Beyle and Dalton 1983; Gray and Eisinger 1991; Radin and Boase 2000). Despite these differences, however, there are general trends that managerial demands have become more and more dominant, while the leadership potential of governors has tended to decrease (Wright 1982: 277).

Growing demands towards politicians as service providers accompanied by the fragmentation of individual government units does not assist IGAs in strengthening their profile as vehicles for political representation and policy coordination. In the opposite, the situation provides direct incentives for IGAs to respond to managerial-professional demands of their members as public officials and support them in fulfilling their specialized roles. Accordingly, IGAs have developed a strong 'non-political' component. All three state IGAs provide a wide range of services to their members as professional groups. Although generalist IGAs in Canada and Switzerland also engage in the provision of expertise, they do not primarily serve particular types of public officials, but serve whole government units. Thereby information provision and the generation of expertise remain tied to the political functions of IGAs. They are directed towards political position-formation and policy coordination and support the provision of collective goods. In the United States, IGAs' services are directed towards individual members to reduce the likelihood of exit. The pressure to do so is strong since the 'political costs' of exiting IGAs are minor compared to other federal systems. In Switzerland, for instance, a canton leaving the Conference of Cantonal Executives would lose its access to the core channel in federal–cantonal relations as far as highly salient issues such as reform debates or international negotiations are concerned. No IGA in American federalism has a status comparable to this Swiss conference since none of them can speak and act on behalf of the states.

As a compensatory strategy, the relevance of service delivery in the American intergovernmental arena is enormous as the resources invested indicate. The National Conference of State Legislatures has one office in Denver with about 130 employers and one in Washington, D.C., with 45–50 staff. The function of the D.C. office is lobbying for the legislative representatives and their staff. The bigger office in Denver is focused on service provision: publishes a newsletter, answers questions, conducts research for legislators, and supports legislative staff. While the Canadian Council of the Federation and the Swiss Conference of Cantonal Executives have by far fewer staff, they are still more strongly directed towards supporting political negotiations between their members. Politics is increasingly demanding as a business in terms of the skills and expertise expected from office holders and staff; American IGAs responded readily to these demands. The National Conference of State Legislatures provides technical assistance and opportunities for policy makers. The Center of Best Practices of the Governors' Association specializes in the provision of expert advice. Further, it is a general feature of generalist arrangements that they try to provide professional training. Some assign formal certifications in order to increase the value of membership (Arnold and Plant 1994: 36–7). Among the three state IGAs, the service dimension is the most pronounced in the Council of State Governments. The majority of its research staff try to identify long-term trends which affect state policy-making such as demographic changes and these changes' driving forces. They also try to identify key innovative policies (in terms of executive programs or legislation) able to respond to these trends. Correspondingly, the time horizon of the staff of both the National Governors' Association and the National Conference of State Legislatures is different from that of Council staff. Due to their lobbying activities, the former are oriented towards the national legislative agenda for the current year rather than long-term developments.

The 'double face' of IGAs as political bodies and service providers is certainly nourished by the strong professionalization of American politics as compared to Canadian and Swiss politics. Nonetheless, systemic features clearly shape the particular nature of the institutional make-up and the functional orientation of IGAs. Due to intense competition from public and private interest groups alike, IGAs in the United States cannot assure that their members' interests will be at all considered in the federal arena, while major intergovernmental channels in other countries can usually at least assure that they are heard. One rational response to this weakness is to emphasize a second function, a function which can prove the usefulness of the arrangement more reliably. Building political coalitions within and outside the arrangement is complex and often contingent on time-specific factors. Service provision for individual members, by contrast, can be fully controlled by the IGA and is less dependent on the cooperation of outside actors. It can function as a more reliable means of maintaining support. In this sense, the weakness of IGAs as bodies for collective state-representation is compensated by the strengthening of individualized membership services.

Compulsory power-sharing structures invite the disaggregation of state units along the specific functions of public office-holders in the first place. The adaptation of IGAs to this situation – a strong focus on the professional features of their members – makes sense. Parties are organizationally too weak to provide a counterweight to these tendencies by, for instance, unifying government units or branches along ideological or programmatic lines. Furthermore, weak party linkages and permeable organizational boundaries imply a low degree of loyalty of office holders to their parties as organizations. As a side effect, office holders are free to employ any source of expertise or use any possibility to develop professional skills outside their party. Bipartisan IGAs which specialize in the needs of particular office-holders address such needs.

Returning to the range of interaction modes introduced in Chapter 1, within these highly institutionalized bodies, co-decision is dominant. IGAs provide a platform on which collective positions are regularly discussed and updated. IGAs can speak on behalf of their members. For instance, staff can give testimonies in Congress and can help to identify common ground. This transcends the role of staff in Canada operating within much weaker intergovernmental infrastructures. At the sametime, American IGAs are not able to act on behalf of state government as political entities, and therefore do not support the drafting of informal agreements to coordinate policy on a voluntary basis, attempts observed in both Canada and Switzerland. We need to keep in mind that the different modes of interaction are likely to be linked to particular structural environments in terms of institutionalization. Different levels of institutionalization, however, do not imply particular sets of functions towards which intergovernmental processes are directed.

On the regional level, we find a striking reproduction of the national patterns. While IGAs are not as strongly institutionalized and weaker in terms of resources, this finding clearly rules out the argument that the great diversity between the states is a major reason why IGAs cannot unify states effectively. If this were the case, we should find stronger rather than weaker bodies with a regional scope. Each of the three state IGAs has several regional pendants. Most of the regional governors associations and the four regional conferences of legislators are staffed by the Council of State Governments which also has four regional offices of its own.[6] These bodies have their own secretariats and their members meet regularly. They are at least institutionalized on a medium level and mainly differ in the rule applied to make decisions. Some of the arrangements need consensus in the executive committee in order to issue a resolution (indicating a medium level of institutionalization). In others a qualified majority is sufficient (indicating high institutionalization). Reflecting the functional orientation of national IGAs, they focus on promoting regional interests at the national level.

These bodies are under considerable pressure to emphasize their regional profile and to specialize accordingly. As soon as issues are picked up at a national level, it is hard for them to pursue an independent strategy along with or even against their national counterparts. The national arena decides what is left to the regional level. While regional arrangements are largely engaged in

---

[6] They are located in New York, Atlanta, Sacramento, and Lombard.

lobbying, they also try to facilitate policy coordination between their members as a second function. The New England Governors' Conference, for instance, runs committees and working groups of state officials in areas of particular interest such as energy, environment, or economic development. As on the national level, structures and processes are strongly structured along policy lines and the annual meetings of the governors or legislators are supplemented by policy-specific meetings of experts. Meetings usually lead to resolutions on best practices or joint letters that articulate shared goals and positions on federal initiatives. Those resolutions directed towards interstate coordination articulate advice each state is free to reject later onwards. They do not generate political commitments imposing constraints on the individual state. Again, we find co-decision as dominant interaction mode, but processes are directed towards collective position-taking, rather than collection action.

HORIZONTAL FEDERALISM: THE CHALLENGE OF COORDINATING POLICY

'Horizontal federalism' refers to interstate relations without the involvement of the federal government, a topic which has attracted little scholarly attention in its own right. In a sense, the empirical weakness of the state level has been strikingly reflected in the American IGR literature. It focuses overwhelmingly on federal grants and the implications of the conditions attached to them (Trench 2006: 228). From the outset, states are perceived as lobbyists for more funding instead of as governments eager to protect their autonomy and able to solve their problems collectively without federal intervention. This reactive position of the states is usually taken as a given without exploring the structural patterns underlying it. Looking back at the range of generalist IGAs, competition between executive and legislative arrangements for federal influence on the national level naturally complicates attempts to coordinate policy across state borders. Different from lobbying, where each branch can engage in separate efforts, policy coordination usually presupposes coordination between executives and legislatures. To push for executive or legislative interests successfully, if necessary against the other branch, is difficult to reconcile with efforts of policy coordination. Federal dominance in IGR and the weakness of 'horizontal federalism' are two sides of one coin that reinforce each other. The disunity among the states in the cross-jurisdictional coordination of state policies allows Congress to legitimize own action within state jurisdiction since it can point to the failure of the states to do the job independently (Derthick 2001: 38–9).

But where does the coordination of policy take place if those IGAs oriented towards federal policy do not do it? We have seen in Canada and Switzerland policy coordination is mainly dealt with by policy-specific arrangements such as ministerial councils or meetings established in those policy fields which are important to lower level governments (usually this is the case if they have own competences). The American picture looks considerably different. One does not find a similarly homogeneous type of structure set up across the range of policy fields to handle whatever cross-jurisdictional problems occur in the respective area. In most policy fields it works the other way around. Once a problem occurs, states might respond by using an instrument to coordinate policy which is considered adequate for this particular case. Instruments available for horizontal cooperation span a considerable continuum in terms of formalization. The most formal instrument, the interstate compact, has constitutional status and can be used to create compact commissions to which the states assign a particular task they want to handle collectively. Next to it, we find a range of mechanisms such as memoranda of understanding and ad hoc commissions which provide for more flexible pathways of interstate coordination up to a range of advisory bodies trying to facilitate policy diffusion and learning across the states. The less formal pathways are often attractive because they avoid legislative involvement ex ante and allow executives to respond to cooperation demands more flexibly. Examples are memoranda of understanding between individual governors bypassing their legislatures. Also measures such as model laws supporting policy diffusion are unproblematic since they leave it to each individual state whether to adopt a particular law or not.

Most of these instruments are underpinned by an IGA promoting (yet rarely controlling) its application. These IGAs are highly institutionalized which corresponds to our theoretical expectations. Yet, in the United States, form and function go together differently than in other systems. In the United States, we find a range of highly developed IGAs – each handling a particular instrument. In Switzerland, directors (i.e. department heads or ministers) are continuously embedded in voluntarily created yet highly developed IGAs, discuss on a regular basis where collective action would be adequate and after having decided that action is necessary in a certain issue area they choose the instrument to address the problem. State actors, by contrast, can 'pick and choose' depending on the problem and receive institutional support on an ad hoc basis instead of being constrained by an institutional arrangement. Exceptions are few. Again, the Council of State Governments is an arrangement with a more encompassing approach. It runs secretariats promoting interstate compacts – the most binding instrument – as well as the unilateral adoption of uniform law – the least binding one. A similar structure we find in environment. The highly institutionalized and sector-wide Environmental Council of the States is the national association of state environmental agencies[7] and was founded in 1993 within the framework of the Council of State Governments (Grees 1996: 60). It has two general meetings per year in addition to numerous project meetings. It runs a secretariat composed of an executive and six policy-specific standing committees and it resembles closely policy-specific structures in our other two countries. However, these are exceptions. Therefore, the following section is structured along the instruments applied in interstate cooperation (instead of starting out from infrastructures) and discusses cross-sectoral differences accordingly. It starts with the most binding and finishes with the least binding of these.

Interstate compacts

The most formal mechanism for interstate cooperation is the interstate compact, a contract device that is specified in Art. I, Section 10 of the U.S. Constitution. The constitution contains no restrictions on the subject matter of a compact and is silent about the process by which states may enter into compacts. The only exception is that compacts require the (usually implicit) consent of Congress and can only be entered if a compact does not change the power balance between the federal government and the states and does not violate federal prerogatives.[8] If entered by a state, a compact supersedes conflicting laws that a state might pass later on as long as this state does not formally leave the contract. The level of obligation and with it the state's individual autonomy loss when entering a compact is very high. Whenever one partner violates it, the contract partners can issue litigation. As a consequence, these compacts tend to be used to back up resource-sharing arrangements which are particular sensitive. In these cases, the 'insurance' resulting from the high level of formality of the compact compensates for the loss of autonomy which follows from a state's entry. Interstate compacts can respond to very different problems and therefore take quite different forms. Three forms can be distinguished: compacts that are self-executing such as border compacts, compacts run by the respective bureaucrats in the states, and finally those that set up an administrative agency – compact commissions – to deal with a regulatory problem or a particular problem area. These compact commissions vary considerably in their scope of competences. Sometimes they function as advisory bodies and issue recommendations for shared regulations or statutes to the member states and facilitate information exchange.

---

[7] For details see Environmental Council of the States, Organizational Structure and Bylaws, As Amended through 12 August 2003.

[8] In principle, the federal government can join interstate compacts. In fact, from the 1980s onwards the interstate compact has also become a mechanism for introducing federal participation in regional programs while limiting federal authority (Elazar 1984: 197). However, in numerical terms, the majority of compacts are struck without federal involvement.

Alternatively, they function directly as regulatory bodies which implement contract provisions.

Compacts are collected by the National Centre for Interstate Compacts, a secretariat run by the Council of State Governments which also actively promotes the creation of new compacts. As a form of interstate law, compacts are formal and highly specific. The secretariat assists this process through the provision of expertise. It is also actively involved in the negotiation period and tries to increase support for the final ratification of compacts when a proposal is finalized.[9] Despite this support, in many cases states prefer less formal instruments (Zimmerman 2001: 2–3; see also Nice 1987).[10] This has less to do with their formality per se. As expressed in the high institutionalization of IGAs, due to the nature of intragovernmental structures in the states, the sensitivity towards power sharing is comparatively low. It is the time needed to set them up. Despite the considerable support of the secretariat, in 2005, the average time to set up a compact from the first idea to the final enactment was 18–24 months. Furthermore, compact negotiations fail on a regular basis (Zimmerman 1990: 145). Most of the compacts are initiated on the bureaucratic level. Only rarely do governors issue initiatives directly, a factor which reflects the technicality of this instrument. During the negotiation phase each state is represented by a legislative actor, while representatives of state agencies bring in the different executive viewpoints on the topic under discussion. Finally, different stakeholders concerned by and interested in the future compact are heard. The latter are important to gather information and to foster support for the final compact which demands legislative approval. Despite this extensive process, compacts often lack promotion during the enactment phase because they do not have enough legislative sponsors. Although individual legislators take part in the compact discussions, the states are most strongly involved through the agency level since bureaucratic actors usually have to handle the compact afterwards. Hence, the finalization of a draft does not signal that the major obstacle of ratification has been overcome.

IGAs such as the Council of State Governments hardly influence the ratification process by individual state legislatures. This process is contained within a state's boundaries. Here again the separation between the branches becomes manifest. As noted previously, compared to executive actors, legislatures are eager to protect legislative state autonomy. Since compacts heavily restrict individual state autonomy and compact commissions are usually run by administrators, enactment is considered to be the most difficult step. This barrier is much less pronounced in the Swiss case where the branches are connected by party linkages.

---

[9] See the list of compacts available on the CSG website. Note that it also includes compacts to which only one state is a party (http://ssl.csg.org/compactlaws/comlistlinks.html).

[10] Unfortunately, there is no common register of informal agreements between states which makes it extremely difficult to specify how dense horizontal networks are (Zimmerman 2001).

Research has indicated that the separation of power structure in America invites that intergovernmental processes are predominantly handled on the administrative level. IGR are considered less politicized than in parliamentary federations such as Canada (Smiley 1987). The mechanisms leading to the dominance of inter-administrative relations in the United States have not been specified. One answer is that executive actors try to avoid legislative involvement. Quite evidently, legislative agreement is much more difficult to assure in a system with strong, independent legislatures. In parliamentary contexts, executive and legislative interests converge considerably since executive–legislative linkages are much stronger both in constitutional and in party-organizational terms. This situation allows executives to act on behalf of their governments including the legislative branches.

Interstate compacts highlight this tension most clearly since they impose severe costs on the legislative branch. Where uniform law is adopted in the form of a compact, legislatures give up their individual law-making power. Individual legislative autonomy is traded against collectively shared regulatory power, power controlled by administrators, not by legislators. In a separation of power structure, legislatures will try to avoid these costs and thus avoid the use of these mechanisms. As a result, compacts merely fill a vacuum and are rarely used. Compact negotiations as well as their enactment usually involve a restricted set of states only. Often only few states sign directly after a draft is completed. Others join later, sometimes decades after the compact has entered effect. In 1998, 175 compacts were in force of which 25 are self-enforcing border compacts (Bowman 2004*a*: 539). Of the 150 non-boundary compacts in force, 60 are bilateral. Only two have all 50 states as members. Also in Switzerland, we find a tendency to use the concordat (the corresponding mechanism to create inter-cantonal law) on a bilateral basis (three-fourth of all concordats are bilateral). Yet given 733 concordats overall, we find still considerably more of them (Bochsler et al. 2004; Bochsler 2006).

In sum, the fact that interstate compacts are at all entered indicates a considerable willingness on the part of state actors to share power and invest in strong intergovernmental bodies. As a result of power sharing which reduces the political costs of cooperation as well as the relative autonomy losses involved, the corridor of adaptation is wide. However, interstate cooperation is very hard to achieve given inter-branch divides if legislative approval is needed which explains their low number. Thinking of Canada, the problem is exactly the reverse. The use of such formal contracts is hard to imagine given the highly autonomy-minded provinces – though it would be much easier for a provincial executive to enter a deal and make sure that it is approved by its parliamentary majority at home. The system in which intragovernmental incentives work most favourably, where the willingness and the capacity to engage in intergovernmental cooperation often go together, seems to be Switzerland.

The use of compact commission

As pointed out before, compacts can be set up to settle specific problems such as border disputes. Once an agreement is in place, the problem is solved. Alternatively, they can be used to set up compact commissions through which states handle ongoing problems collectively. Before exploring the use of compact commissions across eight policy fields as in the other two case studies and drawing some conclusions about the patterns of policy-specific institution-building in American IGR, one might wonder whether these commissions are directly comparable to policy-specific arrangements as we found them in Switzerland and Canada. It is argued here that commissions represent functional equivalents to IGAs since they are used to engage in collective action between the states. Once in place, they are formalized and what commissions do can have binding force – depending on how they are set up by the states. Whether to initiate the creation of these commissions in areas of state competence and how these commissions look like, however, is completely up to the states.[11] It is their choice and there is no formal pressure to choose that route. Therefore, these arrangements can be assessed in the same way as voluntarily created policy-specific IGAs in Canada and Switzerland.

Compact commissions can be categorized along our continuum of interaction modes which allows for a systematic cross-national comparison. Commissions are neither vehicles for ad hoc coordination as Canadian IGAs nor for co-decision as Swiss IGAs. Paradoxically, they either favour unilateral adaptation or supragovernmentalism, (two interactional modes which are located on opposite ends of the continuum) or in particular cases both. Some commissions are set up to provide expertise for their states to facilitate interstate cooperation in a particular policy field such as the Education Commission of the States. They give advice and provide expertise without formally compromising legislative authority of individual states nor do they help to create political commitment as implied by ad hoc coordination or co-decision. They inform states about best practices in other states and give recommendations, yet leave it completely to the individual state to decide whether to implement such a policy at some point or not. They support unilateral adaptation, the least constraining mode of interaction. Most commissions, however, deal with narrowly defined, regulatory issues. As indicated above, the scope of their activity is very restricted since the legislatures oppose to give up too much of their decision-making power. By constituting formal interstate authorities they correspond to 'supragovernmentalism'. It is the most constraining interaction mode since individual decision-making power of the participating states is transformed into collective authority. The question is why,

---

[11] The need for Congressional consent is rarely an issue. Usually implicit consent is sufficient.

TABLE 5.1. *Interstate compacts and compact commissions until 1998*

Policy Fields	Compacts	Compact Commissions	Competence Distribution[a]	Institutionalization
Economic and trade policy	0	0	Shared	Low
Financial and tax policy	1	1 sector-specific	Concurrent	Low to medium
Health policy	2	0	Concurrent[b]	Low
Social policy	3	0	Concurrent	Low
Transportation	8	6 issue-specific	Shared	Medium
Justice and crime control	19	2 issue-specific	Shared	Medium
Education	11	7 sector-specific	Exclusive	High
Environment	58	43 issue-specific (13: environment, 27: water, and 3: parks)	Shared	High

Note: This table is based on a collection of all interstate compacts and commissions until 1998, published in the National Center of Interstate Compacts.

[a] The categories are based on Watts' classification (1999a).
[b] Implied federal power in the provision of welfare and medical services Art. 1 Section 8 (Schram 2005: 388).

while serving similar functions as IGAs in other federal systems, the structural pattern looks so different.

Table 5.1 indicates that neither compacts nor commissions are used frequently, a finding that points at the weakness of policy coordination in American federalism more generally. This weakness originates in compulsory power-sharing between the branches complicating cooperation, a problem occurring across the range of policy fields analysed. Furthermore, the table points to the considerable lack of sector-wide structures (thus, a stronger fragmentation along issues), and with it, a higher diversity of structural patterns than in the other two systems. Policy-specific variables seem to make more of a difference for institution building in the American context.

Since commissions rarely span whole sectors, it is reasonable to consider the range and scope of commissions to judge the sector-wide level of institutionailzation in addition to the indicators introduced in Chapter 1 (using them exclusively, any commission ends up being highly institutionalized given its formal character irrespective of how narrow its focus). Using this stricter yardstick, we see that structures in concurrent areas tend to be weaker than in shared or exclusive areas. Concurrent areas are particularly dominated by federal legislation which overrules state law. The leeway for the states to engage in horizontal coordination is likely to be more restricted than in exclusive and shared jurisdictions. While this makes intuitive sense, note that in Switzerland highly institutionalized IGAs exist in concurrent areas as well. The argument does not travel across countries. Similarly, cooperation in economic and trade policy as well as in financial and tax policy is scarce, most likely a consequence of heavy redistributive implications in these policy areas. Yet again, in Switzerland, we found high institutionalization in such areas as well. And even in the United States the picture is not that clear-cut. Although states are heavily influenced by federal tax policy, they actively use their taxing power as one of their core competences and compete along these lines. Still, the Multistate Tax Commission as the only compact in place is quite exceptional in several respects and justifies classifying the policy field as low to medium. While the number of commissions is indeed very low, the one commission in place is highly institutionalized[12] and has with twenty member states a quite considerable scope. Although, substantially, the Multistate Tax Commission's scope does not cover a whole policy field, it is active in an important sub-field in which interstate competition is particularly pronounced. Interstate commerce belongs clearly in the high-conflict category in which states can directly benefit from imposing costs on other jurisdictions – an area in which cross-jurisdictional cooperation is difficult to achieve. Nevertheless, states decided to set up the Commission to deal with multistate taxpayers.[13] While one core function is to gather expertise and draft recommendations for uniform law (falling under unilateral adaptation), the commission also has the authority to audit businesses on behalf of the states (falling under supragovernmentalism). Compared to Canada, where finance ministers refuse to issue any collective statements after they have met – not to speak of setting up an institutional back-up – the extent of cooperation among the states in this policy area is considerable. In environmental policy, we find the highest number of compact commissions fulfilling regulatory tasks, yet mostly addressing very specific issues. States not only have a long history of cooperation in water-related issues (Gerlak 2006), but have also become active on other issues such as clean air standards (Conlan 2006). Also in transportation, commissions are used comparatively frequently, as environment an area with a strong spatial dimension. Finally, one finds a sector-wide commission of (nearly) national scope in education policy, an area were the states have far-fetching competences.[14] The Education Commission of the States has 47 members and is paralleled by a range of regionally based education commissions. Again we find the tendency that in policy fields in which lower level governments have the most to loose, institution building seems particularly worthwhile.

The mode of competence distribution and the relative level of conflict help us to some extent to comprehend the relative differences across policy fields within the system better. However, as already has become clear when analysing Canada and Switzerland, neither of the two policy-specific variables give us a convincing account for the patterns of institution building across different federal countries.

---

[12] The Streamlined Sales and Tax Agreement is a similar compact which has been adopted recently by a considerable number of states.

[13] http://www.mtc.gov/MTCBylaws10-17-02.pdf

[14] This should not imply that federal intrusion cannot be observed. The recent federal initiative 'No Child Left Behind' is one good example.

The U.S. findings do not change this picture. But does this line of argument save the given approach claiming intragovernmental relations to be a core factor underlying institution building? Even if we can argue that certain policy variables do not lead us very far when trying to understand institution building both across policy fields and across political systems, we still need to ask why cross-sectoral differences are more pronounced in the United States than in Canada and Switzerland. Why does institutional choice seem relatively more responsive to policy-specific factors in the United States? One answer leads us back to compulsory power-sharing.

The full extent of the fragmentation of American IGR across policy fields and issues can only be captured by looking at intra-executive divides: compulsory power-sharing on the level of state executives. Looking at the internal structure of state executives more closely, governors have to share power not only with other elected officials such as directly elected department heads, but also with numerous semi-autonomous boards and commissions (Dye 1985: 32–3; Gray and Eisinger 1991: 141). As a consequence, the governors' program, the legislative program, and that of independent agencies are distinct and none of them dominates the picture (Beyle 1983: 134). Already facing an independent legislature, this intra-executive fragmentation prevents the governor from dominating executive agencies and disciplining program specialists through integrated state programs (Esman 1984: 29). Neither are departments internally integrated nor are cross-departmental ties in place. The direct election of state attorneys in more than 40 states complements this picture (Provost 2003: 37). Simply put, governors control neither of the branches in 'their state' since other state actors not only enjoy formal independence but often are democratically legitimized as well.

Compulsory power-sharing within state executives fragments processes within and across state departments. This, in turn, nourishes the stronger consideration of policy-specific factors when it comes to engaging in intergovernmental cooperation which contrasts with the considerable homogeneity of institutional choices in Switzerland and Canada where departments are more cohesive and linked to each other. The lack of cohesion within state executives adds to the 'functional pattern' along which American IGR evolves and can help to explain why subject matter specialists are free to form coalitions with their counterparts on the federal level. These administrative expert coalitions which operate with considerable independence are bound to emphasize policy specificities also when it comes to intergovernmental cooperation. The leeway of Swiss and Canadian administrators is far more limited by ministerial priorities or those of the core executive. Simultaneously, inter-branch divides motivate agency creation along these lines which reinforces the tendency to divide up sectors and delegate narrow subsets to such specialist bodies. While legislatures tend to create independent boards to circumvent the executives, the executives prefer agencies they hope to control more effectively than their legislature. Overall, bureaucracies have never developed a cross-cutting set of loyalties capable of tying departments together and connecting them to a hierarchical superior (Muchmore 1983: 188; Chubb and Peterson 1989: 12–16).

In sum, the high level of fragmentation across and within individual departments privileges specialists over generalists in American IGR and gives intergovernmental exchanges their strongly administrative character. The stronger role of specialists favours that policy characteristics play a more important role when it comes to the usage of the particular instruments of interstate cooperation than in both Canada and Switzerland. Simultaneously, it invites institution building along issues, since specialists tend to organize around issues rather than covering whole policy fields. Instead of cohesive executives which impose a 'governmental' logic able to tie issues and departments together, we find a 'functional' rationale. This 'functional rationale' shapes internal state politics and, since intragovernmental processes feed back into IGR, the nature of interstate cooperation as well.

Flexible mechanisms of interstate cooperation

Moving on to more flexible mechanisms, memoranda of understanding tend to be used more often than compacts since they are less constraining and frequently circumvent the legislatures. They are signed by individual governors, department heads, or senior officials and are effective only while the signing official is in office. The advantages are clear. Unlike compacts, which take an average of two years to establish, memoranda of understanding are relatively easy to obtain, since only executive officials need to agree. They thus allow state executives to respond to current problems much more immediately than compacts do (Purcell 2007: 92–93). Unfortunately, existing research offers little insight into theses agreements. The core problem for research on inter-executive and administrative agreements is 'the lack of a central repository in any state' of written or verbal agreements (Zimmerman 2002: 164). Interviews confirm this situation. Often actors such as officials working in the governor's office who are engaged in intergovernmental processes know little or nothing about these agreements entered by some subunit of their own government. This situation reflects the general nature of IGR as laid out above. There is hardly coordination and communication between governmental and administrative units indicating a striking lack of hierarchy. At best, memoranda were collected in the respective department responsible for the subject matter addressed in them.[15]

The memoranda which were accessible were highly specific and set up directly by the respective departments. While due to the above-mentioned problems the

---

[15] In contrast, in provincial governments in Canada memoranda with other provinces were centrally stored by the government involved.

documents analysed did not constitute a representative sample of memoranda, existing literature supports this finding (Zimmerman 2002). On the one hand, they are worked out by officials to tackle very specific problems, and tend to be technical. On the other hand, they are not presented to, or accessible by, the public. Thus, the need to keep a memorandum vague for political reason is very limited.[16] Negotiations leading to memoranda are neither mediated nor supported by IGAs. The immediate participants – mostly state officials – get in touch and enter agreements whenever particular problems demand it. This is rather unusual. For any other instrument considered we find some sort of institutional backup.

Policy diffusion is the least formalized and most indirect form of 'horizontal coordination'. It is considered extremely important by intergovernmental actors including officials and IGA staff. States have long emulated each other's policies and do so significantly more often than engaging in formal interstate compacts or other 'explicit agreements' on the executive level. Diffusion does not involve a negotiation process. Rather, it denotes a voluntary adoption of innovative legislation realized in other states and thus falls in the category of unilateral adaptation.[17] Several IGAs try to support these diffusion processes: To improve information exchange and to support the diffusion of innovation, the Council of State Governments publishes a selection of 40 to 50 innovative state laws each year. On average, between two and four are adopted by a wide range of states. This figure does not give a realistic indication of the degree to which states emulate individual policies. However, it does show how diffusion processes are backed up by IGAs. Regional, generalist IGAs also consider the facilitation of interstate cooperation as an important task besides lobbying. However, they equally emphasize that they do not give advice which kind of legislation or measure to adopt. In contrast to arrangements such as the Council of State Governments which actively proposes model legislation, they restrict themselves to providing a platform for discussion.

Since 1892, the 'National Conference of Commissioners on Uniform State Laws' has been actively pressing for equal standards across state borders. The commission is composed of attorneys, judges, and law professors, as well as legislators. The conference attempts to develop uniform state laws in areas where states wish to act independently of the federal government, but where nationwide uniformity is desirable. Between 1896 and 1983, approximately 150 model acts have been drafted and submitted to the states. This is a rather modest number and, not surprisingly, much fewer have been adopted (Elazar 1984: 196). This process suffers from a similar problem as compact negotiations

---

[16] Chapter 7 will show that in Canada this is quite common.

[17] Which factors drive diffusion processes is debated. Relevant factors are territorial closeness, various policy-specific factors, and the ideological position of previous adopters (e.g. Gray 1973; Grossback, Nicholson-Crotty, and Peterson 2004).

since each uniform act is years in the making and it is often difficult for the commissioners to defend an act in their home state where it needs to be approved by the legislature.[18] Clearly, the implications of adopting standardized legislation are less severe than entering a compact since state legislatures are free to pass a new law after having adopted the model law. Nonetheless, also here enactment is difficult, in the face of state legislatures eager to defend their power.

SUMMARY

The dominance of compulsory, constitutionally defined power-sharing structures unbridged by the organizational ties of political parties has enhanced the high institutional development of individual IGAs. More precisely, the incentives generated by power sharing within the states – low electoral pressure and autonomy losses, and the limited impact of alternation and of party-based conflict across the states – facilitate the investment into highly institutionalized IGAs. These findings demonstrate the pervasiveness of power sharing in American federalism which creates a heavy need for cooperation (Elazar 1991: 75). Paradoxically, the compulsory nature of power sharing has equally contributed to the severe fragmentation of the intergovernmental landscape. It provides incentives for inter-institutional competition between IGAs rather than their mutual integration since each IGA represents the 'state interest' only partially. No IGA can rely on being 'the' channel to voice state interests or 'the' forum for federal–state negotiation. Equally, the latent competition between IGAs for influence on the federal government undermines the unification of the states as one level of government. The executive–legislative divide can be identified as driving force underlying these tendencies both on the regional and on the national level which showed remarkably similar patterns of institution building.

The divergence between executives and legislatures impacts on horizontal coordination in several ways. It complicates compact negotiations as well as the enactment of uniform law. Compulsory power-sharing leads to a strong emphasis of 'institutional interests' because it creates a distance in orientation between executive actors (who focus on policy delivery) and legislative actors (who want to protect legislative autonomy). The resulting tendency towards predominantly inter-executive or inter-administrative interaction on the horizontal, interstate level delimits states' capacity to cooperate. Legislation-based instruments (which tend to be more forceful mechanisms for harmonization and delimit the leeway for federal intrusion) are only applied infrequently. Overall, horizontal

---

[18] http://www.nccusl.org/Update/DesktopDefault.aspx?tabindex = 0&tabid = 11

cooperation fails to provide a feasible alternative to national legislation. Nor does it lead to a strong defense of state rights.

Overall, IGAs in the United States do not function as mediators for collective state action in the sense of generating and channelling political commitment to coordinate policy. They cannot generate political constraints on member governments. At best, IGAs actively support the drafting processes of formal compacts as the Center for Interstate Compacts. The high level of institutionalization of generalist IGAs allows for regular co-decision with regard to the formulation of collective positions. However, since they only represent the interest of particular state actors, as opposed to the states as political units, co-decision cannot be directed towards cross-jurisdictional policy-coordination. This quite naturally decreases the relevance of IGAs for their members. To maintain continuous member support, they provide professional services and expertise to their members perceived in their professional role rather than in their political function. The following chapter will develop the argument further showing that this orientation towards functional rather than political demands leads to a structural and strategic convergence of IGAs with private interest groups.

Looking at IGAs oriented towards policy coordination more specifically, American IGAs show a peculiar pattern. Some IGAs actively support the drafting of interstate law and the creation of interstate authorities – *supragovernmentalism*. As the high institutionalization of generalist IGAs, the set-up of highly formalized compact commissions expresses the willingness on the part of state actors to share power and invest in strong intergovernmental bodies constraining individual state action. Both reconfirm a favourable impact of power sharing within the states on intergovernmental institution-building. Simultaneously, compulsory power-sharing leading to a strong emphasis on institutional interests often undermines agreement between the two branches. Since state legislatures are eager to protect their law-making power, as a consequence, formal compact commissions rarely capture whole sectors and are used infrequently.

Alternatively, IGAs are located on the other end of the continuum and simply provide information to support the *unilateral adaptation* of policies, a process which is completely controlled by the individual state and more common than engaging in interstate compacts. Unlike IGAs in the other two federal systems, they rarely engage in political negotiations or the generation of informal yet collectively binding agreements presupposing IGAs able to represent, thus, speak and act on behalf of the states as cohesive government units. Reinforcing the fragmented nature of American IGR, compulsory power-sharing on the level of state executives leads to the stronger role of specialists unconstrained by an overall political rationale imposed by a cohesive core executive. This allows for a greater impact of policy characteristics on IGR, more specifically, on the choice of cooperation mechanisms and thereby on the policy-specific pattern of institution building.

INTERGOVERNMENTAL INSTITUTIONALIZATION IN CANADA, SWITZERLAND, AND THE UNITED STATES: SYSTEMIC CONVERGENCE – FUNCTIONAL DIVERGENCE

The three country studies confirmed that intragovernmental incentives shape the patterns and structures of IGR. They have also demonstrated that overall the patterns of institutionalization vary to a stronger degree across political systems than across policy fields within them. Intragovernmental incentive structures generated by power concentration and power sharing motivate intergovernmental actors to invest in IGAs of different strength and type. They shape corridors of adaptation delimiting informal institution-building by imposing political costs on intergovernmental actors in their home arenas. Depending on the cost intensity, they harm or facilitate intergovernmental institutionalization. Supporting the first core hypothesis put forward in Chapter 2, compared to polycentric Canada, in the two power-sharing democracies, intergovernmental institutionalizations has proven higher on both the national and regional levels.

Putting the three cases next to each other also reveals that similar levels of institutionalization of IGAs do not lead to their orientation towards the same functions. This issue will be assessed in greater detail in Chapter 6, when the nature of intergovernmental agreements in the three systems is examined. Table 5.2 sums up the main functions (not all functions) which the range of national IGAs deals with.[19]

Although institutionalization and the functional orientation of IGAs are not directly linked, a higher level of institutionalization allows a body to engage in a comparatively greater number of functions. In contrast to the other generalist IGAs, the First Ministers' Conference is mainly focused on one function; the Council of the Federation on two. Furthermore, we find certain country-specific differences. A strong focus on the provision of services is clearly a functional orientation favoured by the American context and can be considered as a response to the given inter-institutional fragmentation. IGAs are concentrated on lobbying with the exception of the Council of State Governments, which focuses on horizontal relations. Note, however, that although it supports the set-up of interstate compacts through a staffed secretariat, it is not involved in political negotiations such as the Conference of Cantonal Executives, the First Ministers' Conference, and the Council of the Federation re-emphasizing a core weakness of American IGAs.

In addition to increasing an arrangement's capacity to serve several main functions, a high level of institutionalization increases the capacity to shape government interaction. While both the Conference of Cantonal Executives and the Council of the Federation are directed towards collective position-taking

---

[19] The category of information exchange has been excluded because it is a natural function of any IGA.

TABLE 5.2. *Main functions of generalist arrangements on the national level*

	Canada		Switzerland	United States		
	First Ministers' Conference[a]	Council of the Federation	Conference of Cantonal Executives	National Governors' Association	National Conference of State Legislatures	Council of State Governments
Degree of institutionalization	Low	Medium	High	High	High	High
Provision of expertise	No	No	Yes	Yes	Yes	Yes
Professional services	No	No	No	Yes	Yes	Yes
Position taking/lobbying	No	Yes	Yes	Yes	Yes	No
Negotiation/policy coordination	Yes	Yes	Yes	No	No	Yes

[a] FMC denotes the meetings of the Prime Minister and the Premiers only. It does not include ministerial councils.

and intergovernmental negotiation, the weakly institutionalized Council is hardly more than the sum of the individual wills of its members. It is completely driven by the momentary constellation of office holders. Staff of the Conference of Cantonal Executives, by contrast, can play a proactive role in shaping government interaction. In all three systems, IGA staff point out that issues are avoided if collective agreement is very unlikely ex ante. Some common ground is a general precondition for an issue to be handled in an intergovernmental forum. However, staff of the highly institutionalized Swiss conference can raise issues and have sufficient resources and the neccessary standing to justify own initiatives. In the Council of the Federation taking initiative is a privilege of the provincial and territorial premiers, while the staff solely functions as bureaucratic support. Government representatives are mandated in the Conference of Cantonal Executives and in First Ministers' Conferences. Hence, in both arrangements, the leeway to change opinions during discussions is limited. Still, the staff in the Swiss context can play a mediating role, as is also the case for staff of the three highly institutionalized American IGAs. IGA staff in the United States point to the identification of common ground between their members as a major task. This is mostly done in policy-specific committees that attempt to bridge conflict. This too is distinct from the Canadian Council of the Federation and the First Ministers' Conferences. In Canada, IGAs are explicitly not considered as bodies which are thought to bridge conflict between members since individual government interests are by definition paramount.

The results presented in the three case studies substantiate the theoretically developed claim that intragovernmental incentives directly affect intergovernmental institutionalization. Furthermore, they emphasize the need to distinguish clearly between an IGA's functional orientation and its institutional capacity to effectively deal with the functions which are assigned to it. In fact, summing up the results of Chapter 3 through 5 already shows the need to consider institutionalization and integration simultaneously in order to understand the role of IGAs in the intergovernmental arena of each system fully. The following chapter will examine the integration between IGAs in the three systems, and will put the findings on institution building – so far focused on the development of individual IGAs – in a systemic perspective.

6

Intergovernmental Integration in Canada, Switzerland, and the United States

After having specified the structural features of individual arrangements and the impact on their internal working, we now move to the 'system level' of IGR and look at the linkages between the different IGAs more closely: their mutual integration. Intergovernmental integration is a core variable in federal analysis. It affects the capacity of lower level governments to act efficiently as one unified group towards the centre and thereby helps to account for the macro-dynamics prevalent in a multilevel setting. While collective action is not necessarily the optimal strategy for each individual lower level government under any circumstances, it is crucial to know whether governments have the capacity to do so when they share a common interest. In this regard, particular attention needs to be paid to intra-horizontal relations. Whether the lower level governments really form one 'order or level of government' expressed through concerted behaviour is an open question. In much of the literature, it is taken for granted that 'multilevel settings' consist of two or more levels. Horizontal cooperation within the various levels is often taken as a given instead of being subject of empirical analysis. As this chapter illustrates, the interaction on the horizontal dimension of federal systems shows remarkable variety.

Acting as one 'level of government' becomes manifest in two ways. First, in the capacity to form common positions with regard to federal plans and policies which, for instance, transfer financial burdens to lower levels or intrude in spheres of lower level jurisdiction. In this case, horizontal collaboration is vertically oriented and serves collective opposition. Second, it can become manifest in the capacity to deal with demands for the cross-jurisdictional coordination and harmonization of policy in lower level jurisdictions without the direct involvement of the federal government. This horizontal coordination can be as crucial for the power distribution in a federal system as position taking directed against the centre. If lower level coordination is ineffective in those jurisdictions where cross-jurisdictional solutions are considered to be necessary, national initiatives become a likely response and with them authority migration to the centre. So far, comparative analyses of intergovernmental bodies and their linkages are rare, particularly so regarding horizontal exchanges. Vertical federal–state relations have been considered as a core aspect in the assessment of federal dynamics (e.g. Downs

1998; Grande 2001). Broadening this perspective, this chapter demonstrates that to fully understand vertical IGR, we also need to understand horizontal dynamics within subnational levels of government.

To recap the indicators introduced to measure integration: Integration is *absent* when inter-institutional relations are characterized by distrust, when IGAs actively avoid being associated with each other. *Weak* integration presupposes that there are detectable and voluntary contacts between the core IGAs. Contact is established ad hoc when shared problems occur, yet actors tend to shy away from or do not see a need for regular meetings. A *medium* integration is assumed, as soon as the respective IGAs meet regularly in order to be informed about their respective objectives or priorities. Setting up regular meetings indicates an active interest of IGAs in establishing a stable channel of communication among them in order to coordinate positions or common activities whenever considered necessary. Finally, integration is *strong* when the relationship between different bodies and the respective responsibilities are specified by statutes. Such statutes stabilize inter-institutional relations because they reduce conflicts by clarifying each body's sphere of authority. The crucial aspect is the willingness to clarify their relationship on a written basis. By agreeing to such a document, actors create an external, neutral reference point which can be referred to whenever conflict occurs in the future.[1]

The analysis of integration in the three federal systems will evolve along the following categories reflecting the different types of IGAs analysed one by one in Chapters 3 through 5. When looking at the *horizontal dimension* of a federal system, an analysis of integration has to take into account the linkages between the following sets of IGAs:

- Linkages between generalist IGAs of multilateral/national scope
- Linkages between generalist IGAs of multilateral/national scope and policy-specific IGAs of multilateral/national scope
- Linkages between generalist IGAs of regional scope
- Linkages between generalist IGAs of multilateral/national and regional scope
- Linkages between policy-specific IGAs of multilateral/national and regional scope

When looking at the *vertical dimension*, the major linkages to consider are the following:

- Linkages between generalist IGAs of multilateral/national scope and the federal government
- Linkages between policy-specific IGAs of multilateral/national scope and the federal government

[1] IGAs and linkages which are legally imposed by the federal government do not fall into that category since then, institutionalization or integration do not indicate any readiness of the side of the lower level governments to interact.

- Linkages between generalist IGAs of regional scope and the federal government
- Linkages between policy-specific IGAs of regional scope and the federal government

Although this list does not include all logically possible types of linkages, it already depicts a considerable complexity and provides a detailed picture of inter-institutional linkages in the three countries. Empirically, the situation is often simpler since not all types of arrangements are necessarily in place in any federal system. For example, there might be very few regional IGAs with a policy-specific profile such as in Canada or only one generalist IGA of national scope, such as in Switzerland. The major focus will be, first, whether there is regularity of contact between IGAs of different type and scope, second, whether there is competition between IGAs located on different levels over the same issues (or, alternatively, we find an implicit or explicit distribution of labour between the levels), and, third, whether there is an explicit specification of inter-institutional relations between the variety of IGAs.

Again, we start with Canada. Due to its majoritarian government dynamics, it can be expected to be weakly integrated since the cooperation-undermining incentives generated by power-concentrating governments should affect integration as negatively as they affected institutionalization. Then we move on to the two power-sharing cases. The comparison of the latter is crucial since according to the second core hypothesis developed in Chapter 2 the level of integration depends not only on the absence of power concentration but also on the particular type power-sharing. Thus, the degree of integration should differ between the two.

CANADA: POWER CONCENTRATION AND INTERGOVERNMENTAL INTEGRATION

In order to obtain a systematic view on integration in Canadian IGR, this section explores first the vertical dimension – the relations of IGAs with (or including) the federal government – and afterwards the horizontal integration involving lower level governments only.

Vertical integration: the dominance of bilateralism

One important feature of Canadian IGR is its weak vertical integration. Although the First Ministers' Conference includes the federal government and the subunits as equal members (in contrast to the other two federal systems), the implications on the process level are minor since the arrangement has remained weakly institutionalized for decades. Vertical interaction between provinces and the federal government occurs predominantly ad hoc and often bilaterally. These are exchanges in which IGAs do not play a role. As a reflection of these patterns, multilateral agreements engaging in policy harmonization are rare. Even more importantly, if policy-specific agreements are set up by First Ministers' Conferences they are not self-sufficient. Usually, after such an agreement has been signed, additional bilateral negotiations between the centre and each province are necessary. The latter negotiate the particular conditions in order to assure the final implementation of an agreement because multilateral frameworks tend to be too unspecific (Cameron and Simeon 2002). Thus, free-floating bilateral exchanges dominate over multilateral exchanges framed by IGAs. Vertical interaction tends to occur outside IGAs because flexibility is paramount for the actors involved. There is only a weak incentive for them to strengthen intergovernmental bodies and to invest in stable linkages. This tendency is most pronounced in the stronger provinces (which can often achieve their goals unilaterally), but equally present in the weaker provinces and territories.

Another major reason for the limited potential for the development of the First Ministers' Conference is the unequal control of the two orders of government over it. As the core multilateral-vertical linkage in the system, the conference is called by the federal government. Since this occurs only on an irregular basis depending on whether it is useful to the federal government, the degree of *vertical integration* in the system as a whole is weak. The federal government controls when the arrangement comes into play, nourishing a critical attitude of provinces and territories towards it. They perceive it as a platform in which the federal government 'announces' its plans. As indicated before, problem-oriented discussions tend to be rare. Blame-shifting strategies, position taking, and the strong drive for autonomy protection have clearly an unfavourable impact on the interaction in this IGA. This feeds back directly to the degree of integration because it does not generate a stable institutional context in which the two levels can bridge their differences.

The recent strengthening of the Council of the Federation as an exclusively horizontal body reinforces the given lack of integration on the vertical dimension of Canadian federalism. The Council strengthens the horizontal level as counterweight to the centre instead of providing for any linkages to the federal level. Providing a forum for interprovincial and provincial–territorial discussion presupposes the absence of dialogue with the federal government. The fact that the reform of the former Annual Premiers' Conference into the Council of the Federation was paralleled by the decline of the First Ministers' Conference indicates that there is no continuously increasing formalization of intergovernmental processes. On the contrary, the increasing weakness of the First Ministers' Conference as a body for intergovernmental concertation seems rather to have supported the foundation of the Council. Note again that the original proposal made by the Québec Liberal Party for the foundation of the Council of the Federation included the federal government as a member but this was rejected by the other provinces (Québec Liberal Party 2001: 91–4). The endeavour to form an IGA that primarily facilitate position taking against the federal government has proven to be the more dominant orientation on part of the provinces.

As mentioned in Chapter 3, the federal government profits from bilateral interaction on an ad hoc basis, in which it is usually the stronger part, and therefore has no interest in stronger integration. In light of this, it is a plausible interpretation that, ultimately, medium institutionalization of the Council of the Federation was achieved only *because* the centre was excluded from this process, thus vertical integration was not pursued. This seems also plausible because the federal government regularly tries to play one province off against the other. Consequently, in its current form, the Council is directed towards the formulation of common positions against the federal government in order to defend provincial interests (Meekison, Telford, and Lazar 2002: 16). The following statement of a member of Council staff clearly captures the conflict between a strengthening of the arrangement actively supported by the provinces and the establishment of a dialogue between the Council and the federal government:

> The secretariat is not so much involved in communication with the federal government. I try to build a relationship of trust with the provincial governments and this is the most important in this first period and not primarily with the federal government. If the federal government calls and wants to know something *it is important that the provinces know that no communication will take place*. The chair changes every year and it is up to him how the Council works because he can put his stamp very much on that. The chair also speaks with the federal government. The other governments of course can also speak to the federal government and do that if they want.[2]   (Author's emphasis)

If the Council secretariat can build trust only when avoiding contact with the federal government, stable horizontal relations and stable vertical relations are mutually conflicting. Any integrative endeavour is likely to cause critical reactions on the side of the provincial and territorial members. Consequently, it would be counterproductive for the staff to make such efforts since it is likely to weaken the capacity of the Council to build up and maintain its status as a forum for interprovincial communication. On top of that, the role of staff is by far too restricted to take the initiative to build up connections with the federal government in the first place.

This is even more crucial in a period in which the Council secretariat still needs to build up its reputation and demonstrate its usefulness since immediate failure could easily motivate provinces to abandon it. The niche it tries to

---

[2] IGA I Can, 7 April 2005: 1.

occupy besides the First Ministers' Conference is the one of a forum that more effectively coordinates provinces and territories. And since it is the actual chair of the Council who decides when and whether to have contact with the federal government, these contacts are at best irregular and fluctuate with the respective office-holder. This corresponds clearly to the findings of Chapter 3 emphasizing a high dependency of IGA activities on the preferences of the current office-holders and a heavy impact of government alternation. Instead of stable inter-institutional linkages, interaction between IGAs is characterized by strategic manoeuvring. This becomes most visible in the Council scheduling meetings as strategic preparations shortly before the First Ministers meet in order to find a common line and push for it most effectively in the later negotiation.

Horizontal integration: strategic manoeuvres and the spillover of conflict

In Canada, integrative efforts are hardly present amongst nationwide, generalist IGAs. The same dynamics are present in the contacts of *generalist* IGAs with *policy-specific* arrangements. The contacts of the Council of the Federation with policy-specific ministerial councils depend on the actual priorities of the premiers in office. Also here integration is weak. Since its foundation, a major focus of the Council has been health policy. This led to the announcement of a 'Health Council' of the ministers of health in the Council's founding agreement. Due to changed priorities in response to successful negotiations over health funding this council is now inactive. More recently, post-secondary education and training have become important issues for the premiers. Accordingly, staff of the Council of the Education Ministers expect more intensive contacts with the Council of the Federation in the future – as long as the premiers want to focus on these issues. Again, the dominance of the momentary interest configuration and the rapid change in priorities makes the set-up of closer institutional ties unprofitable because strong ties could reduce the room for manoeuvre to adapt to such changing priorities. This creates problems on both the highest political and the lower administrative level. Naturally, there tends to be more continuity on the latter because officials are replaced less frequently. However, due to the denser interaction, newly incoming un-experienced officials can cause more severe drawbacks in intergovernmental cooperation than politicians, who meet less frequently. Whenever changes occur, previously settled cross-jurisdictional issues need to be renegotiated. This slows down processes considerably. Again the empirical findings indicate that denser interaction does not simply indicate more collaboration, it can make collaboration more demanding, especially if former achievements are not backed up institutionally and exist on an exclusively informal basis.

If we turn to the more institutionalized *policy-specific* IGAs such as the Council of the Education Ministers or the Environmental Council and their *relations to other policy-specific arrangements*, their staff point out that there are neither regularized nor formalized linkages between them. Closer ties between specific councils tend to be a result of personal overlap, not institutional ties. For instance, the Labour Council has long been considered as the 'twin' to the Education Council because ministers have provincial often been responsible for both areas, a constellation which necessarily creates closer ties and a better handling of cross-cutting issues. However, this does not change the fact that the basic patterns of interaction evolve ad hoc. Simply speaking, the intensity of interaction rises when particular issues are salient and declines again afterwards without having any long-term impact on the nature of processes and structures on the macro level.

This lack of integration is problematized by the staff of ministerial councils who run the daily business of IGR. Since policy issues do not always fall clearly in one council's area of responsibility, they see a need for stronger linkages in order to handle cross-cutting issues more effectively and to achieve greater synergy between the works in separate yet related fields. As staff of the Council of the Ministers of the Environment indicates, political dynamics restrict the scope to set up stable institutional ties:

> Decision-making needs to be integrated. There is no effective mechanism for cross-cutting issues. We have an arrangement with the health departments because we share areas of interest. There is a significant long-term impact on health. We are working on a long-term arrangement here. On the political level, however, this is more difficult. Biodiversity would be another area in the fields of environment and fishery, but it is not well developed.... There are not many formal arrangements between councils. In this area the problem is to find means on the political level. On the officials level this is a matter of routine. But effective co-management is not very well organized at least on the political level.[3]

Ministers remain first of all part of their particular government which shapes the capacity to integrate different policy-specific IGAs. They try to improve their bargaining position in their council by threatening that their government will block negotiations in other policy areas. Such manoeuvring clearly weakens the impact of factors otherwise favourable to integration such as overlapping interests in different policy arenas, shared responsibilities, the potential for synergies, or the complexity of issues. The tight link between ministers and their cabinet is mirrored on the bureaucratic level since intergovernmental officials – although less driven by political motives – are responsible to their governments. Correspondingly, Canadian officials consider decisions upon relative priorities to be the responsibility of politicians, rather than their own responsibility as public officials (Peters 1998: 17).

As Table 6.1 shows, the absence of a secretariat organizing the ministers as a collective in weakly institutionalized areas makes integration across policy fields

[3] IGA Can IV, 2 November 2005: 3.

TABLE 6.1. *Institutionalization and integration of ministerial councils*

Policy Fields	Institutionalization	Integration
Economic and trade policy	Weak	Weak
Justice and crime control	Weak	Weak
Education	Medium	Weak
Environment	Medium	Weak
Fiscal and tax policy	Weak	Weak
Health policy	Weak	Weak
Transportation	Medium	Weak
Social policy	Weak	Weak

very difficult. For the Council of the Ministers of the Environment to maintain regular contacts with the ministers of health as a collective, for example, means maintaining regular contact with each individual provincial and territorial health department both on the political and administrative level. Although the number of government units is smaller than in the Swiss or American case, this is still a resource-intensive process. And even between medium institutionalized IGAs linkages remain fluid and ad hoc.

Competitive regional representation

The regional dimension of intergovernmental representation underlines the picture drawn so far. While we find two regional IGAs with a generalist outlook, in most sectors we do not find policy-specific regional pendants to the national ministerial councils. As between the Council of the Federation and First Ministers' Conference, there is no formal clarification about the respective tasks of the Council of the Federation, the Council of Atlantic Premiers,[4] or the Western Premiers' Conference.[5] They coexist but – beyond the provinces' overlapping membership in them – there is no indication of regularized interaction patterns. Just as the Council of the Federation meets before the First Ministers to agree on a common strategy, the two regional arrangements meet before Council meetings in order to coordinate positions regarding regional issues. They do so to gain a greater weight in the nationwide meetings and release regional positions in order to influence the national agenda. The two largest provinces, Ontario and Québec do not participate in regional IGAs. Due to their considerable strength within the federation, there is no need for them to gain weight through regional coordination efforts. Their behaviour re-emphasizes the predominant bilateral dynamics on the

---

[4] Members are Nova Scotia, New Brunswick, Prince Edwards Island, and Newfoundland and Labrador. The Council of Maritime Premiers (CMP) is formed by a subgroup of the CAP (Nova Scotia, New Brunswick, and Prince Edwards Island).

[5] Members are British Columbia, Alberta, Saskatchewan, Yukon, Northwest Territories, Nunavut, and Manitoba.

vertical and on the horizontal dimension of Canadian federalism. Most simply, they do not need regional support to influence the agenda of the Council of the Federation and often they do not even need the Council to insist on their interests towards the federal government.

SUMMARY

We already saw in Chapter 3 that the incentives generated in power-concentrating governments nourish these governments' disinclination towards strong institutionalization. These incentives equally weaken integration. Starting with the Council of the Federation, even weak vertical integration is problematic since distrust dominates its relations with the federal government. The establishment of strongly developed intergovernmental structures seems to be as far off as constitutional revision (Lazar and McLean 2000; Meekison, Telford, and Lazar 2002). Executive federalism as currently operating in Canada is acceptable exactly because it is weak and does not touch upon the different governments' constitutional privileges. If horizontal IGAs on the national and regional level are strengthened by the provinces and territories, this is done to defend interests against the federal government, again weakening any incentive to support the integration of the intergovernmental system as a whole. Even if IGAs serve collective opposition only, lower level governments still refuse to be embedded in a strong infrastructure. These dynamics also lead to a weak integration across policy fields in which we rarely find secretariats stabilizing cooperation between ministers in the first place, not to speak of institutional ties between such secretariats. This situation is considered counterproductive by administrators prioritizing effective policy-making over governmental autonomy protection. The political rationale nourished by intragovernmental dynamics, however, dominates.

Interaction between IGAs on the horizontal and vertical, national and regional level is driven by strategic manoeuvring. The two regional IGAs time their meetings before upcoming meetings of the national IGAs. The Council of the Federation in turn schedules meetings to prepare the First Ministers' Conference. Overall, generalist IGAs engage little in cross-jurisdictional policy-harmonization. Whether the formation of a common front is successful mainly depends on the internal capacity of the respective body to speak with one voice and the willingness of premiers to stick to this position in later negotiations with the federal government. Clearly, whatever collective position an IGA issues, there is no obligation for the individual government to comply later on. Given frequent alternation, new governments can easily deviate from a position which its predecessor – often the rival party – supported.

Interest aggregation in the Canadian federal system follows a 'bottom–up logic'. Issues are transferred to the higher level when interest convergence between governments is given ex ante. When moving up from a regional IGA to the Council of the Federation, only few issues are likely to remain on the agenda. Note that a regional handling or individual government responses can be the better choice depending on the issue. The problem, however, remains that, given the dominant incentive structures, issues are likely to remain unaddressed because individual governments oppose it for strategic reasons. IGAs do not moderate this tendency. At best they provide administrative support while common concerns are identified by government representatives without the active interference of the intergovernmental staff (if there is staff at all). Obviously, the lack of linkages does not mean that relations between IGAs are uncoordinated. The form of this coordination, however, re-emphasizes the competitive nature of Canadian IGR, the paramount importance of individual flexibility and the pressure to gain short-term advantages in one's electoral arena.

SWITZERLAND: VOLUNTARY POWER-SHARING AND INTERGOVERNMENTAL INTEGRATION

In Switzerland, we expect a very different picture. Given voluntary power-sharing in the cantons, IGAs should be strongly integrated. Again, we start out with an analysis of the vertical integration of the Swiss federal system, followed by its horizontal integration.

Mechanisms of vertical integration

All major IGAs in Swiss federalism are purely horizontal, thus the federal government is no full member. Nonetheless, a variety of vertical linkages are in place. Looking at the linkages of the Conferences of Directors to the federal level, a delegate of the respective federal ministry is usually invited either to executive meetings or to plenary sessions, an invitation which is often accepted. Although these federal representatives have no formal voting right, this practice facilitates cantonal–federal communication and allows the federal government to raise issues, formulate positions, and gather information about cantonal plans and positions. On a need basis, working groups are formed with federal officials and other policy-specific conferences. The Conferences of Directors have frequent contact with the department on the federal level responsible for the same policy field. Federal officials describe the relations with IGAs very positively and appreciate their work in coordinating the cantons. From their perspective, it is easier to find a common basis when dealing with one instead of 26 counterparts.

It has already been mentioned that the foundation of the Conference of Cantonal Executives in 1993 was accompanied by a growing perception that the federal *Ständerat* – the second house of parliament whose members are directly elected – do not adequately pursue territorial interests. Moreover, the contact commission between the federal government and the cantons (*Kontaktgremium Bund-Kantone*), another vertical link in place at that time, was considered a 'creature of the federal government,' in which no dialogue between equals could take place. Given this situation, the Conference of Cantonal Executives was created on the initiative of a number of cantonal officials. The immediate reaction of the federal government was to dissolve the 'contact commission' and to avoid any contact with the newly formed body. In particular, the federal executive, the *Bundesrat*, was advised by its staff not to participate in the plenary sessions of this new conference to which its members were regularly invited. However, with the strengthening of the Conference of Cantonal Executives, the federal government had to accept the new situation and nowadays considers the Conference as constructive communication partner that is able to bundle the diversity of cantonal interest successfully. This shift facilitated cantonal–federal exchanges and strengthened the cantons as governmental level considerably.

The most noticeable success of the Conference of Cantonal Executives took place in 2003 when a cantonal referendum succeeded in blocking federal plans for a tax reform that would have introduced heavy financial burdens on the cantons. It was the first time this instrument was successfully applied since its introduction in the federal constitution in 1874. The cantons had to agree to its initiation within a period of three months – a very narrow time frame given the number of cantons and their heterogeneity. Agreement could be achieved with support of the Conference of Finance Directors and the Conference of Cantonal Executives which pushed the cantons to unify on this issue and to oppose the reform package (Braun 2004). More generally, the federal government had to notice that through the support of the conferences, especially the Conference of Cantonal Executives, it has become much more difficult to divide the cantons. And as one federal official put it, the former strategy 'divide et impera' is much less effective. Nowadays, federal institutions such as the federal parliament and the federal executive need to pay more attention to cantonal demands.

As one response to the changed situation, the federal government assigned an official in the federal Department for Finance the particular responsibility to handle federal–cantonal communication. Cantonal officials have been working in the federal administration in the framework of particular projects such as the most recent federalism reform or the *Schengen* agreement for some time. The phenomenon of a federal official being responsible for federal–cantonal exchanges, by contrast, is entirely new. That such a post is established first in the finance department is no surprise. As in all federal systems, federal budget cuts or cost shifting to lower governmental levels are one of the most sensitive topics in federal–cantonal relations. Discussing federal plans with cantonal officials before they are discussed in the press helps avoiding the escalation of conflicts and enables the federal government to respond to cantonal sensitivities before new legislation is proposed officially.

Despite the claim of the federal government that such means also serve the cooperation with the Conference of Cantonal Executives, the conference itself does not appreciate such innovations. It emphasizes that particular contact persons in the federal administration are not necessary and prefers the use of direct channels to members of the Federal Council on the political level. Evidently, if the federal government improves its immediate communication with the individual cantonal administrations, the capacity of the conference to unify the cantons against the federal government and to speak as the representative of the cantons as a collective might be questioned. Again, we do not find a natural inclination towards the strengthening of cooperation as often associated with Swiss political culture. In the opposite, the Conference of Cantonal Executives has a clear perception of the loss of influence when parallel channels are set up which might undermine its efforts to maintain a linchpin position in federal–cantonal relations.

To strengthen its position as major vertical channel, the Conference of Cantonal Executives itself has made active efforts to integrate the Federal Council in its meetings. Over the years, the federal executive has been regularly invited to the plenary sessions, invitations which only were accepted in more recent years. More crucially, federal–cantonal meetings take place on a regular basis through the 'federalism-dialogue' (*Föderalismus-Dialog*), a committee composed of Bundesrat delegates and a delegation of four to five representatives of the Conference of Cantonal Executives which deals with specific policy areas and issues common papers. In the last 16 years, the Conference of Cantonal Executives has become the central IGA channelling general inter-cantonal and, increasingly, also federal–cantonal transactions.

In December 2001, the Conference of Cantonal Executives and the Conferences of Directors agreed upon a general framework which clarifies the respective responsibilities and attempts to facilitate coordination between the IGAs and the federal government. This represents an attempt to integrate the horizontal and the vertical dimension of Swiss IGR.[6] The federal government does not support the framework officially – it can only be 'invited' by the cantons to follow the framework (Trees 2005*b*: 35). It uses the framework – but does so inconsistently. Depending on the issue, it first contacts individual cantons or the Conference of Cantonal Executives. However, the federal government is willing to accept the framework as a point of reference which is already significant, especially considering its initial refusal to have contact with the newly

---

[6] Zusammenarbeit der Kantone mit dem Bund: Rahmenordnung über die Arbeitsweise der KdK und der Direktorenkonferenzen bezüglich der Kooperation mit dem Bund, Konferenz der Kantonsregierungen, Fassung vom 3. Oktober 2003.

founded Conference of Cantonal Executives. Despite occasional tensions, we find a tight network of considerably formalized relations. Vertical integration – both of the generalist as well as the policy-specific IGAs – can be therefore considered as strong.

Mechanisms of horizontal integration

Starting with the Conferences of Cantonal Directors, the contacts between the different policy-specific arrangements vary according to the proximity and overlap between the areas for which they are responsible. Apart from the Conference of Cantonal Executives, the profile of the Conference of the Directors of Finance is the most overarching. It enjoys contact with a wide range of policy-specific conferences. While the secretaries of the national directorial conferences and of the Conference of Cantonal Executives meet regularly once a year, exchanges to address concrete problems also take place in between. According to the actors involved, the exchange between the policy-specific arrangements works well. From time to time positions of different conferences are not in line, thus not all discrepancies can be avoided. However, conflict can usually be resolved on an informal basis. Policy-specific arrangements in Switzerland make strong efforts to avoid these conflicts since they weaken the cantons' position towards the federal government. In addition to the meetings of secretaries of national IGAs, the secretaries of the four generalist conferences on the regional level and their national pendant meet twice a year. The conflict potential between them is more limited than between the various national bodies since the regional bodies focus on issues of regional interest, which the Conference of Cantonal Executives usually does not pick up. Here too, additional contacts are established on a need basis.

The fact that IGA staff meets regularly already indicates a medium integration of Swiss IGR. Looking at formal indicators for integration beyond the regularity of meetings, the framework (*Rahmenordnung*) mentioned previously clarifies the respective responsibilities and attempts to facilitate cooperation between the policy-specific conferences.[7] Its impact on horizontal integration is considerable. The Conference of Cantonal Executives was assigned the responsibility to resolve conflict between different Conferences of Directors whenever the latter disagree on which of them is in charge of a particular issue (Jahresbericht CH Stiftung 2001: 9–11). As a cantonal official noted, it is not yet an automatic reflex to refer to the framework in cases of conflict. However, the staff of policy-specific conferences are clearly aware of the framework and, where there is doubt about how to proceed, they use it as an external reference point.

---

[7] Zusammenarbeit der Kantone mit dem Bund: Rahmenordnung über die Arbeitsweise der KdK und der Direktorenkonferenzen bezüglich der Kooperation mit dem Bund, Konferenz der Kantonsregierungen, Fassung vom 3. Oktober 2003.

The framework functions as a back-up for those situations which cannot be resolved informally.

The Conference of Cantonal Executives is supposed to play the role of an arbiter which, however, is not unambiguously welcomed by the directorial conferences. Initially, intergovernmental actors hardly welcomed the establishment of the Conference of Cantonal Executives in the first place. Not only the federal government and the *Ständerat* (the second house of parliament) were critical, but also the Conferences of Directors (Minger 2004: 10). Although it was clear that a generalist arrangement representing the governments as a whole – not only individual departments as the directorial conferences – is likely to strengthen the cantons, the Conference of Cantonal Executives was also perceived as a competitor for influence in the intergovernmental arena. This was less the case regarding its function as a new policy-specific conference responsible for foreign affairs. There was agreement that this gap needed to be filled. Yet the growing ambition of the Conference of Cantonal Executives to handle topics of overarching, cross-sectoral relevance in general, for example issues related to the distribution of cantonal–federal competences, nourished suspicion on the part of some policy-specific conferences. When years later the Conference of Cantonal Executives managed to formally take over a core position in inter-institutional coordination, further doubts that the conference might in the end get too powerful arose.

Another source of criticism refers to the composition of the Conference of Cantonal Executives. While the executive uses a formula of regional representation, it is perceived as unrepresentative in terms of its partisan affiliations and in terms of the directorial conferences it represents. On the one hand, the executive is perceived as predominantly conservative. On the other hand, a considerable number of its members have also been members of policy-specific IGAs either in the area of finance or in the area of crime control, justice, and police. Only few of them came from policy-specific arrangements dealing with health or social policy. During the negotiations over the federalism reform and the bilateral negotiations with the EU, the Conference of Cantonal Executives dealt strongly with financial and judicial issues and in this context such a 'bias' had its advantages. At the same time, the under-represented Conferences of Directors feared the generalist conference to become dominated by other policy-specific IGAs which nourished further reservations. To avoid such criticism in the future, the Conference of Cantonal Executives declared intentions to represent the major policy-specific bodies more evenly.

Though not free from tensions, the working relations between the Conference of Cantonal Executives and the directorial conferences are overall productive. They work very closely together whenever it is in the cantonal interest, as was the case throughout the recent federalism reform. Furthermore, policy-specific conferences are aware of the contribution of the generalist Conference of Cantonal Executives to the strengthening of cantonal interests in the federal system and value the rich flow of information gathered by it, information which particularly smaller cantons cannot obtain independently. Nonetheless, critical voices remain, reflecting the endeavour of the individual IGAs to maintain their relative weight in the system. Although the Conferences of Directors are firmly established bodies in IRG for several decades, they have no formal status and this is perceived as a constant threat. Without constitutional protection, they are under pressure to demonstrate their usefulness to their member cantons that finance them. Accordingly, any body which weakens their status and continuously gains influence in the intergovernmental arena is perceived as problematic. These dynamics affect inter-institutional relations, although the various Conferences of Directors consider themselves as cantonal representatives who, in principle, favour an overall increase of cantonal power to which the Conference of Cantonal Executives strongly contributes.

The ambiguity of evaluations indicates that the efforts to further integrate inter-institutional relations through the framework agreement between the various Conferences of Directors and the Conference of Cantonal Executives was not a formalization of already settled relations (hence a formal expression of a pre-existing informal agreement). In the opposite, the framework addresses tensions between different IGAs as well as the IGAs and the federal government. In principle, cantonal actors are open towards reforms strengthening the given infrastructures and organizing the relations between IGAs more efficiently due to intragovernmental incentive structures favourable to such long-term oriented choices. Nonetheless, they are aware of potential power losses. Both cantonal representatives as well as staff of cantonal IGAs oppose integration efforts which visibly shift the balance of power in the system into a – from their individual viewpoint – unfavourable direction. They assess the possible costs in terms of power and autonomy losses and are ready to reject efficiency-increasing reforms violating their institutional self-interest too considerably. Hence, new initiatives to enhance cooperation are not self-enforcing. They will be made subject to a cost-benefit analysis before being embraced or rejected.

This becomes particularly visible when looking at the most recent initiative by the Conference of Cantonal Executives to strengthen its integration with the various Conferences of Directors – their merger in one 'House of Cantons' located in Berne. This project was initiated by a report discussed in the plenary session in 2001 and confirmed by the executive in 2004. In the end, in June 2005, the plenary session confirmed the project in a much 'lighter' version than the staff of the conference would have preferred.[8] Though willing to work door on door to improve communication and generate synergies, the directorial conferences insisted that each body be represented separately and maintains its

---

[8] Medienmitteilung vom 24. Juni 2005, Ja zum Haus der Kantone, http://www.kdk.ch/int/kdk/de/mm.html

institutional autonomy. For the Conference of Cantonal Executives, by contrast, the concentration of the conferences under one roof is preferably only a first step. The fusion of all conferences in one institution is envisaged. At this scenario, the Conference of Cantonal Executives would have core coordination responsibilities like a general secretariat and stabilize its position as the linchpin of Swiss IGR linking cross-sectoral and sectoral as well as vertical and horizontal coordination mechanisms. An idea related to that scenario, which was rejected, involved the reduction of the directorial conferences from ten to four to five, each responsible for broader policy sectors, a reform which would have facilitated inter-institutional coordination and increased integration considerably. However, it would also have abolished some of the Conferences of Directors as autonomous entities. As one might expect, the latter were not willing to accept what they consider as their own dissolution in an overall cantonal institution with the Conference of Cantonal Executives as the highest instance. The cantons themselves – sensitive to what they perceive as centralizing tendencies – did not find such a development desirable and the original proposal was revised. Most importantly, the individual Conferences of Directors remained in place and still decide upon their political moves and questions of personnel independent from each other and without interference of the Conference of Cantonal Executives (Trees 2005*b*: 80).

Mechanisms of intra-regional and national–regional integration

Reconfirming the overall picture, we find linkages between the generalist and the policy-specific conferences within the same region, albeit with different intensity and formality. The relations of the Conference of Central Switzerland to the regional directorial conferences are the most integrated among the four regions. This region pretty much mirrors the situation on the national level. Integration is based on comprehensive formal statutes that clarify responsibilities and structure their joint work. The Conference of Eastern Switzerland comes close to this level of formalization. So far the relations are based on a framework which specifies joint work in areas of shared interest (Trees 2005*b*: 27–8). In both regions, inter-institutional relations fall in the category of high integration. The Conference of Northwest Switzerland cooperates with regional directorial conferences informally, a formalization is currently under discussion. Integration is therefore on a medium level. Linkages are weakest in Western Switzerland, where cooperation is infrequent. Again, there are plans to change this situation in due course (Trees 2005*b*: 28). To achieve a higher integration between IGAs in Western Switzerland is no easy process since similar tensions came up as observed between the various national conferences. The regional policy-specific conferences showed resistance against further integration, rejecting intrusion into what they consider to be their spheres of responsibility. The strongest linkages are in those two regions which set up generalist IGAs already in the 1960s (the conferences of Central and Eastern Switzerland) and, having become part of the intergovernmental landscape, found it easier to establish linkages to other IGAs. In the two other regions generalist IGAs were established later and linkages to policy-specific IGAs are so far comparatively weak. However, given favourable intragovernmental incentives in the participating cantons, one can reasonably expect that the difficulties to set up stronger linkages between the various bodies will be overcome in the long run.

Turning to national–regional integration, it is noticeable that there is no simple hierarchy between the national and cantonal levels. Regional bodies do not try to avoid national issues or necessarily specialize on very narrow regional problems. This contrasts with the dominant pattern in the United States where regional IGAs participate in meetings of the national bodies in Washington D.C. and gather information about the national agenda, an agenda which prescribes the distribution of labour between the two levels. In Switzerland, the situation is much more balanced. There national staff try to keep informed about lower level activities since they do not control the activities of regional arrangements. At the same time, the secretaries of the generalist IGAs on the regional level meet regularly with the secretary of their national counterpart, the Conference of Cantonal Executives, to avoid clashes of interests.

Overall, national–regional integration is on a medium level. It is intense but without the backing of an elaborate, written framework. While the Conference of Central Switzerland is mainly focused on policy coordination within the region, the other three regional conferences focus on the representation of regional interests in the federation as a whole (Trees 2005*b*: 104). To avoid clashes, the Conference of Cantonal Executives is sensitive to regional divisions and avoids issues on which the regions compete. Vice versa, it is unusual that generalist-regional IGAs take positions on issues where a nationwide consensus already exists.

Policy-specific IGAs on the regional level are linked to their national pendants through contact on a need basis, through the exchange of protocols or, and this constitutes the most formal mechanism, the participation of national IGA personnel in regional conferences. Although contradictory position-taking towards the federal government is often avoided, in those policy fields where bodies coexist on different levels, it is not uncommon that a regional policy-specific conference takes a position where a national position has already been issued. Where national solutions are paramount in a policy field, such as fiscal policy, national proposals will finally integrate regional demands. In other areas such as education, different regional positions can prevail.

To sum up the overall dynamics, although the national IGAs are stronger in terms of resources and were established earlier, regional arrangements can still provide a counterbalance to national ones. The regional level tends to be strongest in those areas touching upon cultural issues which do not allow for compensation through side payments.[9] By contrast, despite the high potential for conflict in fiscal policy, the national level tends to be the major platform. Putting these findings in a comparative context, in terms of national–regional integration, Canadian IGR can be described as a bottom–up process, American IGR as a top–down process, while the Swiss situation comes closest to a national–regional balance.

SUMMARY

Starting out with vertical integration, the linkages to the federal level of government, both the Conference of Cantonal Executives and the Conferences of Cantonal Directors evaluate the relationship with the federal peak institutions as productive. The Conference of Cantonal Executives is much more than a platform to form a front against the federal government and provides an intra-horizontal channel for exchange and conflict resolution. The integration between national and regional IGAs as well as between cantonal arrangements located on the same level is, on average, medium to high. IGAs consider it necessary to specify their respective tasks and have established mechanisms for conflict resolution in order to fulfil their respective functions adequately. They try not to weaken each other to maintain a strong position towards the federal government and are aware that a rising number of strong IGAs increases the complexity in Swiss IGR and thereby the costs of integration, a challenge they actively try to counteract.

Simultaneously, setting up these linkages may result in tensions between IGAs. IGA staff are very aware of their institutional self-interest and attempt to defend their sphere of influence. As with institutionalization, integration has proven far from self-explanatory within a supposedly 'cooperative culture', a finding which supports the assessment of IGR through a rationalist lens. Integrative efforts are driven by two rationales which are, at times, conflicting: The endeavour to set up more efficient relations to strengthen the lower level collectively, while trying to maintain one's individual status and power in the intergovernmental arena. From a cross-national perspective, the latter rationale has a relatively weak impact, which roots in the low political costs of institution building generated by voluntary power-sharing in the individual cantons.

---

[9] One example is conflict over which language is to be taught as first foreign language in school, French or English. Obviously, there is no middle solution which can satisfy all regions.

UNITED STATES: COMPULSORY POWER-SHARING AND INTERGOVERNMENTAL INTEGRATION

Building on the findings presented in Chapter 5, this section substantiates the claim that one crucial cause of the states' surprisingly limited resistance against central dominance is the coordination failure within and between the states rooted in compulsory power-sharing. Most strikingly, these coordination problems are reflected in the weak integration between IGAs representing individual state actors. In scholarly work, the United States is in part portrayed as a federal system in which bargaining networks are essential while command–control relationships are alien (e.g. Elazar 1991: 75; Radin and Boase 2000: 80). This position is contested by those emphasizing the increasingly coercive nature of federal–state relations in which the centre can dictate policies on the states due to its superior spending power (e.g. Kincaid 1990; 2003). Contributing to this – so far unresolved – debate on the nature (or the various natures) of American IGR, this chapter shows that the predominance of power sharing cannot be equated with a balance of power between different government units or levels of government.

Following Derthick (2001), one of the 'enduring features of American federalism' is the weakness of the states. Indeed, federal–state relations have changed over time and there is no doubt about that. Nonetheless, as Derthick rightly emphasizes, it is still remarkable that the states – despite a political rhetoric defending state rights – have never forcefully opposed central intrusion into state jurisdictions. While other features (e.g. the judiciary) clearly play a role, research on American IGR pays insufficient attention to one core element which systematically affects the nature of intergovernmental structures and patterns of interaction: the unequal capacity of the two governmental orders to coordinate internally. This constellation contributes considerably to the observed imbalance among the two levels in the American system. While both the federal government and the states have to overcome internal constitutional divisions, the centre does not need to organize support outside its own boundaries. To act as one 'order of government' against the central government and to successfully defend own authority, concerted interstate interaction is a prerequisite to allow for even and balanced federal–state interactions. However, since intra-state unity is already difficult to achieve, interstate unity is even more so. Consequently, the states perceive the potential of collective resistance to prevent the federal government from intruding into their jurisdictions as fairly limited. The following sections highlight that compulsory power-sharing has two countervailing effects. As Chapter 5 has shown, it sets overall incentives in favour of institutionalization. Simultaneously, it contributes to intra-horizontal divisions: IGAs are unable to bridge their differences which undermines inter-institutional integration.

Inter-branch divides and the dilemma of competing autonomies

One crucial feature of the American intergovernmental landscape is the coexistence of generalist IGAs which reflect the division between the branches, most notably the National Governors' Association and the National Conference of State Legislatures. These arrangements have several regional pendants with partially overlapping constituencies introducing a high degree of complexity in the intergovernmental arena. To arrive at a systematic picture of the level of integration between the multitude of IGAs, this section first looks at the horizontal divides on the national level – horizontal integration between IGAs of national scope – in greater detail. Second, it analyses the vertical relations between these national arrangements with their regional pendants. To a considerable degree, if not completely, these bodies are directed towards getting their member interests recognized in federal policy and lack a clear distinction of labour, which results in an ambivalent oscillation between mutual information-sharing and competition.

Note that in contrast to the analysis of the other two cases, there is no specific section which assesses the vertical integration between the federal government and IGAs. The reason is simple. IGAs have frequent contact with national-level institutions, be it Congress or the federal bureaucracy. We find issue-specific federal–state commissions set up on an ad hoc basis which assure communication between federal and state actors. While interaction is intense, it is also unstructured and dependent on federal goodwill. So are the linkages between federal-level institutions and state actors or IGAs embracing the latter which implies that the vertical integration with federal institutions – when measured in structural terms – remains weak.

Looking at the horizontal integration between national IGAs, already the mere multitude of IGAs devalues the state level's status as a major layer in the American federal system. This renders the formation of an interest profile of a state as one coherent unit and, more so, of the horizontal level composed of states extremely demanding. Logically, the more IGAs are in place, the more difficult integration becomes, in particular if they represent separate state institutions (e.g. state legislatures) that are only weakly connected to other institutions inside the individual state unit. The low level of horizontal integration between national IGAs, in turn, provides one explanation why the federal government has much more leeway to pick and choose who to deal with when interacting with the 'state level' than in other systems. In federal systems where one IGA plays the role of the main communication or interaction partner for the federal government when it comes to major intergovernmental matters (such as the Conference of Cantonal Executives in Switzerland), the capacity of the federal government to steer IGR from the outset is more limited. The weakness of vertical and horizontal integration in the United States – as vertical and horizontal dynamics of IGR more generally – are connected.

Furthermore, in American federalism, the high institutionalization of IGAs and the resources related to it stabilize inter-institutional divisions instead of being used to overcome divisions as in the Swiss context. This does not mean that IGAs made no integrative efforts. The three state IGAs have moved to the same building in Washington, D.C. – the 'Hall of the States' where a multitude of other association is located. On an informal basis, their directors see each other in the monthly 'Big 7' meeting. Within the 'Big 7', as the major IGAs in American federalism are called,[10] the state associations are more closely linked than the others in the group. They have shared memberships in certain boards and the common origin of the National Governors' Association and the Conference of State Legislatures from the Council of State Governments indicates a certain 'natural linkage' between the three state IGAs. At the same time, it is clear that if interest convergence had been strong enough, institutional separation would not have been necessary in first place. This becomes evident in efforts of the governors and the state legislatures to create 'founding myths' emphasizing their institutional autonomy. The representative of the National Governors' Association, for instance, dated the arrangement's foundation back to 1908 when Roosevelt, who was governor at that time, called the first meeting of governors to talk about IGR. Neither the governors' nor the legislatures' representative mentioned the Council of State Governments when talking about the origin of their institution (a behaviour correctly predicted by the representative of the Council of State Governments in an earlier interview). The endeavour to distinguish one's IGA from other IGAs is pronounced. This process of 'institutional emancipation' reflecting constitutional divides only starts out at the national level. As discussed later, the same pattern is reproduced regionally which points to the pervasive impact of compulsory power-sharing independent of the relative diversity of the given state configurations.

Although the three state IGAs are linked through 'broad bands', these bands are far from indicating shared interests. Since regular meetings take place, integration between the three major state associations is on a medium level. However, as pointed out, they represent only a subgroup of state-related IGAs which are located on the horizontal level. The effect on the overall degree of integration is necessarily limited. The pressure to cooperate in order to gain more weight in the system conflicts with the IGAs' autonomy which led to their philosophy of 'cooperate not merge' (Arnold and Plant 1994: 105). Interviews with the personnel of a range of national IGAs have confirmed their general willingness to cooperate, a feature which is rooted in state-internal power-sharing structures. They are aware that divides decrease the overall impact on federal action – of the states as

---

[10] The Big 7 consists of the three state IGAs and, in addition, the following four arrangements: the National League of Cities; the National Association of Counties; the United States Conference of Mayors; and the International City/County Management Association (Cigler 1995: 135).

collective and of their own arrangement. Simultaneously, they emphasize the practical difficulties involved in finding common ground and point to a 'natural tension between the branches' which complicates the relations between the arrangements considerably.

As laid out in Chapter 5, this conflict of interest becomes visible in the legislatures' strong resistance to federal mandates and the much more pragmatic approach towards federal intrusion pursued by the governors and is generated by the diverging institutional interests of the two branches. This difference in orientation accounts for the absence of any strong and coherent mobilization of the 'states' as political units against central encroachment. Legislative and executive IGAs both intend to protect 'autonomy' but when referring to 'autonomy' they mean very different things. While legislative actors attempt to protect their law-making competences, executive actors are interested in securing as much leeway as possible in the implementation phase in order 'to get things done'. As long as the centre gives funding with sufficiently loose strings attached, the intrusion into spheres of state authority is not of overriding importance from an executive point of view. As a consequence, funding is hardly ever rejected just for the sake of protecting the states' legislative authority. This orientation goes back to the disparate nature of the states as political units. Since executives lack an internal (constitutionally supported or party-based) linkage to the legislatures, they are more interested in the capacity to deliver services than in maintaining the state's right to decide unilaterally upon precisely which service ought to be delivered. Evidently, from a cross-national point of view, it is ironic that in the United States the direct participation of the legislatures in the intergovernmental game turns out to be an expression of the weakness of legislative autonomy protection.

Substantial vertical coordination that transcends mere lobbying and deals with policy occurs but through different channels, for instance through bilateral federal–state working groups that are created ad hoc to develop solutions for specific problems and are dissolved afterwards. Similar observations can be made about the implementation stage, where state agencies deal with the corresponding federal agencies when problems arise that require collaboration. During the stage of policy formulation, the focus of this book, most executive associations tend to prioritize their individual impact on federal legislation. Legislative IGAs can hardly compensate for that and integration remains insufficient.

As detailed in Chapter 5, when it comes to policy-specific IGAs, American IGR are structured along the repertoire of different instruments available for interstate exchanges. Examples of nationwide IGAs promoting such an instrument are the National Conference of Commissioners on Uniform State Laws or the National Center for Interstate Compacts. They try to support the adaptation of uniform laws and regulations across state boundaries. As a consequence of this functional division of labour and high level of specialization of IGAs backing up particular instruments, the creation of stable inter-institutional linkages does not constitute a major issue. Horizontal integration among IGAs favouring different forms of policy coordination remains weak. Most IGAs try to promote the use of their 'own instrument' to maintain their niche instead of pooling their collective weight through stronger structural ties between them. The Council of State Governments which tries to form an umbrella connecting IGAs and which promotes the use of several instruments again forms an exception but cannot make up for dominant tendencies.

These findings are reinforced when looking at policy-specific IGAs such as compact commissions. There are indeed contacts between generalist and policy-specific IGAs – yet only ad hoc. Due to their very different nature and the specific functions assigned to them, their relations are unproblematic and less contentious than relations between generalist IGAs of different scope. Generalist and policy-specific IGAs tend to coexist rather than interact. Completing the picture, linkages across policy-specific bodies are weak as well. Policy-specific commissions tend to mostly work with state administrators who are specialists in dealing with the particular issue at hand. Mirroring the dominant patterns of generalist IGAs, policy-specific IGAs are weakly integrated yet for different reasons. While the relations between policy-specific arrangements are free from competition, given their narrow profile (itself a consequence of the inter-branch divisions described above) there is only limited need to establish stable ties to bodies handling very different issues. For most parts, they simply do their own thing, while information exchange evolves informally whenever necessary.

In sum, the integration between most of the national IGAs – be they generalist or policy-oriented – is weak. Although the three generalist state IGAs – the National Governors' Association, the National Conference of State Legislatures, and the Council of State Governments – meet regularly and therefore reach medium integration, this hardly counterbalances the overall level of fragmentation.

Fragmentation across branches and government levels

Moving on to the relations between the national and regional state IGAs, the overall weak integration in American federalism is emphasized further. State IGAs face a trade-off between flexible and informal relations to a multitude of private and public interest groups which they can exploit on an ad hoc basis and the creation of reliable linkages to a limited number of bodies. In an environment in which the stronger arrangements as well as stronger states 'fend for themselves', IGAs tend to resort to the former strategy.

Although their constituencies overlap, regional IGAs of governors and legislators are independent from their national pendants. There is no 'natural link' between those bodies representing the same governmental branch. Most of the regional governors and the four regional conferences of legislators are staffed by the Council of State Governments which also has four regional offices of its own.[11] Despite its overarching activities, the Council's coordination achievements are limited. They neither lead to a close integration between IGAs representing different branches active in the same region nor between those representing the same branch in different regions.

Mirroring developments on the national level, most (albeit not all) regional governors' arrangements formerly belonged to the Council of State Governments' regional offices yet became independent to create their own platform for executive representation. Furthermore, there are no regular meetings between the staff of the National Governors' Association and the staff of regional IGAs. Although the former has two meetings a year and 'allows the regional associations to meet there',[12] the biannual meeting is not used for the vertical coordination between national and regional IGAs but for the drafting of national policy-resolutions between the governors on a national level. The mere presence of regional representatives cannot be considered as an equivalent to the specific meetings of regional and national directors as set up for instance in the Swiss context. The latter are explicitly directed towards facilitating national–regional communication and coordination which is clearly distinct from what we find in the American context. The following comment by the staff of a regional governors' arrangement illustrates the nature of national–regional relations:

> The National Governors' Association ignores regional associations until they have an office in D.C., they do not ignore you then because you pay rent and you have more media access. This is our weakness that we do not have an office in D.C. and are not there. I have recommended the National Governors' Association to meet 2–4 times a year with the regional associations to have a working dialogue. But the National Governors' Association has become the *Romans* and we are only *Galls* [italics by author]. Only the Romans get better treatment but we are only Galls. They say in D.C. that whenever we want to communicate we should contact them, that anytime we can communicate. But it is so painful to arrange it. And what happens regularly, if a regional association causes too much irritation the National Governors' Association tells the governors: tell them to back off. The incentives to prevail against the National Governors' Association are not given. This mutes the enthusiasm and often there are jurisdictional ties. It is said that we only deal with the regional issues and the National Governors' Association with the national ones even if they have a regional basis. If one is not in the Hall of the States, the communication is not good.[13]

The comment highlights two important points. First, although the regional associations represent partially the same constituencies as the National Governors' Association and one might therefore expect at least an interest in smooth inter-institutional relations, executive IGAs located on different levels compete for influence over issues and members. Overlapping membership tends to complicate

---

[11] They are located in New York, Atlanta, Sacramento, and Lombard.
[12] IGA XI, 6 December 2005: 2.   [13] IGA US IX, 30 November 2005: 3–4.

matters rather than it helps to create common ground. Since the national branch is stronger in resources and in prestige, it dominates interaction as soon as conflict occurs. Since the National Governors' Association does not depend on the cooperation of regional arrangements, it has no incentives to engage in regular contact or information exchange, not to speak of mutual coordination. Thus, the imbalance between centre and periphery is not only clearly reflected in federal–state relations but also in the relations between national and regional IGAs. This argument is substantiated by a second important aspect revealed by the comment. The function of the 'Hall of the States' is not limited to facilitating coordination between IGAs. Evidently, the shared location of dozens of IGAs increases efficiency of information exchange and allows for flexible ad hoc coordination between them. This already presupposes that arrangements are interested in such exchanges which is overall correct. Note, however, that this readiness differs markedly according to the issue at stake and the size and resources of the individual IGA. Analogously to large states, which are often able to pursue their interests independently without actively engaging in an IGA, large arrangements show little interest in cooperating with small ones – be there an overlap in constituencies or not. In fact, the 'Hall of the States' expresses the inequality between those IGAs located in the building (or at least in Washington D.C.) and those which are not. IGAs with their headquarters outside the capital are easily disqualified as second-best channels of influence. From this angle, the 'Hall of the States' indicates the centralization of IGR rather than the strengthening of intergovernmental integration in the American federal system.

As a reaction to the given imbalance, regional arrangements try to carve out their own 'functional niches'. They specialize on policies which are closely rooted in the very profile of their region. For example, they emphasize their role in international coordination with the bordering Canadian provinces in order to justify their own existence. Simultaneously, they avoid conflict by stepping back from issues whenever a national initiative is expected – ex ante accepting and thereby reinforcing a hierarchy between the national and the regional level. As another member of a staff of regional IGA points out:

> If they can reach consensus on the national level, then the NGA [National Governors' Association] position is crucial. There are two situations when the regions get nevertheless active, first, when one position affects the different regions in different ways. A second situation is when the NGA cannot reach consensus. Usually, however, we come in when the NGA does not intervene because it is not interested.[14] [insertion by author]

To pursue this strategy of conflict prevention or 'one-sided adaptation', information about which issues are likely to enter the national agenda is required. This strategy is most feasible for IGAs with a Washington office due to their

---

[14] IGA US XI, 6 December 2005.

privileged information access. Regional associations with staff in Washington D.C. can attend the weekly meeting of the National Governors' Association with the individual state offices[15] in the 'Hall of the States' to gather information about the National Governors' Association and about its regional pendants which also attend. Vice versa, it is only of limited importance for the National Governors' Association to meet regional representatives. Its main objective is to build internal consensus by convincing staff of the individual governors' offices of joint initiatives. This objective presupposes that regional divides are overcome, which is different from assuring inter-institutional compromises acknowledging regional differences in the first place.

In sum, the regional associations and the National Governors' Association are integrated on a medium level because they meet (more or less) regularly. However, due to their overlapping constituencies, their relations remain ambivalent. Although channels of communication exist between national and regional IGAs located in Washington, D.C., staff continuously emphasized their informal character. Most notably, channels tend to have a 'top–down' character and relationships between arrangements are often characterized by competition, with the National Governors' Association playing the dominant role. Usually a wide range of intergovernmental actors participate in the meetings of the National Governors' Association meetings which, however, do not constitute a proper basis for inter-institutional exchange. It complements the picture that there are no separate meetings among regional groupings and that there is very little direct contact between the actual regional offices outside Washington. The integration between regional governors' arrangements remains weak. All in all, the more internally unified the National Governors' Association, the less there is leeway for regional initiatives. The relationship between these IGAs is clearly characterized by a trade-off in which national interests dominate regional voices.

On the side of the legislative IGAs the situation looks very similar. Contact between them occurs on an ad hoc basis. Since the justification of these IGAs equally hinges upon maintaining a particular niche, regional associations of state legislatures try to emphasize own issues and, more generally, their independence from other arrangements. Again, the different status of associations with and without an office in Washington indicates an imbalance between regional IGAs which is supported by the absence of stable horizontal linkages between them. Again relations are competitive. A staff member of a regional branch representing the Western legislatures even points to the 'legitimating division' between regional associations: '...opposition from other regions is good because if they have their issues, we have ours'.[16] Since IGAs justify their own necessity through their distinctiveness from national and from regional arrangements, strong link-

---

[15] Most states run an office to represent individual state interests.
[16] IGA US VIII, 29 November 2005: 2.

ages between them are counterproductive. Similar to the regional governors' arrangements, the regional conferences of the legislatures are free to attend the annual meeting of the National Conference of State Legislatures. Yet their attendance varies from year to year. Legislative arrangements do not take shared positions simply because they represent the same branch in order to increase their individual weight. Instead, competitive dynamics in the system undermine any incentive to develop strong structural linkages across branches as well as across regions.

Finally, legislative and executive IGAs active within the same region reproduce the national situation between the branches on a smaller scale. IGA staff clearly indicate that there are natural limits to cooperation when one body represents executives and the other legislatures, despite covering the same territory. The two groups are distanced further since legislators deal with a wide range of issues, whereas executives have access to specialists in their administrations and therefore tend to specialize more. Linkages are loose and constantly open for strategic reorientation (Gage 1992).

SUMMARY

Summing up the overall patterns of integration in American federalism, IGAs compete for access to the federal government or, alternatively, for influence over their partially overlapping memberships. This constellation undermines stable inter-institutional linkages, which in most cases leads to weak integration among IGAs of different type and scope. As a consequence of compulsory power-sharing in the states, we find many highly institutionalized IGAs but we do not find a system of IGR able to generate concerted state behaviour. We neither find stable, structural channels between the federal and state level of government. Looking at national–regional linkages between different types of state IGAs, integration is mostly weak and information tends to be transported from the higher to the lower level without adequate feedback mechanisms in place. As federal–state relations are centrally dominated, so are inter-institutional relations.

One effect of this notorious competition between IGAs in the American system has already been touched upon in Chapter 5. IGAs try to compensate for this weakness by serving their individual members as professional service-providers. This implies a convergence of public and private interest groups in the American intergovernmental area (Cigler 1995), a tendency which finds reflection in a web of informal ties between IGAs and lobbyists. Indeed, the former tend to invest in and rely on contacts with private interest groups as an information resource more than on other IGAs. The rationale behind this strategic choice becomes clear in the following statement of an IGA staff:

The NGA [National Governors' Association] only meets two times a year. The Democratic Governors' and the Republican Governors' Associations meet much more often.... the goal is to raise money for the election of higher numbers of Republican and Democratic governors.... There more political information is exchanged, the gossip, problems people have, more political and more personal relations are set up. There are 20 governors each with two to four members of staff and 300 lobbyists in attendance who go to both.... The single biggest network outside the legislature is the lobbyist community.... If I want to know something from the other regions regarding telecommunication, I call the guy from AT&T who has been at both meetings and he has notes and this is very effective. I can ask what did you hear about x, y, z. However, these relations are time-consuming. You cannot just call someone after months to get some information.[17] [insertion by author]

Obviously, the majority of IGAs is not only *functionally* similar to private interest groups in their nearly exclusive focus on vertically oriented lobbying and service delivery to their members. They also adapt *strategically* by engaging in close networks with private interests in order to profit from their superior material resources and their access to fora which the public, in particular the bipartisan arrangements, cannot enter directly. As one IGA staff put it, 'business' contacts with a lot of lobbyists are normal. The only body with whom contacts are denser still is Congress. These channels differ in their main functions yet supplement each other. While the channel to lobbyists is used to receive information, the channel to legislators is used to exert influence through providing information.

The strategic adaptation of state IGAs as an answer to the multiplicity of competitors has immediate consequences for intergovernmental integration. While in Switzerland strong formal as well as dense personal ties coexist and are clearly compatible, in the United States the establishment of formal linkages appear alien to the predominant 'networking practices'. Since American IGAs are pressed to compete for influence on the federal government and for their members' loyalty, the establishment of formal ties could easily delimit their capacity to freely form coalitions and freely access various sources of information. The informality of linkages tends to increase the number of channels a body can exploit and, hence, maximizes its freedom to manoeuvre. A similar picture appears regarding the relations of regional IGAs with more policy-specific public interest groups. Just like national IGAs, they pursue contacts and collaboration on an ad hoc basis. Such a conflict between formalization and collaboration does not exist in the Swiss context since IGR are less fragmented and less shaped by divergent institutional interests. Most importantly, Swiss IGAs represent whole governments and, as a consequence, can represent the cantonal level of government more effectively.

Scholars have argued that American state actors accepted the 'realism of the administrative state' and cared less about competence distribution than about

---

[17] IGA US IX, 30 November 2005: 4–5.

the 'realities' of funding, implementation, and coalition building around concrete programs (Arnold and Plant 1994: 106; Esman 1984; Wolpe and Levine 1996). One crucial part of the 'reality' which feeds this acceptance is the unequal capacity of the two governmental levels to coordinate internally. On the vertical dimension, this coordination failure is institutionally underpinned by intra-state divides, most notably by branches defending different ideas of state autonomy. Compulsory power-sharing structures on the state and executive level have been impressively projected outside state boundaries and coined intergovernmental institution-building in the United States. From the state executives over the legislatures to individual states and cities lobby separately in Washington for their genuine interests (Cigler 1995: 142) like any private interest group. Relations between IGAs resemble relations between interest groups as described by Salisbury – as often friendly but generally unstable (1992: 349). Correspondingly, the pre-emption of state and local authority enacted by Congress and the conditions attached to grants have increased dramatically in the last few decades (Kincaid 1990; Zimmerman 1990: 48–49). With the continuous growth of national funding, interest groups have started to focus more and more on Washington and especially public interest group have multiplied enormously, while at the same time wielding increasingly less influence over policy results (Salisbury 1992: 339). State IGAs – already established for decades – reacted to such an environment by becoming involved in flexible networks with private interest groups, instead of setting up a system of IGR based on stable ties with IGAs to increase their collective weight. This reaction reinforces national clientilism and centripetalism and heightens the pressure on state and local actors to compete for national funding (Kenyon and Kincaid 1991: 91, 111), a reaction which makes structured interstate cooperation even less likely.

Although informal interstate relations abound in scope and variety, these activities are too fragmented to lead to a coordinated and internally consistent action of lower level governments as one 'order of government' (Cigler 1995: 150). Since the states are confronted with steadily growing demands in the delivery of policies and services, it is unlikely that they will escape the dependency stimulated by federal funds, which at the same time reinforces the effects of compulsory power-sharing that in itself impedes integration. At the same time, the centre's propensity to fund people rather than places exacerbates the formation of alliances along territorial lines (Cigler 1995: 150). The federal government encourages intergovernmental cooperation along functional lines which tends to erode the ability of the states to develop coherent policies that integrate their various programs and activities on a statewide basis (Elazar 1984: 186). Failing interstate cooperation, in turn, strengthens the dominance of the federal government since national regulation is easily justified if states are unable to address cross-jurisdictional problems effectively. After a rise in the 1960s, the number of compacts declined later on with the rise of federal pre-emption (Zimmerman

1990: 58–60, 141–2). Although horizontal coordination is an alternative path to federal pre-emption and state governments try to push for the adoption of uniform laws to avoid the latter (Bowman 2002: 12–13, 16), success has been limited so far. Over the last decades, American federalism has become increasingly centralized (Kincaid 2001: 147). Unlike the Canadian provinces or the Swiss cantons, the American states do not manage to guard their jurisdictional power through concerted action, a dilemma rooted in the very nature of compulsory power-sharing in the states which has been resisting ideological surges and reform attempts.

CONCLUSIONS: INTERGOVERNMENTAL INTEGRATION IN CANADA, SWITZERLAND, AND THE UNITED STATES

Overall, the findings confirm our theoretical expectations. Intergovernmental integration is weak in Canada and in the United States, while it is strong in Switzerland. In all three cases, intragovernmental incentive structures play a major role to account for the respective patterns of institution building.

Rooted in the strong power-concentration in the Canadian provinces, interaction between generalist IGAs on the horizontal and vertical, national and regional level is driven by strategic manoeuvring. The two regional IGAs time their meetings before upcoming national meetings of the Council of the Federation and the First Ministers' Conferences. Whether the formation of a common front is effective highly depends on the often temporary willingness of premiers to stick to positions in later negotiations with the federal government. Due to the internal cohesion of lower level governments in Canada, conflict often spills over from one policy field to the other. Ministers try to improve their position in intergovernmental negotiations by threatening that their cabinet colleagues will boycott negotiations in a related policy fields should their demands fail to be met. In terms of interest aggregation, the process is structured bottom–up. Issues are only transferred to the higher level when interest convergence between the governments involved is given ex ante. IGAs at best provide administrative support, while the identification of these issues is controlled by government representatives without the active interference of the intergovernmental staff (if there is staff at all). Obviously, the lack of linkages does not mean that relations between IGAs are not coordinated. Yet the way they are coordinated emphasizes the competitive nature of Canadian IGR rooted in intragovernmental incentive structures which push governments towards short-term oriented, strategic manoeuvring.

As with institutionalization, the Swiss picture is very different. Swiss IGAs are strongly integrated both vertically and horizontally. Given voluntary power-sharing within the cantons in the form of oversized party coalitions, neither executive–legislative divides nor intra-executive divides affect IGR negatively. The given intra-cantonal party-cooperation has two effects. First, it ties executives and legislatures together. Second, the oversized governments neutralize negative effects of party competition on IGR since intra-executive compromise moderates positions brought into the intergovernmental arena ex ante. IGAs are involved in both position taking and policy coordination. The strong efforts to coordinate horizontally in an efficient manner (by assigning responsibilities to different policy-specific IGAs and establishing the Conference of Cantonal Executives as a coordinating body) contribute to the strength of the cantonal level of government and help prevent authority migration to the centre. Since the Conferences of Directors are actively involved in policy coordination, the formal framework agreement between IGAs was considered as functionally necessary to increase efficiency and avoid responsibility conflicts. Finally looking at national–regional integration between IGAs, in contrast both to the United States and Canada, we find not only generalist IGAs of regional scope. In the core policy fields of cantonal competence we also find policy specific ones. The relations between regional and national IGAs – both generalist and policy-specific ones – tend to be balanced in the sense that conflicting action is mutually avoided with neither level strongly dominating the other.

In the U.S. case, the impact of the executive–legislative divide – a consequence of compulsory power-sharing – has been the most pervasive feature when assessing the linkages between generalist and policy-specific IGAs. At the heart of this divide lie different understandings of autonomy ascribed to by the different branches: the autonomy to decide and to implement. This divide feeds a lack of integration as well as competitive relations between IGAs. These dynamics in turn reduce the capacity of the states to defend collective interests towards the federal government. As a consequence, American IGR is much more centrally dominated than the Canadian and the Swiss system. This imbalance between federal and state level is mirrored by the dominant pattern of national–regional linkage between the IGAs themselves. In the United States, we find top–down dynamics between generalist IGAs on the national and regional level. National IGAs define which issues are national and therefore fall within their own responsibility to which regional IGAs respond passively. In contrast to Canada, there is considerable information exchange between IGAs. These processes, however, tend to be one-sided. The national arrangement plays the dominant part.

Most notably in the United States, it is not the two 'levels of government' that cooperate. The federal government mostly interacts with the individual states or individual state actors supporting a kind of 'fend for yourself federalism' from which the federal government profits the most. The competition between

IGAs creates the opportunity to play the states off against each other. In its interplay with the superior federal spending power (a challenge for lower level governments in each of the systems analysed in this study, as in virtually any federal system), the coordination failure rooted in compulsory power-sharing creates a vicious circle that in the end further nourishes federal dominance. In American federalism, intergovernmental dynamics on the horizontal and the vertical dimension reinforce each other in an unfortunate way, with the same source underlying: compulsory power-sharing. On the vertical level, the incapacity of a strong IGA or a strongly integrated group of IGAs to unify the states as political units necessarily prevents the formation of a strong collective front against federal intrusion. Moreover, executive–legislatives divides on the state level and on the level of state executives complicate horizontal policy-coordination between them and motivate a resort to softer instruments of executive and administrative coordination. Since these softer instruments are less effective than national regulation and dominated executive actors (who care less about the protection of legislative autonomy), vertical and horizontal disintegrations are mutually reinforcing to the disadvantage of the states as political units. To compensate for their politically weak status, IGAs are increasingly oriented towards the functional needs of their members as professionals instead of members' political demands as state representatives. This orientation nourishes the institutional and strategic convergence of IGAs and private interest groups.

We end up with the following results as summed up in Table 6.2. In both Canada and the United States, integration is weak, yet it is weak for different reasons. In Canada, patterns of interaction between IGAs boiling down to strategic manoeuvring and weak integrative linkages clearly reflect competitive pressure generated in power-concentrating governments and the instability of interest configurations between them. In the United States, the institutionalization of generalist IGAs is strong and cooperative endeavours are made by numerous bodies on various levels reflecting the cooperation-favouring impact of power-sharing structures within the states. However, regarding integration, the nature of power sharing plays the decisive role. Diverging institutional interests within each state undermine the political representation of the states as coherent government units. In Switzerland, this divide is bridged by party linkages, thus by voluntary power-sharing. Efforts to integrate IGAs have been fruitful although the system shows a broad variety of different IGAs which considerably increases the costs of integration.

Concluding with the overall dynamics of IGR in the three systems, we arrive at the following picture. In Canada, processes evolve bottom–up. Driven by strategic calculus, governments usually cooperate based on the smallest common denominator. This implies that most issues never make it to the national level and are dealt with within regional IGAs or are handled by lower level governments individually. In the United States, we find strong 'top–down dynamics' between IGAs. Nationwide IGAs define which issues are national. In order to prevent conflict, regional IGAs usually try to avoid

TABLE 6.2. *Intergovernmental integration in Canada, the United States, and Switzerland*

	Canada	United States	Switzerland
Federal–State Integration (overall)	Weak	Weak	Strong
Generalist	Weak	Weak	Strong
Policy-specific	Weak	Weak	Strong
National–Regional Integration (overall)	Weak	Medium	Medium
Generalist	Weak	Medium	Medium
Policy-specific	—	Weak	Medium
Horizontal Integration (overall)	Weak	Weak	Strong
Generalist/generalist	Weak	Medium	Strong
Generalist/policy-specific	Weak	Weak	Strong
Policy-specific/policy-specific	Weak	Weak	Strong
Institutional Main-Weight (resources)	National	National	National
Major level for horizontal coordination (without federal involvement)	Regional	Regional	Regional
Mode of Intergovernmental Interest Aggregation	Bottom–up	Top–down	Federal–regional balance

such issues altogether or drop issues once they attract the attention of national IGAs. In Switzerland, generalist and policy-specific IGAs exist on both levels and have considerable leeway to issue positions on topics of their own choice, despite active attempts to avoid conflict. Although the national level is more strongly institutionalized, in contrast to the other two systems, there is neither a clear bottom–up nor top–down logic. In terms of intergovernmental interest representation, the Swiss case comes closest to a national–regional balance.

7

Intergovernmental Institutions and the Nature of Intergovernmental Agreements

Whether intergovernmental structures are highly institutionalized or not, in most federal systems lower level governments – one way or the other – discuss federal plans of common concern or boundary-crossing policy problems inside or outside of IGAs. These discussions might result in an agreement, a common accord, or a communiqué.[1] The capacity to arrive at collective agreements has important implications for the potential of lower level governments to influence the federal government or, alternatively, to coordinate policy horizontally. Quite naturally, the quality of these agreements differs which brings us back to an assumption this book started out from: namely that the institutional development of IGAs affects the quality of agreements drafted within them. This chapter questions this assumption and examines the various 'so what' questions confronting the presented approach. Does institutionalization really matter for the quality of intergovernmental agreements? Does it affect the output of intergovernmental interaction, and if so, how? The existing case study literature clearly emphasizes the relevance of the institutional make-up of IGAs (e.g. Armingeon 2000*a*; Lazar 2000; Skogstad 2000; Richter 2005). The interviews conducted for this study also pointed to considerable differences in the degree to which governments comply with agreements across the three systems analysed. Finally, the analysis could show that the processes generated within and between IGAs, especially the impact of IGA staff on intergovernmental processes, vary with their institutional development. All these findings indicate that informal intergovernmental institutions shape the outputs of intergovernmental cooperation. Still, there is a dearth of comparative studies relying on the same set of indicators to examine agreements' quality across several systems. In an attempt to address this gap, this chapter assesses how far the level of institutionalization affects the capacity of intergovernmental agreements to constrain individual governments. Methodologically speaking, institutionalization changes its status from a dependent variable to an independent variable in order to examine whether the institutional structures of an IGA affect the

---

[1] In the case study literature on Canada the terms accord, communiqué and agreement are used interchangeably. Compacts and concordats refer to formal treaties in the American and Swiss system, respectively. I will use 'agreement' (formal or informal) as an overall category.

quality of agreements which governments voluntarily enter to address collective problems.

After systematizing the variety of instruments for cross-jurisdictional cooperation available in the three countries, I compare non-binding agreements produced within generalist and policy-specific IGAs in 2004 and 2005. The reason for the restriction to non-binding agreements is simple. Mirroring the overall patterns of institutionalization, in the two power-sharing democracies Switzerland and the United States, lower level governments can enter formally binding agreements. They constitute formal interstate legislation, are highly problem-specific and impose legal constraints on the participating governments. In Canada, such an instrument is unavailable. Thus, taken all types of agreements into account, agreements are likely to be less constraining in Canada. Thus, a cross-national comparison including formal and informal agreements would introduce a bias in favour of the two power-sharing democracies and, with it, in favour of the approach put forward in this study. Therefore, the analysis of this chapter focuses on the constraining capacity of non-binding agreements. It explores which functions agreements serve and in how far they formulate concrete positions or address concrete problems. Such an analysis cannot deliver a final evaluation of agreements' effectiveness in terms of policy outcomes, hence agreements' actual implementation. Nonetheless, an analysis of the written output of IGAs indicates the extent to which governments are willing to commit themselves to collectively generated solutions and whether the institutional context in which they do so contributes to the drafting of more constraining agreements. Simply put, if principles, which are supposed to guide government behaviour, formulated by an agreement are too vague to detect non-compliance of individual governments, the fact that the agreement has been signed is unlikely to have strong effects.

The following sections empirically specify the concept of intergovernmental agreement, compare the variety of agreements in the three countries and introduce the criteria for assessing agreements' capacity to commit and constrain individual governments. The final section presents the results and their implications for the question whether institutionalization really matters.

INTERGOVERNMENTAL AGREEMENTS: TOWARDS A COMPARATIVE ANALYSIS

An intergovernmental agreement is defined as a document which the necessary number of government representatives in an IGA have agreed to, as required by the given decision-making rule. To be included in the analysis, an agreement demands explicit intra-institutional confirmation.[2] Moreover, the final document should be publicly accessible. Although the publication of information material, analyses, and reports help facilitate intergovernmental interaction and presupposes the investment of resources, it does not impose any constraints on the behaviour of IGA members. The explicit confirmation of each government representative tightens the link between procedural agreement and substantial collective commitment. The criterion of public accessibility is important since it indicates that whatever the contents, participants are in principle ready to be publicly associated with a collective initiative.

The variety of agreements is vast within and across federal systems, both in terms of formality and content. They can find expression in resolutions commenting on federal legislation. Alternatively, intergovernmental actors can choose constitutionally based interstate compacts to coordinate policy across jurisdictions. Breach of the latter may result in litigation since they explicitly rule out contradicting lower level legislation. Formalization is low when agreements have purely political character and no legal force. The specification of how these agreements can nonetheless generate a sense of obligation is essential since non-binding agreements are by far the most frequent output of intergovernmental processes.

While covering a considerable range of instruments, the following analysis has some unavoidable and necessary caveats. Oral agreements cannot be included in the analysis. First of all, they are unlikely to be formally channelled through IGAs, thus are likely to be arranged between governments without institutional mediation. Since the goal is to compare IGAs' outputs, such agreements play therefore a limited role. This is not to say that they are irrelevant in practice and clearly it would be interesting to know the extent to which problems are solved outside of IGAs. The same holds for policy diffusion or the adoption of uniform law which tends to be based on unilateral action of individual governments (although model legislation might be drafted by IGAs like in the United States). Further, memoranda of understanding struck directly by ministries are not included because, as oral agreements, they do not allow for conclusions about the impact of IGAs' institutionalization on governments' coordination capacity. As a consequence, this chapter does not assess the relative relevance of oral, written, non-binding, and binding agreements. Nor does it give an indication of the overall coordination capacity or activity of the federal systems under analysis. Instead, it is interested in whether the level of institutionalization in a federal system adds to the capacity to solve problems collectively.

---

[2] This decision-making rule may or may not be specified in written statutes. The absence of a written rule usually means that decisions are made by consensus.

Clearly, the more IGAs are involved in the formulation and the negotiation of written agreements, the more these structures will help to address cooperation demands within the respective multilevel systems (given their activities do not offset each other). If IGAs were completely irrelevant, actors would not bother to invest in such infrastructures in the first place. Furthermore, the sense of obligation generated by written agreements should be more considerable than generated by non-transparent inter-administrative deals. Written and publicly announced agreements provide a better indication of how active and willing actors commit themselves to shared positions and cross-jurisdictional policy-making. We gain insights into the impact of different levels of institutionalization of IGAs on their 'production' of agreements of a particular type and of a particular quality. To give an overview, the following section shortly runs through the variety of agreements available to create collective commitment in Canada, Switzerland, and the United States.

Intergovernmental agreements in Canada are not legally binding. No legal framework governs them. Although there have been some debates whether executives can 'de facto' be bound by agreements, it is a widely shared conviction that a legislative assembly can always legislate and put an end to a contract, be it between the executive branch and a private citizen, a company, another government, or a foreign power (Poirier 2004: 436). This was reconfirmed in 1991 in a classical interpretation of the doctrine of parliamentary sovereignty by the Supreme Court of Canada in the Canada Assistance Plan Reference. Based on this ruling, this doctrine can only be restricted by two elements: the constitutional distribution of legislative powers and the charter of rights. Consequently, all agreements are political commitments whose implementation is highly dependent on the momentary interests of the governments involved. Due to frequent alternations, these interests change rapidly. Interestingly, Poirier found out that the majority of civil servants she interviewed were convinced that the agreements they were working with were binding, while a majority of senior officials claimed the opposite (2004: 442). Evidently, the penetration of bureaucratic processes by political dynamics is stronger on higher levels of the administration which easily explains this difference. Political dynamics are immediately felt when decisions transcend mere technicality and, as a consequence, are transferred to higher levels. As we will see later in detail, the nature of agreements equally reflects the predominance of flexible ad hoc coordination as dominant interaction mode.

Compared to the Canadian repertoire, the range of mechanisms available in Swiss and American IGR is – regarding their level of formality – much wider. They are applied in contexts in which collective interaction is regularized, thus co-decision is the dominant interaction mode. Starting with Switzerland, the output of intergovernmental conferences can be guidelines, benchmarks, recommendations, and concordats. Each of them can be used to coordinate policies across cantonal borders and they vary in the degree to which they commit and constrain individual governments. The concordat is the most formal instrument and is considered as binding 'inter-cantonal law' (Abderhalden 1999). The most extensive (but not complete) database covers concordats from the beginning of the nineteenth century up to 2002 and includes 733 of these inter-cantonal treaties. Usually, however, informal mechanisms such as recommendations and guidelines are preferred to address collective problems since they interfere less in cantonal autonomy. Alternatively, recommendations can be issued to comment on or amend federal plans or legislation. Below the level of the Conferences of Directors, which negotiate over both concordats and recommendations, we find a layer of committees able to issue working guidelines directly sent to the cantonal administrations. The development of codes of good practice is not exclusively initiated on the political level nor does it presuppose political ex post confirmation.

The role of interstate compacts as the most formal instrument in the United States has been described already. Still, it is important to emphasize again that while the drafting of compacts is supported by the National Center for Interstate Compacts which is run by the Council of State Governments and involves a variety of different state actors, a successful drafting process does not indicate the later ratification by individual state legislatures. (In Switzerland, in contrast, a concordat to which the executives agree usually passes the cantonal parliaments due to the stronger executive–legislative linkages in place.) Furthermore, there are formal administrative agreements between state executives which need not be confirmed by the state legislatures. However, as with memoranda of understanding in Canada, IGAs are not involved in the drafting of the former. Therefore, they are not included in the examination. The generalist state IGAs formulate policy positions on federal policies in a wide range of areas and these are updated at their annual meetings. Moreover, they issue testimonies on current federal legislation presented in Congress.

Table 7.1 indicates a wider range of agreement types in the two power-sharing democracies than in polycentric Canada. The respective repertoires systematically vary which is already an interesting finding. In Canada, power-concentrating dynamics do not only dominate intergovernmental processes, but are also paralleled on the constitutional level by the doctrine of parliamentary sovereignty which conflicts with the idea of formal intergovernmental agreements. Theoretically, Canadian actors could create formal instruments through constitutional reform. Swiss actors, for instance, did so and established new legally binding instruments for inter-cantonal cooperation. In Canada, however, constitutional change is unfeasible exactly because lower level governments were unwilling to risk a shift in the overall power-distribution in the system, reflecting the same orientation undermining the set-up of a strong intergovernmental infrastructure.

TABLE 7.1. *Agreements in Canada, Switzerland, and the United States*[b]

	Canada	United States	Switzerland
High formalization legally binding agreements	—	Interstate compacts	Concordats
Low formalization/ informal agreements	Conference communiqués and releases (Council of the Federation, First Ministers' Conferences, Ministerial Councils, and Regional Conferences)	Policy resolutions and testimonies (National Governors Association and National Council of State Legislatures)[a]	Recommendations and collective positions (Conference of Cantonal Executives and Conferences of Directors)

[a] The Council of State Governments is not included since it mainly supports the unilateral adoption of model laws or states' engagement in interstate compacts which are not considered in the analysis. Furthermore, testimonies are not included since they usually consist of parts taken out of policy positions. Hence, their inclusion would overrate the productivity of the respective IGA under analysis.
The table only covers institutionally channelled agreements.

[b] The following analysis will focus on the range of informal agreements only. The main IGAs covered are listed in brackets.

INFORMAL INTERGOVERNMENTAL AGREEMENTS: CLASSIFICATION AND OPERATIONALIZATION

Non-binding intergovernmental agreements address the challenge of generating individual government commitment in an environment without external enforcement mechanisms. This configuration in which neighbouring governments cooperate within a voluntarily established infrastructure corresponds to the configuration of international regimes which try to create binding agreements in an anarchic environment (Scharpf 1997: 142). Consequently, if the regime concept is applicable within federal states, one might expect that the tools for assessing international agreements should also be applicable to intergovernmental agreements. If one looks more closely at the two constellations, however, applicability proves to be limited.

International agreements are usually analysed as tools of policy coordination (Downs et al. 1996: 383; Scharpf 1997: 142). Agreements drafted in IGAs, by contrast, fulfil a variety of functions. They frequently engage in collective position-taking or the formulation of demands towards the federal government as the upper tier of government. These demands might form part of federal–state negotiations (corresponding to international negotiations between nation states) but often simply push for changes in federal legislation. A constitutionally induced and stable line of opposition as typical for federal systems does not exist in the international system since there is no upper tier. In order to assess the capacity of intergovernmental agreements to generate constraints on individual governments, we need to differentiate along the range of functions different agreements might fulfil. At the same time, a sound comparison of IGAs' overall impact on the nature of agreements presupposes criteria which capture the constraint implied by an agreement irrespective of its function which further reduces the applicability of tools developed for international agreements.[3] The latter tend to presuppose that agreements serve coordination purposes, while in the national sphere this agreement type forms only a minority.[4] While this literature can be used as a starting point, to address this problem, the next section will distinguish three basic agreement functions. Furthermore, it proposes a way of assessing precision and substantial depth as two criteria applicable to the different agreement types, which help to estimate the relative degree of government commitment across the range of functions intergovernmental agreements might serve.

How to constrain governments through non-binding agreements

An agreement can (*a*) formulate collective demands or positions; (*b*) aim at the coordination of policy measures to arrive at concerted action between different jurisdictions; and (*c*) try to establish a particular process or procedure of interstate or federal–state interaction. The distinction between a demand and a procedural initiative is sometimes fine. The request issued by an IGA that the federal government should cooperate more with lower level governments when it comes to the implementation of particular federal programs is not yet a procedural initiative that binds the group of IGA members in any sense. It might only refer to bilateral federal–state interaction between the federal government and individual lower level governments. The demand to involve the lower level governments as a group in the process of international treaty negotiations, by contrast, clearly implies a collective involvement and is therefore counted as a procedural initiative. In general, procedural initiatives can range from the intention to meet again (which is only useful in an environment in which meetings are not yet regularized) to agreement provision laying out monitoring requirements or specific mechanisms for resolving conflicts.[5] It is further necessary to distinguish clearly between

---

[3] An alternative would be to use different criteria to assess the content of each agreement type and then weight the respective types differently to construct an overall index for each IGA. However, such a procedure would be very complex and any result would be heavily influenced by a range of choices. Although it leads to a rougher picture, a less demanding strategy is therefore preferable.

[4] Downs et al. operationalize the depth of cooperation of an international treaty as 'the extent to which it requires states to depart from what they would have done in its absence' (1996: 383). If agreements simply state collective positions, the definition is not applicable.

[5] Kennett points to the necessity of setting up interprovincial or federal–provincial mechanisms in Canada to compensate for positive and negative externalities and enforcement mechanisms against non-compliance (1998: 52–7). However, sanction and enforcement mechanisms are usually not part of informal agreements since compliance towards agreement provisions remains a matter of choice.

procedural and coordination initiatives. If, for instance, the premiers mandate their ministers to explore ways of collaboration in the area of internal trade policy, it is considered procedural. If they mandate their ministers to collaborate to find collective solutions to core problems in the area of internal trade, it is considered as coordination initiative. Coordination initiatives do not focus on processes but on policy problems or problem areas in which collective action is considered desirable.[6] Comparing the constraints each agreement type implies, proposals of policy coordination tend to be most constraining for government behaviour, followed by procedural initiatives, again followed by collective demands. The following section presents the criteria for assessing the commitment capacity of these agreements further.

Irrespective of the given function, a collective statement can be formulated in a general and abstract or in a precise and concrete manner.[7] Following Kennett, '...one cannot assume that agreement to vaguely worded commitments will trigger a virtuous circle of self-reinforcing and increasingly specific cooperative measures'. It can also reinforce a negative circle of unilateralism (Kennett 1998: 43). If the participating governments insist on their individual leeway as a result of intragovernmental incentives, this inclination should reduce the precision of agreements since precision narrows the scope for reasonable interpretation by unambiguously defining the conduct of participants (Abbott et al. 2000: 412).[8] This ambiguity delimits what can be achieved in written form even if actors in principle consider a common solution as useful. We therefore need to assess whether collectively shared positions or goals are stated in the form of vague principles or, alternatively, as concrete goals which can guide the future actions of each individual participant. If the agreement is a shared position, for example, the question is whether the individual government sticks with this position later on. For this to become evident, the position must be sufficiently concrete. When

[6] Cases in which ministers give mandates to cross-jurisdictional working groups of officials to explore ways of collaboration are only counted as a coordination initiative if this group is supposed to report the results back to the ministerial forum. Otherwise it does not express a commitment to deal with the issues collaboratively.

[7] Note that one of the three aspects which constitute the 'constraining capacity' of agreements, namely their precision, has already played the role of an indicator for institutionalization as operationalized in Chapter 1. This does not lead to circularity since the indicator 'precision' refers to binding and non-binding agreements alike. This means that as soon as an IGA successfully engages in the drafting of formal agreements, precision can be classified as high. Since the following examination looks only at non-binding agreements circularity is avoided.

[8] The criterion precision has been taken out of the debate on the legalization of international relations. Besides precision, two further dimensions have been specified in this literature: obligation (the legal character ranging from non-legal norms to legally binding rules [*jus cogens*]) and delegation (the degree of delegation of legal authority to implementing institutions) (Abbott et al. 2000: 403–5). I do not refer to the latter two dimensions in my assessment of intergovernmental agreements since they can only be applied to coordination initiatives and make only limited sense regarding position taking and procedural initiatives. Furthermore, delegation of non-binding intergovernmental agreements is mostly low and therefore cannot usefully map the differences between these agreements.

the agreement is a coordination initiative, governments may agree on the general attempt to achieve less unemployment as a goal. Alternatively, they may attempt to achieve the reduction of carbon dioxide emission below a certain level. Although the latter goal does not point to any necessary measures on the part of the individual members to achieve such a reduction, the range of government responses is restricted insofar governments take the goal seriously. This commitment has therefore stronger implications for the actual behaviour of the governments than proclaiming the reduction of unemployment. The precision of an agreement has also implications for the capacity of mutual monitoring. Simply speaking, if non-compliance is hard to detect because the collective goal is not sufficiently specified ex ante, there is no way for governments to mutually control whether others stick to agreements and to potentially sanction non-compliance by retaliatory actions.

The second criterion refers to the substantial depth of a collective statement which is assessed in the following manner. Regarding collective positions (e.g. demands towards the federal government to withdraw from a legislative project or to change it), the question is whether an amendment proposal is made. Regarding coordination initiatives the question is whether the participants agree not only on a shared goal but also on the best instrument to obtain it.[9] Finally, regarding procedural initiatives, the question is whether simply more collaboration is proposed or whether it is explicitly directed towards a particular purpose. To make this distinction clearer, lower level governments can, for instance, agree to oppose some piece of federal legislation. The precision of such a demand is necessarily high since it refers to a current legislative proposal. To simply oppose the latter requires neither substantial concertation nor significant expertise. It is therefore crucial to distinguish between an agreement's precision and its substantial depth. Mere collective opposition is not equivalent to a collectively supported alternative to achieve a preferred legislative output or a better problem-solution. It boils down to insisting on the status quo.

Precision and substantial depth are assessed in a dichotomous way. The categories are consciously kept simple which has the following advantages. First, agreements are easier to classify. A more fine-grained conceptualization would leave greater leeway for interpretation and be less reliable. Second, the categories deliver an overall picture of the nature of the agreements that governments enter

---

[9] A good example of this distinction is the Canadian provinces' and territories' demand towards the federal government to solve the problem of fiscal equalization. While there is agreement among the lower level governments on the general goal and the fact that this issue needs to be put on the agenda, experts expect the coalition to fall apart as soon as the federal government agrees to discuss concrete solutions. This is because any concrete measure to reform the equalization scheme will affect the individual provinces and territories very differently. Therefore, so far, collective positions on the general goal to address fiscal imbalance have been issued but without any means of how to do so being specified.

into and these agreements' constraining capacity which can be systematically compared across federal systems. In specifying agreements' function and assessing each subgroup's precision and substantial depth, allows pinning down whether the agreement can be expected to serve its respective function adequately or not. The following section elaborates on how institutionalization is expected to affect the nature of agreements.

Institutionalization and the creation of constraining agreements

As pointed out previously, in contrast to Canada, in Switzerland and the United States interstate cooperation can be backed up by formal horizontal contracts. Since concordats and compacts establish interstate law, their precision and their substantial depth will naturally be high. Moreover, non-compliance can be legally sanctioned as long as the respective government does not exit the agreement according to the given termination rule. The fact that these agreements are actually drafted within or with the help of highly institutionalized IGAs already tells something about the usefulness of the latter. It is at least doubtful that the weak Canadian infrastructure could effectively do so even if a formal instrument as in the two power-sharing democracies was available. Leaving formal agreements aside, the comparison of non-binding agreements represents a stricter and more interesting examination of whether institutionalization has an impact on agreements since non-binding agreements are struck much more frequently. If institutionalization is one major factor to influence the capacity to draft constraining agreements, we can expect the following:

- If increasing institutionalization raises the capacity to produce constraining agreements, the constraining character of non-binding agreements should be weaker when produced in weakly institutionalized IGAs than in highly institutionalized ones.

Highly institutionalized IGAs are expected to have the resources to develop more elaborate drafts and, moreover, to generate an environment, in which government representatives are willing to raise conflicting issues and overcome conflicts of interest. It has already been demonstrated above that the modes of agenda-setting and IGAs' functions systematically differ across the three systems reflecting the given level of institutionalization. Nevertheless, the above hypothesis can be challenged. Processes in a highly institutionalized environment facilitating 'co-decision' might not per se be more conducive to the development of constraining agreements than 'ad hoc coordination' framed by a weak infrastructure. It is equally possible that actors' increased investment in agreement negotiations and the collective capacity to find a solution is to a much stronger extent a matter of will than of context. As some Canadian officials argued, Canadian politicians simply do not think they need a strong intergovernmental infrastructure to get things done. They think they can achieve their goals satisfyingly without investing in IGAs which restrict their individual flexibility. If this holds, a weaker institutionalization of IGAs does not indicate a lower problem-solving capacity. The constraining character of an agreement would be unrelated to the institutional development of the arrangement in which it has been produced.

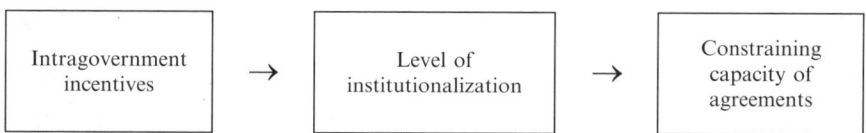

FIGURE 7.1. Institutionalization as major impact on agreements' constraining capacity

The two questions guiding the following analysis are whether the type, precision, and the substantial depth of intergovernmental agreements vary (*a*) with the level of institutionalization of an IGA; (*b*) with the political system in which the IGA is embedded; and (*c*) with the type of IGA (generalist or policy-specific). As demonstrated previously, the level of institutionalization is rather homogenous within each system under analysis. Yet since we still find some intra-country variance, we can disentangle the impact of intragovernmental incentives and of institutionalization as two separate factors. Figure 7.1 assumes an impact of intragovernmental dynamics on institutionalization and, in a second step, of institutionalization on the capacity of agreements to constrain individual participants.

Alternatively, intragovernmental incentives could affect both the level of institutionalization and the nature of agreements simultaneously as depicted by Figure 7.2. As far as the level of institutionalization and intragovernmental incentives coincide, it is not possible to disentangle whether it is really the impact of institutionalization which affects the nature of agreements or whether it is the intragovernmental incentives which affect negotiations and their output simultaneously. This problem can be addressed by comparing not only across systemic contexts but also different institutionalization levels within the same systemic context. Since intragovernmental incentives drive actors' choices in favour or against IGAs' institutionalization, it is reasonable to expect that they also affect the output of intergovernmental negotiations directly. More concretely, if institutionalization

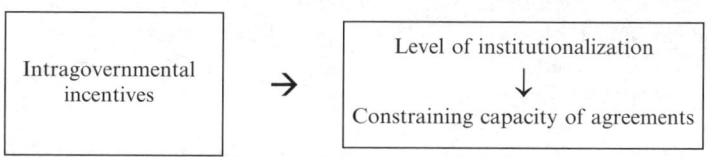

FIGURE 7.2. Intragovernmental incentives and institutionalization as simultaneous impacts on agreements' constraining capacity

has an independent effect on the capacity to generate agreements with particular features, we should see systematic differences in the output of Canadian IGAs which are weakly institutionalized compared to Canadian IGAs which are institutionalized on a medium level. The same can be argued regarding Swiss IGAs. Therefore, Swiss policy-specific IGAs of high and of medium institutionalization and Canadian IGAs of medium and of low institutionalization are included into the analysis, instead of deliberately choosing a homogeneous group of arrangements for each country.

Such an intra-country comparison should further control for the type of IGA. Generalist and policy-specific IGAs should be treated separately since in many federal systems we find a distribution of labour between them regarding their respective functions. Output differences between generalist and policy-specific IGAs are interesting since they indicate the extent to which the distribution of labour between arrangements shapes the output, in particular agreements' predominant function. It is reasonable to expect that this distribution of labour is more visible the higher the level of institutionalization of IGAs in a system. More highly developed IGAs tend to defend a rather clearly defined institutional self-interest in terms of own spheres of responsibility. In the following sections, the material covered and period of examination are specified and the results are presented. On this basis, I start with an analysis of the output patterns of generalist IGAs in the three countries. The more complex picture of policy-specific arrangements will follow.

MATERIAL AND PERIOD OF EXAMINATION

To examine the impact of institutionalization on intergovernmental agreements, I look at the informal agreements struck in the framework of the major national generalist bodies and of a range of policy-specific bodies during the two-year period 2004–5. To take a very recent time period increases the actuality of the comparison which is a merit in itself. Moreover, it allows for the inclusion of the Council of the Federation which was founded only in 2003 and shows a higher level of institutionalization than its predecessor, the Annual Premiers Conference. At the same time, since its predecessor, the Annual Premiers Conference, was composed of the same members, basic practices to negotiate agreements have been established for decades. Hence, the output of the Council of the Federation can be reasonably compared with the output of older IGAs. Focusing on 2004 and 2005, we also avoid looking at the Conference of Cantonal Executives, set up from scratch in 1993, in its formative years.[10]

---

[10] The period has the additional virtue that, by then, it was rather difficult for the positive impact of institutionalization on the nature of agreements to show. First, regarding Swiss IGR, it takes into consideration that in 1999 the Swiss constitution underwent reforms (Fleiner 2006). Among other

Although a two-year period delivers only a snapshot of the different ways IGAs work, it is sufficient to provide an insight into the basic cross-national patterns. This is particularly the case in the power-sharing democracies in which procedures display a considerable degree of routine and issues are clearly assigned to different arrangements. In Canada this is less the case. The fluctuations in output are likely to be more considerable. Since there is often only one ministerial meeting a year in weak IGAs, a higher number of IGAs are included to broaden the scope of the analysis.[11] According to IGA staff, the types of agreements struck during these two years are representative for the working of the various IGAs in the long run. The following types of non-binding agreements are considered:

- *Switzerland*: Recommendations/releases of the policy-specific Conferences of Cantonal Directors (education; fiscal policy; health; justice, police, and crime control; and planning and environment) and the generalist Conference of Cantonal Executives
- *Canada*: Conference communiqués of policy-specific ministerial councils (education; finance; environment; health; internal trade, social policy; and justice),[12] the generalist Council of the Federation, Western Premiers' Conference, and First Ministers' Conference
- *United States*: Policy positions of the National Governors' Association (executive committee, standing committees on education; health; environment; and

---

changes, the constitution now recognizes inter-cantonal cooperation which increases its legitimacy. This favours formal cooperation which should decrease the need for very precise informal agreements after 1999. A similar point can be made about the NFA reform (*Neuer Finanzausgleich*) which was passed in 2004 and, indeed, triggered a huge debate about the need to increase formal inter-cantonal cooperation. Second, regarding Canadian IGR, during these two years Canada was ruled by a Liberal minority government on the federal level. Due to this constellation, the federal government was particularly vulnerable to provincial pressure which provided incentives for the provinces to exploit this situation. This might have functioned as a trigger to push more actively for concrete collective demands in the context of the Council of the Federation, while the approach underlying this study expects rather vague collective agreements on the side of the provinces and territories due to weakly institutionalized structures.

[11] Internal Trade is also considered since it represents a policy area in which a major agreement has been struck (the Agreement on Internal Trade) setting up a secretariat for bureaucratic support despite the low institutionalization of the area of economic and trade policy as a whole. In order to prevent a central impact of the market clause in the Canadian constitution, the Constitutional Court distinguished interprovincial and international trade which is a responsibility of the federal government from intraprovincial trade which is a responsibility of the provinces (Simeon and Papillon 2006: 106).

[12] Note that in Canada the fluctuation of meetings varies quite considerably over time, and with it the number of agreements. Looking at the distribution of meetings between the premiers and the premiers with the federal government from 1974 to 2000, the number in the year 2000 is average (Simmons 2004: 288). However, fluctuations do not pose a problem since the mere quantity is not very telling. It might well be the case that some IGAs publish numerous vague agreements, while others publish a few of high precision, which is considered in the way agreement as a concept is operationalized.

justice and crime control) and the National Conference of State Legislatures (standing committee on budget matters and finance; education; health; environment; and justice)[13]

Policy-specific IGAs have been chosen to maximize the variance of relevant policy-specific features. As Table 7.2 shows, the mode of competence distribution and the conflict potential in the selected policy fields vary within and across countries. If we find systematic patterns, these factors are unlikely to provide a convincing alternative account.

Capturing the range of IGAs whose output is covered in the later analysis, Table 7.2 differentiates between generalist and policy-specific IGAs in each system. This is straightforward in both Canada and Switzerland. The U.S. picture is again more complex. While compact commissions handle interstate matters in a variety of policy fields, thus qualify as policy-specific IGAs, they do not support explicit yet informal agreement between its members – neither to coordinate policy informally nor to formulate positions on federal legislation (they fell either in the category supranationalism or unilateral adaptation). In American IGR, collective policy-specific resolutions are issued by policy committees embedded in the National Governors' Association and the National Conference of State Legislatures. This again highlights the patterns of institution building strongly structured along policies and issues, which shape the major generalist IGAs internally. Given a focus on informal agreements, these resolutions represent policy-specific agreements (although being issued by a policy-specific committee embedded within a generalist IGA) and are therefore included in the analysis. Accordingly, the resolutions of the executive committee of the National Governors' Association represent resolutions with cross-jurisdictional profile. They are classified therefore as generalist. In contrast to the other standing committees, the executive committee is not restricted to particular policy fields. It has general authority over all policy issues and primary jurisdiction over issues involving federalism, homeland security, the federal budget, and federal tax policy.[14]

Finally, Table 7.2 indicates that agreements drafted in regional IGAs are not considered for each of the three cases. One might consider this as problematic since, as indicated by Chapter 6, given different dynamics in intergovernmental interest representation, the number of issues that reach national IGAs is likely to differ across the three regimes. The bottom–up dynamics observed in Canada make it more difficult for issues to travel upwards than in the two power-sharing democracies, which are more nationally oriented. Due to the observed bottom–up logic, the regional level might be a particularly important tier for intergovernmental cooperation in Canada. Analyses looking at national IGAs might underestimate

---

[13] Besides a general statement which outlines the basic principles of policy of the National Conference of State Legislatures, all other resolutions are assigned to a particular policy area. As a consequence, this conference is only included in the analysis of policy-specific agreements.

[14] http://www.nga.org/portal/site/nga/menuitem.bc322e700246bc1c28dcbeeb501010a0/?vgnextoid=70ad6eb58fda0010VgnVCM1000001a01010aRCRD

TABLE 7.2. *Intergovernmental arrangements and their level of institutionalization*

	Canada[a]	Switzerland	United States
Low institutionalization	*Policy-specific ministerial councils:* • finance • justice and crime control • social policy • health *Generalist IGAs:* • First Ministers' Conference • Western Premiers' Conference	—	—
Medium institutionalization	*Policy-specific ministerial councils:* • environment • education • internal trade *Generalist IGA:* • Council of the Federation	*Policy-specific conference of cantonal directors:* • environment	—
High institutionalization	—	*Policy-specific conferences of cantonal directors:* • education • health • justice, police, and crime control • finance *Generalist IGA:* • Conference of Cantonal Executives	*Policy-specific committees of National Governors' Association and National Conference of State Legislatures:* • education • health • justice and crime control[a] • budget and fiscal policy[b] • environment *Generalist committee:* • National Governors' Association executive committee[c]

[a] Note that the range of IGAs considered is deliberately in broader Canada given the higher instability of processes.
[b] In contrast to the National Conference of State Legislatures, the National Governors' Association has no committee in the area justice and crime control.
[c] In contrast to the National Conference of State Legislatures, the National Governors' Association has a standing committee in this area which, however, issues no resolutions.
[d] The National Conference of State Legislatures has no generalist executive committee in charge of cross-sectoral issues.

the productivity of IGAs if most cooperation occurs on a regional level. While national agreements might be vague and constrain governments little, regional agreements or positions could be very elaborate and address concrete policy problems. In order to check for this, I also consider agreements drafted by the Western Premiers' Conference. Since the Conference of Atlantic Premiers is exceptionally highly developed and not representative for the overall level of institutionalization in Canada, its analysis would not help to identify a potential bias in the selection of Canadian IGAs. The Western Premiers, by contrast, operate in a weakly institutionalized setting as the First Ministers do. It can therefore provide a valid check for whether the types and range of issues handled at the respective level plays a role independent of the given level of institutionalization which is kept constant. In the two power-sharing democracies, such a check is not considered necessary given that the constraining character of agreements in nationwide IGAs is expected to be high anyway. It is more difficult to bridge differences between all lower level governments in a federal system than between a subset. Thus, if we find a connection between institutionalization and the quality of agreements on the national level, this can be expected to hold in less complex configurations as well.[15]

THE ANALYSIS OF GENERALIST AGREEMENTS

Comparing the output of generalist IGAs, overall, institutionalization seems to support the drafting of constraining agreements. Yet as one might expect, the picture is more complex once one looks at the components agreement type, precision, and substantial depth separately. In essence, highly institutionalized IGAs do not produce a better output on all three dimensions. They do so only regarding precision and substantial depth, while the agreement type depends on the integration of IGAs as well. To analyse the findings in greater detail, I start out with an overview over the degree of precision and substantial depth and continue with the distribution of agreement types comparing weakly with highly institutionalized IGAs. The section concludes with a closer look at the five generalist IGAs (the Council of the Federation, the First Ministers, the Western Premiers, the Conference of Cantonal Executives, as well as the executive committee of the National Governors' Association) and their interplay with other IGAs in their respective system which allows for a better understanding of the distribution of agreement types.

---

[15] This reasoning gains plausibility when looking at the inclusiveness of concordats (formal intercantonal treaties). Only very few of them include all cantons indicating that they are easier to set up than more inclusive agreements. A similar pattern shows regarding interstate compacts in the United States.

TABLE 7.3. *Percentages of precise and substantial agreements issued by generalist intergovernmental arrangements in 2004–5*

	Demands/ Positions	Policy Coordination	Procedural Initiatives	All Agreements
First Ministers' Conference (Canada)	0% N = 3 (0 precise and substantial)	33.3% N = 3 (1 precise and substantial)	33.3% N = 3 (1 precise and substantial)	22.2% N = 9 (2 precise and substantial)
National Governors' Association (United States)	56.4% N = 39 (22 precise and substantial)	100% N = 1 (1 precise and substantial)	40% N = 5 (2 precise and substantial)	55.5% N = 45 (25 precise and substantial)
Conference of Cantonal Executives (Switzerland)	30.7% N = 13 (4 precise and substantial)	100% N = 2 (2 precise and substantial)	50% N = 4 (2 precise and substantial)	42.1% N = 19 (8 precise and substantial)

Note: Shaded area: low institutionalization; white area: high institutionalization.

Starting out with precision, intergovernmental actors are able to agree on specific goals in weakly institutionalized environments (e.g. the First Ministers agreed upon reducing waiting time in health care). However, they do so less often than in highly institutionalized settings. Furthermore, they less often come up with substantial agreements, thus define means or measures to realize these goals less often. The same holds for the specification of processes (often procedural initiatives do not transcend the set-up of one-shot meetings), the presentation of collectively formulated alternatives to federal bills, and the justification of demands for more federal funding. The reason for this is obvious. Although the precision of collectively articulated goals already increases the level of commitment governments are willing to enter, growing substantial depth leads to more concrete implications for the individual government's future actions. Due to the given intragovernmental incentives, Canadian actors try to avoid this and the nature of agreements reflects their strong orientation towards autonomy protection and flexibility. Table 7.3 gives an overview over the percentages of precise and substantial agreements issued by the First Ministers, the National Governors' Association, and the Conference of Cantonal Executives differentiated along agreement types.

The First Ministers produced by far fewer agreements than the more institutionalized arrangements and produced a lower percentage of both precise and substantial agreements. Considering all agreements, only 22.2 per cent are precise and substantial. In each of the categories coordination agreements and procedural initiatives, one agreement was precise (33.3 per cent). Considering the highly institutionalized IGAs in the two power-sharing systems, only one category shows a lower rate than 33.3 per cent – only 30.7 per cent of the collective demands issued by the Conference of Cantonal Executives are precise and substantial (while numerically the Conference still issued more of them in this category (four) than the First Ministers did over all agreement types (two)). Consequently, comparing the Conference of Cantonal Executives and the National Governors' Association, the latter tops the former regarding the number of precise and substantial agreements. There are two reasons for this. First, the National Governors' Association has considerably more staff and resources than the Conference of Cantonal Executives and second, it constantly updates former policy positions at annual meetings instead of drafting completely new positions.[16]

The type of agreements predominantly struck in IGAs (defined by these agreements' function) is crucial if we want to fully capture the possible implications of precision and substantial depth.[17] While the First Ministers struck the same number of agreements, namely three, in each category, the generalist IGAs in the two power-sharing systems concentrated on the articulation of demands and positions towards the federal government. In both cases, demands and positions constitute a clear majority of agreements. In Switzerland, the task of policy coordination is assigned to the various, much older, policy-specific IGAs. The pattern points to a distribution of labour in the system rather than limited capacities of generalist IGAs. This interpretation is supported by the fact that the two coordination initiatives by the Conference of Cantonal Executives are specific in goals and means. One covers recommendations in a range of policy fields about how to integrate foreigners through legislative measures, implementation, and information exchange.[18] Finally, in some cases, collective demands are followed by formally elaborate procedural initiatives. This link between different agreement types reflects the role of this generalist conference as linchpin in the intergovernmental system and its efforts to stabilize IGR and its own role in particular through more formalized inter-institutional linkages.

Moving on to the United States, the one coordination initiative issued by the National Governors' Association expresses its commitment to the Streamlined Sales and Tax Agreement, a formal interstate compact supported primarily by the National Council of State Legislatures and the Center for Interstate Compacts.[19] The governors did not issue a single informal coordination initiative attempting to commit state governments politically without resort to formal–legal means. This reconfirms the pattern observed in Chapter 5. When it comes to policy

---

[16] Position taking on currently debated federal legislation takes the form of testimonies in Congressional committee hearings. However, this instrument does not add any variation in terms of precision and substantial depth. Usually, testimonies are only verbal presentations (either by staff or a governor) of policy positions drafted in policy-specific standing committees.

[17] Note that when comparing agreement types and their frequencies, the category of announcements is not included if not indicated otherwise.

[18] See 'Rechtliche Integrationshemmnisse' (www.kdk.ch).

[19] Through the streamlined Sales and Tax Agreement, states forged a common sales tax system for the Internet age. States developed common sales and use tax systems for remote vendors, negotiating uniform definitions of taxable items, common tax rates, and facilitated administration (Conlan 2006: 673).

coordination, American IGAs promote either unilateral adaptation (e.g. through proposing model laws) or the creation of interstate law. While the demands and positions issued by the National Governors' Association are precise and substantial, IGAs are not engaged in the creation of voluntary commitment which will be further supported by the analysis of agreements drafted in policy-specific committees.

As Table 7.3 indicates, the First Ministers have issued the same number of agreements in each category. While one has to be careful with the interpretation given the low overall number of nine agreements, it is still noteworthy that one-third of the agreements are coordination initiatives. The two other generalist IGAs, the Council of the Federation and the regional Western Premiers' Conference also show a balanced distribution of agreement types. Despite the Council's reputation for supporting the premiers in pressing more funding out of the federal government, in 2004 and 2005 it issued 32.1 per cent of coordination initiatives (nine of 28). Most of them, however, are not substantial reconfirming the pattern revealed by Table 7.3. Among the three IGAs in Canada, the Council has been most productive. Compared to the First Ministers' Conference, this finding was expectable because the federal government is no member of the Council, so one major line of conflict is absent in its negotiations. Compared to the Western Premiers, it is more surprising since the latter have to bridge the interests of six governments only, not of 13. The difference between the nationwide Council and the Western Premiers (28 compared to 19 agreements) can be traced back to the former's medium institutionalization. More importantly, the comparison of the Western Premiers with both nationwide IGAs indicates that intergovernmental activities are unlikely to be underestimated due to a focus on the national level.

The Canadian case implies that under favourable conditions in weakly institutionalized contexts too, governments can agree upon precise and substantial coordination measures. If an issue is salient, sufficient interest convergence is given and coordination is considered to be collectively and individually profitable, governments can effectively generate collective responses to boundary-crossing problems. In these cases, resources are drawn from the government departments in charge of the policy area by assigning a mandate to the ministers to work out a plan. If the momentum behind such an initiative can be maintained until a plan is developed and transferred back to the First Ministers, precise and substantial, publicly endorsed agreements are possible. As soon as government parties change, however, governments easily withdraw from major agreements since 'they' did not agree to them in the first place. And even if there is no alternation, governments which supported an agreement in the first place might withdraw later on for strategic reasons (e.g. due to an upcoming election). As the contrast to the highly developed IGAs shows, while the institutional development of an IGA does not coincide with a particular function or repertoire of functions, it increases an arrangement's capacity to fulfil whatever task is assigned to it by supporting the generation of more precise and more substantial results. Equally, in terms of quantity, the number of issues dealt with by Canadian IGAs in the two years is low on both the regional and the national level (note that these figures are not unusual or particular for the period analysed according to the various interviewees). Canadian intergovernmental actors themselves consider IGAs' capacity to bridge conflict as low. In order to issue a precise and substantial coordination initiative in the Canadian context, the specific circumstances need to be very favourable.

To fully understand the cross-national pattern, we also need to consider the interaction between generalist and policy-specific IGAs. In Canada, generalist IGAs are more actively involved in policy coordination because there are no strong policy-specific councils dealing with this task on a routine-basis. There is no clear distribution of labour between generalist and policy-specific IGAs as we find it in Switzerland. Policy-specific IGAs tend to have no effective institutional boundaries defined by own staff, resources, and explicitly assigned areas of responsibility – a core feature of institutionalization. Tasks and issues constantly travel from one IGA to the other. The generalist IGAs, the First Ministers and the Council of the Federation, include the most powerful actors in the system, the heads of government. They decide which problems remain in the policy-specific councils and which are taken out of these and dealt with on the highest political level. Thus, the hierarchy within cabinets finds reflection in the nature of intergovernmental dynamics. Weakly institutionalized IGAs are unable to provide an effective counterweight to the latter. In the power-sharing democracies, highly institutionalized IGAs defend their institutional self-interest and with it its members' responsibility for a particular set of issues, a dynamic assuring more continuity in terms of who is in charge of what. This is not the case in Canada, where structures and processes are much more fluid. Canadian IGAs are neither functionally differentiated internally nor do they specialize and try to monopolize a certain function vis-à-vis other bodies. That generalist IGAs, especially the First Ministers, are more involved in coordination initiatives than their Swiss and American pendants, does not mean that they are equally productive in a less institutionalized setting. It merely shows that the other IGAs are weak. Whenever ministers are confronted with politicized issues, they depend on a mandate granted by their heads of government to legitimately deal with such an issue collectively. This is complemented by the lack of initiative on the side of IGA staff and their avoidance of critical issues.

In sum, the analysis of generalist IGAs indicates that a higher institutionalization supports the drafting of precise and substantial intergovernmental agreements as well as the production of more numerous agreements.[20] The patterns also

---

[20] Note that issues having been subject to collective debate and decision making have been counted as agreements, not whole documents. A lower number of meetings in Canada did not bias the result. Since releases often treat a bundle of different subject-areas, this strategy avoids underestimating the output of IGAs which release few but detailed documents. Furthermore, it is less demanding to arrive at ten provisions which fall within an individual policy area, than to arrive at ten provisions pertaining to different policy areas. Issues are therefore only counted separately if they belong to

highlight the importance to look at the interplay of the different IGAs in a system to understand the distribution of agreement types.

THE ANALYSIS OF POLICY-SPECIFIC AGREEMENTS

Regarding the precision and the substantial depth of agreements, the two power-sharing polities again confirm the patterns already identified in the section on generalist IGAs yet in a more pronounced manner. Table 7.4 shows the agreements issued in education in 2004–5. The results are representative for other policy areas where similar patterns emerged. Table 7.4 shows that the Canadian education council produced fewer agreements than its American and Swiss pendant. At the same time, however, the difference in agreement number is less pronounced since the Council of the Ministers of Education in Canada is one of the few Canadian IGAs institutionalized on a medium level which bridges the gap between the three IGAs somewhat. Overall, as already indicated by Table 7.3, institutionalization supports the precision and the substantial depth of agreements. Also, precise and substantial agreements are produced in higher numbers in the two more institutionalized IGAs.

Starting out with an overview over the distribution of agreement types in the three systems displayed in Table 7.4, in Canada we do not find a particularly strong focus on policy coordination reconfirming the patterns in generalist IGAs as displayed in Table 7.3. Nonetheless, the distribution of agreement types is less balanced than in the group of generalist IGAs. Policy-specific IGAs show a stronger tendency towards coordination initiatives which points to the general tendency in federal systems to develop a distribution of labour between policy-specific and generalist IGAs. In the overall weakly institutionalized Canadian context, however, it shows less clearly since policy-specific IGAs cannot monopolize a particular set of issue, a problem we return to later.

In the two power-sharing democracies, policy-specific IGAs show very distinct patterns which can be traced back to the different patterns of integration. The policy committees of the National Governors' Association and the National Council of State Legislatures engage extensively in the formulation of demands. Some of them do not issue coordination proposals at all which again points to a barrier that inter-branch divides generate. IGAs do support formal coordination as the Centre for Interstate Compacts which invests

---

different policy-areas or sub-areas, and hence touch upon different interest constellations. A set of provisions all relating to one narrow policy issue (such as in the case of a series of provisions on the emission of different pollutants produced by a particular industry) are counted as one precise proposal. An exception is made if individual issues fall in different functional categories (i.e. one is a procedural, one a coordination initiative).

TABLE 7.4. *Percentages of precise and substantial agreements in education in 2004–5*

	Demands/ Positions	Policy Coordination	Procedural Initiatives	All Agreements
Council of the Ministers of Education (Canada)	40% $N = 5$ (2 precise and substantial)	50% $N = 2$ (1 precise and substantial)	20% $N = 5$ (1 precise and substantial)	33.3% $N = 12$ (4 precise and substantial)
Committee on Education of National Governors' Association (United States)	53.3% $N = 15$ (8 precise and substantial)	50% $N = 2$ (1 precise and substantial)	50% $N = 2$ (1 precise and substantial)	52.6% $N = 19$ (10 precise and substantial)
Conference of Directors for Education (Switzerland)	100% $N = 4$ (4 precise and substantial)	100% $N = 20$ (20 precise and substantial)	100% $N = 3$ (3 precise and substantial)	100% $N = 27$ (27 precise and substantial)

Note: Shaded area: medium institutionalization; white area: high institutionalization.

considerable energy to promote interstate compacts. However, as detailed in Chapters 5 and 6, reflecting the fragmentation within the states, IGAs cannot function as vehicles to generate political agreement to coordinate policy informally between the states and this limitation reflects in the dominant agreement type produced by American IGAs.

In the Swiss case this problem does not exist. The Swiss Conferences of Cantonal Directors predominantly issue coordination agreements. The finding that procedural agreements are rather rare reflects the already strong institutionalization and integration in Switzerland. The need to set up new channels to improve the flow of exchanges between governments or IGAs is limited. When procedural agreements are initiated, they are usually issued by the Conference of Cantonal Executives which tries to strengthen its linchpin position in the intergovernmental arena. The differences between the American and the Swiss situation re-emphasizes that the level of institutionalization affects IGAs' capacity to fulfil whatever functions assigned to them. That the informal coordination of policy and the generation of non-binding agreements belong to these functions presupposes individual IGAs' capacity to represent cohesive governments in the first place, a condition American IGAs do not meet.

Looking now at the cross-sectoral variance in each system and starting out with the Swiss Conferences of Directors, we find that the four highly institutionalized IGAs set up in health, finance, education and crime control, justice and police hardly issued any imprecise or non-substantial agreements (we come back to the medium-institutionalized policy fields below). In 2004 and 2005, the Conference of Education Directors passed 20 coordination and three procedural initiatives, all are precise and have substantial depth. The same is true for the four demands towards the federal government. Health reconfirms this picture, where exclusively precise and substantial coordination and procedural initiatives were issued. The finance directors and the directors in charge of crime control, justice, and police show similar patterns with only a few non-substantial agreements. Despite considerable differences in the personnel available, the differences in terms of output across policy fields are surprisingly small. The directors in crime control, justice, and police passed 34 agreements (31 precise and substantial), although the conference has only 2.9 full-time positions compared to the Conference of Education Directors with around 30 employees dealing with political work.[21] This finding is interesting since it reconfirms the initial decision to operationalize institutionalization as structural development instead of using the allocation of resources to IGAs as a proxy. Clearly, it is still a matter of choice whether the individual canton will finally adopt such recommendations. The table does not measure the effectiveness of the outputs in terms of policy outcome. However, when it comes to coordination initiatives, a director tends to avoid agreeing to any recommendation which, once proposed as legislative draft, risks public opposition at home – in parliament or in the form of a referendum – since such reactions could easily undermine his or her reputation.

Comparing the generalist and policy-specific IGAs in the Swiss context, the difference between the output of the generalist Conference of Cantonal Executives and the policy-specific Conferences of Directors is more likely a result of the political character of the issues left to the Conference of Cantonal Executives (e.g. federal reform affecting the power distribution between federal and cantonal levels) than the result of different institutional capacities. In contrast to the directors, the cantonal representatives sent to the Conference of Cantonal Executives are usually mandated since the final resolutions tend to attract more public attention than those issued by a directorial conference. The less precise and less substantial agreements issued by the Conference of Cantonal Executives leave greater leeway for interpretations and is therefore less constraining for cantonal participants.

Moving on to the United States, the highly institutionalized, policy-specific standing committees (education, justice and crime control, environment, and health)[22] produce even fewer unspecific and non-substantial positions than the generalist executive committee of the National Governors' Association. Mirroring the Swiss situation, many issues addressed in the policy committees are less general[23] and therefore potentially less sensitive. The differences in the precision of positions and substantial depth across policy fields are minor which is not

---

[21] The Conference of Education Directors also runs an information centre whose staff are not included in this figure.

[22] Only the governors run a committee on fiscal policy which, however, does not issue any policy resolutions.

[23] For example, state positions on federal funding policy compared to federal solid-waste facility policies.

surprising since all committees are institutionalized on the same level and structured along the same lines.[24] This overall picture is reconfirmed by the agreements issued by the National Conference of State Legislatures. Its policy committees produce equally precise and substantial positions. Content-wise policy positions of the National Conference of State Legislatures are fairly similar to the policies of the governors. Yet, while both IGAs often plea for more federal funding, a core concern for both branches, this orientation is more pronounced in the National Governors' Association than in the Conference of State Legislatures. The latter more frequently demands greater state flexibility, a pattern which complements the observation in Chapter 5 that the branches have different priorities when it comes to autonomy protection. Furthermore, it is noteworthy that the legislatures explicitly ask for more individual state flexibility as far as justified by the need for regionally or locally specific solutions. It does not refer to the legitimate rights of state government as sovereign units. Whenever its policies request more authority, the prerogative of national responses is already presupposed, while state authority is treated as a residual. Congress is requested to define whether to become active in or stay out of a policy area and whether, as a consequence, states are to gain greater flexibility which reflects the passive role of the states described above.

By and large, Canadian ministerial councils meet less often and, more importantly, less regularly than IGAs in Switzerland and the United States. While environment and education are institutionalized on a medium level, have stronger structures, and more regular exchanges; finance, health, social policy, and justice and crime control are only weakly institutionalized. Taking a cross-national perspective, it comes as no surprise that these IGAs pass fewer agreements. The cross-sectoral pattern is less homogeneous than in the two power-sharing cases. Table 7.5 sums up the precise and substantial agreements issued in Canada categorized along agreement type in seven policy fields.

So far, the analysis has focused on cross-country variance. Table 7.5 brings in the analysis of intra-country variance, in concrete, the effect of medium compared to low institutionalization on the nature of intergovernmental agreements in the Canadian context. Table 7.5 shows that in the weakly institutionalized health and social policy councils, no agreement was substantial within the two years analysed.[25] The two medium-institutionalized IGAs issued five substantial

---

[24] For instance, states take much more collective positions in the area of natural resources than in the area of early childhood and workforce which nicely reflects the findings of Chapter 5: a greater number of interstate compacts have been set up in the former policy field.

[25] Adding the agreements issued by the ministers responsible for seniors (which substantially belongs in the area of social policy), one additional substantial procedural initiative was issued, namely to set up an annual meeting to share experience. However, in all three countries, IGAs responsible for sub-sectors such as forestry and their output are not considered.

TABLE 7.5. *Precise and substantial agreements in Canadian policy-specific intergovernmental arrangements in 2004–5*

	Positions/ Demands	Policy Coordination	Procedural Initiatives	All Agreements
Health	0	0 (2)	0 (1)	0 (3)
Justice and crime control	0 (5)	3 (9)	3 (7)	6 (21)
Social policy	0 (1)	0 (3)	0 (4)	0 (8)
Finance	0 (0)	0 (0)	0 (0)	0 (0)
Environment	0 (0)	2 (3)	0 (2)	2 (5)
Internal trade	0	1 (3)	1 (2)	2 (5)
Education	2 (5)	1 (2)	1 (5)	4 (12)
N	11	22	21	54

Note: Shaded area: low institutionalization; white area: medium institutionalization.

commitments – all of them also specific.[26] To assess the effect of institutionalization on agreements (while keeping intragovernmental incentives constant), however, we need to look at the whole range of policy fields and here the picture is not very clear. The council handling justice and crime control produced with 21 agreements by far the largest number of agreements. What is striking about this area is the heavy reliance on cross-jurisdictional expert-committees on the working level. To a much greater extent than in any other area analysed, ministers are willing to assign comparatively far-fetching mandates to these committees at one meeting and to publicly endorse their recommendations at a later one. The delegation of tasks to lower levels is per se not particular. In other fields, however, ministers tend to ask their individual officials to think about possibly collective solutions or, more vaguely put, ask a group of officials to 'gather information'. Moreover, whether they come back to the issue later on is not sure. The ministers of justice, by contrast, seem to have established comparatively high continuity irrespective of a weakly institutionalized environment on the political level. One reason may be the nature of the subject-matter. The familiarity of the participating actors with legal matters may contribute to the greater willingness to bind oneself to specific recommendations drafted by legal experts (especially when these recommendations concern regulation rather than legislation which are less 'autonomy-threatening'). Furthermore, actors may see a greater need to address rather technical legal problems concretely and fix agreements with considerable precision.

Internal trade is medium institutionalized and produced as many precise and substantial agreements as the environmental council. While the overall area of economic and trade policy is only weakly developed, the existing Agreement

---

[26] Much of the work of the medium-institutionalized environmental council centres around the implementation of the Canada-Wide Accord on Environmental Harmonization of 1998 which delivers guidelines for nationwide standards in a wide sub-field in environmental policy and sets up procedures to improve intergovernmental cooperation.

of Internal Trade, signed in 1995 on the highest political level and leading to the creation of a secretariat on the bureaucratic level, facilitates interaction and supports cross-jurisdictional policy-coordination. Finally, the area of health points to the shifting of issues from one IGA to the other. One of the major First Ministers' projects during the period under examination was a 10-Year Plan on Health issued in September 2004. This is likely to have shifted a range of related issues from the ministerial council to the level of premiers. Simultaneously, instead of being focused on own initiatives, health ministers had a mandate to elaborate on this project issued by their premiers and prime minister. The fluidity of IGR in Canada and the absence of institutional boundaries of IGAs assuring stable 'issue ownership' come into play. Depending on the priorities of the heads of government in a certain period, the activities of higher level IGAs such as the First Ministers' Conference and the Council of the Federation are likely to affect the scope of activities of policy-specific councils. They might do so by either monopolizing certain issues, thus constraining policy-specific IGAs, or by delegating issues to them.

What do these findings tell us about the relative impact of different levels of institutionalization in the Canadian context? Most importantly, cooperation-undermining government dynamics are also felt within the more institutionalized IGAs. Medium institutionalization increases the regularity of meetings and provides expertise gathered outside the individual provincial or federal departments. Considering justice and crime control as an outlier, the more institutionalized IGAs on average produce a higher number of agreements and a higher share of precise and substantial ones. Still, one should not read too much into this. The mixed output patterns indicate that even resource-strong IGAs do not necessarily fare better than weakly institutionalized IGAs when operating in a cooperation-undermining setting. The latter seem to catch up rather easily whenever policy-specific dynamics or momentary developments are favourable which points to a direct impact of intragovernmental incentives on the output of intergovernmental negotiations, which cannot be neutralized by a slightly higher level of institutionalization.

This interpretation gains weight when bringing in a cross-country perspective. Medium-institutionalized arrangements in Canada cannot generate a similar output as achieved by equally institutionalized arrangements in power-sharing contexts, for example, the medium-institutionalized Conference of Directors responsible for Environment and Planning in Switzerland. This implies that an increased institutionalization matters but to different degrees across different systems. Medium institutionalized IGAs are not irrelevant in the long run. Still, in a cooperation-undermining context, they change the dominant interaction mode of ad hoc coordination only to a limited degree. Intragovernmental dynamics do not only establish barriers against more far-fetching institutional developments, but also against the possible impact institutionalization can have. This is particularly crucial whenever a stronger arrangement is chosen than, in principle, supported by the dominant intragovernmental incentive structures, thus is located outside the corridor of adaptation.

This argument gains further leverage when looking at Swiss IGAs[27] and comparing those on a medium and high level of institutionalization – set up in a context where the corridor of adaptation is wide and intragovernmental incentives favourable. The Directorial Conference responsible for Environment and Planning produces fewer agreements than any of the four highly institutionalized IGAs. This is striking because the Conference of Finance Directors, the smallest of the highly institutionalized IGAs, has (while being institutionally more developed) fewer resources than the Conference of Directors for Environment and Planning.[28] The latter also drafted fewer substantial agreements than its highly institutionalized counterparts, yet the two coordination and procedural agreements in environmental policy are both precise and substantial. (The same is the case for its two coordination agreements in planning.) In the cooperation-favouring Swiss context, this conference has the capacity to produce constraining agreements despite its medium level of institutionalization. Furthermore, with one part-time secretary as only staff, it produced more precise and substantial agreements than the equally developed education council and as many as the environmental council in Canada which are far better equipped in terms of resources.

The irony of these findings is that if intragovernmental dynamics affect both the set-up of IGAs and their respective output simultaneously, institutionalization matters most in contexts where the incentives on the micro level are favourable towards strong IGAs in the first place. The variance across Swiss IGAs indicates that institutionalization has an independent impact on the drafting of constraining agreements. However, when comparing Swiss and Canadian IGAs, the same level of institutionalization and much fewer resources still lead to a better output in the cooperation-favouring Swiss than the cooperation-undermining Canadian setting. The reason is simple. In Canada, IGAs need to function as counterweight against intragovernmental dynamics, while in Switzerland, they function as reinforcement mechanisms for a pattern already inherent in the very nature of its composite polity. Referring back to the causal arrow depicted in Figure 7.2, in Canada the nature of processes driven by intragovernmental dynamics seem to exert a strong direct impact on the nature of intergovernmental agreements. A more institutionalized context cannot compensate for this sufficiently. In an ex ante cooperation-favouring environment, by contrast, the reinforcing impact of a higher institutionalization can fully display itself. This implies that institutionalization has rather a reinforcing than a transformative impact on intergovernmental processes.

---

[27] Such an 'internal' comparison is not possible in the United States since the committees are structured along the same lines.

[28] The Conference of Finance Directors has 320,000 Swiss francs per year and 120 per cent full-time positions (*Stellenprozente*). The Conference of Directors of Environment and Planning has 590,000 Swiss francs per year and 80–120 per cent of a full-time position (*Stellenprozente*).

Looking at each system individually, the respective cross-sectoral variance indicated that policy differences shape the nature of agreements struck in IGAs. But they tend to explain the relative difference within a system better than providing an overall account for cross-country differences. The extremely sensitive area of fiscal policy provides an apt illustration of this point. Starting with Switzerland, the Conference of Finance Directors clearly shows output patterns different from other policy-specific IGAs. It engages to a wider extent in position taking on federal legislation and the formulation of detailed amendments. This orientation contrasts with the conferences in charge of education, health or crime control, justice, and police which focus on policy coordination. The differences in resources do not provide a convincing answer. While, with 1.2 full-time positions, the Conference of Finance Directors is the smallest arrangement, the crime control, justice, and police conference has only 2.9 full positions and still generated 13 precise and substantive coordination agreements. In addition to this, the discussion of (unsuccessful) coordination agreements is not visible in the protocols of the meetings between finance directors despite the statement of staff that the conference deals with policy coordination 'half of the time'. The contradiction is resolved when one recognizes that coordination efforts are located on the level of the conference's specialized sub-committees. They are usually not dealt with officially on the level of directors which explains why this activity is not reflected in protocols or official agreements. Most concordats, in fact, fall in the area of fiscal policy (Bochsler et al. 2004)

Parallels emerge in Canada; here the output of the council of ministers responsible for finance stands out as well. Although ministers meet about once a year, Canadian finance ministers refuse to publish agreements. They avoid the proclamation of collective statements altogether. Given the stronger hierarchy in Canadian lower level governments than in the Swiss cantons and their considerable politicization, the leeway for cooperation on lower levels is also limited. As one intergovernmental official put it:

> The finance departments are quite closed to everybody else. Those who go to these meetings work there. It is small delegations. They discuss intergovernmental transfer policy, tax policy. ...Their relationship is different because as soon as governments start to talk about money, funding formulas, etc. they are even more politicized. Finance ministers have different roles in their cabinets than other ministers.[29]

We find similar patterns in the United States. Given the importance of this policy area for the American states, the National Governors' Association runs a policy-specific standing committee. Yet unlike all other of its committees, the committee responsible for fiscal matters does not issue policy positions. This might be partially rooted in the fact that the legislatures have a prerogative on budgetary and fiscal matters. Accordingly, the National Conference of State

---

[29] Fed Can II, 13 December 2005.

Legislatures has a standing committee in this area which issues positions. Given a separation between the branches and their intergovernmental activities, however, it is unlikely that the executives simply 'leave' the issue to legislatures since in this case, a committee would be unnecessary in the first place. Overall, their handling indicates that fiscal matters are particularly contentious for executives which are under pressure to deliver policies, a process from which legislatures are more detached in a separation of powers structure than in a parliamentary system where the branches are tied together. Furthermore, the executive committee of the Governors' Association partially deals with fiscal matters.

The cross-national parallels are obvious. The sensitive nature of fiscal policy reflects in the way exchanges are handled by the respective executives compared to other policy fields. However, the two power-sharing democracies are less sensitive and the impact of policy features is less pronounced than in Canada. In Switzerland, the nature of the policy only restricts the functional orientation of the conference which still issues highly precise and substantial collective demands and positions. In turn, policy coordination is shifted to a lower (more technical, less conflict-intense, and less visible) level. Furthermore, the policy committee of the National Governors' Association, albeit without articulating public positions, provides a forum for regular exchange, while the Conference of National State Legislatures issues collective demands. Only in Canada, where institutionalization is generally low, do we find a complete lack of collective statements of lower level governments. For fiscal matters to be explicitly discussed in the intergovernmental arena, this needs to be initiated by the First Ministers' Conference. This has been shown by the recent debate of equalization and fiscal imbalance, which again mirrors the immediate impact of intra-executive hierarchies on intergovernmental processes in Canadian federalism.[30]

INTERGOVERNMENTAL INSTITUTIONS AND THE NATURE OF AGREEMENTS

We are left with three tentative findings which support the claim that intergovernmental institutions affect the nature of intergovernmental agreements and which indicate how they do so. Given the restricted scope of the analysis, the findings only allow for preliminary conclusions.

---

[30] Note that this finding does not contradict the core finding of Chapter 5 that due to compulsory power-sharing in the states the institutionalization pattern of policy-specific IGAs is much more strongly affected by policy characteristics. On the contrary, it shows that looking at the output of *highly institutionalized* IGAs in the United States, the institutional context indeed moderates policy impacts in contrast to weakly institutionalized Canada.

First, institutionalization increases the capacity of an IGA to fulfil whatever functions are assigned to it. Earlier chapters already pointed to the process dynamics generated by different levels of institutionalization: the increasing capacity to bridge conflict, the strengthening of the corps d'ésprit, the establishing of reliability and routines, the increase of a body's decisiveness, and the provision of expertise gathered outside of the individual member governments. Institutionalization also shapes the nature of agreements as demonstrated by the higher precision and substantial depth of agreements drafted in highly developed IGAs. Although differences across policy fields could be detected, overall, they proved to be less pronounced than differences across systems and levels of institutionalization.

Second, the level of institutionalization does not go hand in hand with a particular functional orientation. Most crucially, IGAs organized along non-compulsory power-sharing structures do not produce informal agreements to coordinate policy because they are unable to represent lower level governments as cohesive political units. They cannot generate political commitment constraining future policy choices of the member governments without a legal backup. The functional orientation of IGAs can be understood when considering the interplay of institutionalization and of integration. Thus, to understand the distribution of agreement types, the systemic environment of IGAs – especially its linkages to other intergovernmental bodies – is decisive. As American IGR indicate, weak integration is harmful towards voluntary policy-coordination when IGAs are strongly developed and reinforce the division between the branches. In Canada, institutionalization and integration are weak. We can observe a shifting of issues from one IGA to the other since a distribution of labour between generalist and policy-specific IGAs is only weakly developed. This situation, however, does not prevent political agreements in the from of coordination initiatives as in the United States since the premiers and prime ministers are able to dominate the process and monopolize issues at any point without facing any institutional resistance at home or by policy-specific ministerial councils. Simultaneously, however, the reliability of participants to stick to these agreements is limited. The shifting of issues across IGAs also implies that we find greater irregularity in the outputs of the respective policy-specific ministerial councils, an effect we find in weakly institutionalized councils as well as in councils institutionalized on a medium level.

Third, the comparison of differently institutionalized IGAs within the same systemic context implied that intragovernmental dynamics affect both the set-up of IGAs and the output immediately. Institutionalization matters most in contexts where the incentives on the micro level are favourable towards strong IGAs in the first place. In polycentric Canada, the process dynamics exert a strong direct impact on the output for which a medium-institutionalized IGA cannot fully compensate. In an ex ante cooperation-favouring environment like Switzerland, the reinforcing impact of institutionalization can fully display itself. Thus, the institutionalization of IGAs has rather a reinforcing than a transformative impact on the dynamics in federal arenas which highlights the likely limitations of federal reform as far as these reforms are supposed to counteract dominant intragovernmental incentive structures.

In sum, while these findings can only be a first step towards more detailed comparative explorations, they indicate that neither the patterns of informal institution-building in a federal system nor the nature of agreements struck between governments can be fully grasped without considering intragovernmental dynamics.

8

Rational Choices in Federal Systems and Beyond

This book has proposed a theoretical framework to explain why political actors in different federal systems choose particular types of institutions to channel intergovernmental processes. It has further explored the impact of these institutional choices on the coordination capacity of lower level governments by analysing the nature of agreements governments enter within different institutional contexts. These two questions are key for any multilevel setting in which governments with decision-making power face boundary-crossing problems (Benz and Papadopoulos 2006). Throughout the last decades, governments in federal systems and international multilevel settings such as the EU have been increasingly often confronted with boundary-crossing problems. Accordingly, the interaction density between governments has steadily increased (see, among others, Hooghe 1996; Börzel 2000, 2001, 2002; Peters and Pierre 2001; Simeon 2001: 145–7; Kincaid 2003). The finding that governments have responded to these growing interdependencies emphasized in a wide range of works is therefore crucial.

In the course of seven chapters, this book has tried to convince its readers that the *nature* of these responses is at least of equal importance. It identified the conditions under which political actors are likely to respond in such a way as to solve the problems they try to address collectively in the intergovernmental arena in an effective manner. To do so, the theoretical framework deliberately shifted the focus from the *quantity of exchanges* to the *quality of the dominant intergovernmental interaction patterns* and *structures*. If informal institutions reflect and, to a certain degree, influence the mode of policy coordination applied by intergovernmental actors and thereby affect the final output of intergovernmental negotiations, we need to know which institutions political actors set up in the intergovernmental arena. We need to know which functions actors assign to these institutions and why they do so. In short, when trying to account for the capacity of intergovernmental actors for institution building, we need to go beyond identifying their mere willingness to intensify boundary-crossing contacts.

Despite the vast literature on federalism and multilevel settings, there has been no systematic approach to why the IGAs governments set up to deal with boundary-crossing problems vary considerably or to what extent institutional differences shape the effectiveness of intergovernmental processes. The rationalist approach presented in this book identifies the incentives generated by the nature of executive–legislative relations in lower level governments as one core factor to account for particular institution-building strategies in the intergovernmental arena. This approach has two analytical starting-points in the literature on empirical types of democracy. While the distinction power sharing versus power concentration constitutes the typology of consensus versus majoritarian democracy (Lijphart 1999), the distinction between voluntary and compulsory power-sharing is rooted in the typology of parliamentarism versus presidentialism. These institutional types describe patterns and structures which cluster in democratic regimes. Despite their lasting prominence, they have increasingly provoked severe criticisms from 'neo-institutionalists' pointing to these approaches' insufficient micro-foundation. Simply ordering macro-structures, they lack an explicit link to those actors located 'below' constitutional structures. The proliferation of actor-oriented rational choice approaches can be considered as a potential remedy (Scharpf 1997). At the same time, this book indicates that we should not dismiss macro approaches such as Lijphart's typology (1999) too readily since these approaches can be substantiated by a micro-foundation. The framework presented in this book which proposed a way to derive hypotheses on the informal institutions to be established in different federal settings is only one example. Structure-based macro-concepts located on the polity level can be refined by specifying their underlying micro-incentives, an endeavour which responds to the neo-institutionalist debate emphasizing the need to specify more properly the causal mechanisms driving macro-dynamics (Scharpf 1997; Peters 1999).

The book argued that internal decision-making dynamics in lower level governments generated by their type of executive–legislative relations influence the capacity of political actors to engage in intergovernmental institution-building. The incentives resulting from these dynamics shape the 'corridor of adaptation' in a system. This corridor constrains the capacity to respond to coordination pressure by building institutions able to facilitate collective problem-solving in the long run. Governments only invest in strong IGAs when they profit from it 'at home'. Following this rationale, the first core hypothesis referred to the institutionalization – the structural development – of individual arrangements: Power-sharing governments favour the institutionalization of IGAs, while power-concentrating governments refrain from it. As the empirical analyses indicates, the presence of power-concentrating governments are linked to high programmatic differences between the governments, unstable government interests over time, strong incentives for blame shifting, and a strong orientation towards autonomy protection. Power sharing invites opposite incentives and thereby high institutionalization.

The second core hypothesis referred to the integration of IGAs, the linkages between these arrangements, which captures the macro-dynamics of the federal system. Different from institutionalization, the level of integration is not only affected by the *degree of power sharing* – power concentration undermines

TABLE 8.1. *Dominant patterns of institutionalization and integration in three federal systems*

Internal Structure of Units	Institutionalization	Integration
Canada: power-concentration	Generalist IGAs: low Policy-specific IGAs: low	Low
United States: compulsory power-sharing	Generalist IGAs: high Policy-specific IGAs: low to high	Low
Switzerland: voluntary power-sharing	Generalist IGAs: high Policy-specific IGAs: high	High

institutionalization as integration – but also by the *type of power sharing* present in governments. Drawing on the literature on veto players (Birchfield and Crepaz 1998), *compulsory* (constitutionally imposed) power-sharing (e.g. presidentialism) and *voluntary* power-sharing (e.g. coalition governments) were expected to have different consequences. In contrast to voluntary power-sharing which is favourable to institutionalization and integration alike, compulsory power-sharing fragments individual governments internally and thereby weakens the linkages between the IGAs. Thus, voluntary power-sharing was expected to favour integration between IGAs, while compulsory power-sharing was expected to undermine it.

The three federal systems Canada, Switzerland, and the United States were chosen for the empirical analysis since they ideal-typically reflect the core configurations power concentration, voluntary power-sharing, and compulsory power-sharing in their lower level governments. The analysis showed that the incentives created by their executive–legislative configurations generated different corridors of adaptation leading to different patterns of intergovernmental institution-building. As Table 8.1 summarizes, due to the dominance of power-concentrating governments, institutionalization and integration of IGAs in Canada are low. Due to voluntary power-sharing in cantonal governments, institutionalization and integration of IGAs in Switzerland are high. In both countries, these patterns showed with regard to generalist and policy-specific IGAs.

Although corresponding to the overall rationale, the United States proved to be more complex. While integration between IGAs is – as hypothesized – generally low due to the fragmenting effects of compulsory power-sharing, the patterns of institutionalization are less homogeneous. Looking at generalist IGAs, we find them highly institutionalized due to power sharing in the individual states. Also among the policy-specific arrangements, we find highly institutionalized arrangements indicating that the corridor of adaptation is broad – as theoretically expected. What we do not find, however, is an equally strong cross-sectoral trend towards high institutionalization as we find it in Switzerland. The reason is the following. Policy-specific IGAs deal with policy coordination (in contrast to generalist IGAs mostly engaged in collective position-taking). Position taking can be handled equally well by whole governments as by governmental subunits such as the individual branches of government. The coordination of policy between several states, in constrast, presupposes the agreement of the executives and legislatures constituting the participating state governments. To form such agreement is easily undermined by divisions between the governmental branches as generated by compulsory power-sharing. In a range of policy fields, this leads to a lower level of institutionalization than one would expect in an environment in general favourable to cooperation. Similar to its effect on integration, the type of power sharing in the American states regularly undermines the set-up of strong policy-specific structures.

The distinction between the two dimensions of institutionalization and integration lies at the heart of this study both conceptually and empirically. These two concepts refer to different units of analysis – institutionalization to the individual IGAs created in a federal system, integration to the relations between them. Furthermore, the distinction allows us to link the empirical findings on institution building in the intergovernmental arena to the range of interaction modes introduced in Chapter 1: unilateralism, ad hoc coordination, co-decision, and supragovernmentalism (see, for a similar approach, Scharpf 2001). These four concepts can be thought as a continuum denoting – in this order – the increasing constraints on individual governments as implied by the respective mode. The interplay of institutionalization and integration defines the structural context which is conducive to particular interaction modes and thereby indicates intergovernmental actors' strategies to address horizontal cross-jurisdictional problems.

Put differently, each of the three federal systems is characterized by a constellation of interaction modes embedded in a particular infrastructure which affects the way governments engage in cross-jurisdictional policy-coordination – as one core function supported by IGAs. *Co-decision* as the dominant interaction mode in the Swiss case found expression in highly institutionalized and integrated structures. Supragovernmentalism through inter-cantonal concordats is also an option but less often used. *Ad hoc coordination* as typical for Canada was accompanied by the weakness of both institutionalization and integration – any coordination mode implying a strong informal or even legal commitment was ex ante excluded. In the United States, the picture is again the most complex. While in the other systems highly developed IGAs serve a variety of functions ranging from position taking to policy coordination, American IGAs tend to specialize much more. On the vertical level, strongly institutionalized and weakly integrated IGAs compete for influence on federal policy. Here *co-decision processes* predominantly serve collective position-taking. Regarding horizontal policy-coordination, one finds a peculiar oscillation between the extremes of *unilateral adaption* and *supragovernmentalism* (e.g. interstate commissions), with unilateral adaptation as the less demanding and thus the more frequent choice. This configuration reflects the incapacity of IGAs to set up voluntary yet politically binding agreements (through either ad hoc coordination or co-decision), an incapacity rooted in the compulsory power-sharing structures within the states. Table 8.2 maps the three constellations.

TABLE 8.2. *Dominant modes of policy coordination and configurations of institutionalization and integration*

	Low Integration	High Integration
Low Institutionalization	*Canada:* ad hoc coordination	—[a]
High Institutionalization	*United States:* unilateral adapation	*Switzerland:* co-decision

[a] For logical reasons, this box remains empty: If structures are institutionally fluid or consist of direct ministerial exchanges, strong integration between IGAs is ex ante excluded.

As emphasized in the introductory chapter, modes of intergovernmental interaction and investments in informal intergovernmental institutions represent two distinct perspectives on IGR which need to be linked in an analysis of federal dynamics. The empirical results demonstrated that particular modes are backed up by corresponding intergovernmental structures which then feed back into the nature of intergovernmental agreements. This is not the same as saying that intergovernmental structures fully *account for* the corresponding mode or vice versa. Instead, the study demonstrates that both interaction modes and actors' institutional choices are to certain extents shaped by *intragovernmental dynamics*. Once in place, however, IGAs support particular interaction modes among those governments embedded in these informal institutions, thus have a reinforcing effect. To validate these claims in further research, Table 8.2 provides a scheme to derive hypotheses about the interaction mode and the infrastructure expected to flow from particular incentives structures within lower level governments. IGR in Spain, for instance, should resemble Canadian IGR, since both are dominated by power-concentrating lower level governments (Bolleyer 2006).

INFORMAL INSTITUTION-BUILDING IN FEDERAL SYSTEMS: GENERAL IMPLICATIONS

Having provided a comparative analysis of three federal systems, the book generates several conclusions which transcend federalism research. They lead to fundamental claims demanding further systematic work in the realm of institutionalism: First, the findings point to the limited impact of institutional reform facing countervailing political dynamics within lower level governments. Second, by capturing underlying micro-dynamics, the findings indicate how IGAs voluntarily set up by intergovernmental actors can affect these actors later on. And third, the findings point to the relevance of the mode of representation underlying and required by different modes of policy coordination applied in multilevel systems.

As Chapter 7 implied, intragovernmental dynamics both influence the institutional set-up and affect IGAs' output directly. This has implications for the likely effects and the effectiveness of *institutional reforms*. Looking at the impact of IGAs' development on their internal processes, the staff in medium institutionalized IGAs in Canada are not supposed to take any form of own initiative. Their role is limited to provide bureaucratic support. In the United States, the staff of highly institutionalized IGAs support the *identification* of pre-existing common ground, thus they are involved in agenda-setting. In the both highly institutionalized and highly integrated Swiss context, staff are entitled to *generate* common ground, to moderate existing differences and actively support processes of non-hierarchical, voluntary policy-coordination. These findings indicate that a high institutional development strengthens the capacity of 'neutral' IGA staff to actively influence the interaction between the governments embedded in a multi-level setting. Putting it in principal–agent terms, once governments have set up a secretariat with personnel, IGAs acquire an own identity. Given medium or strong institutionalization, IGAs constitute an agent separate from the sum of member governments, who is in charge of representing the latter. The empirical analysis showed that lower level governments regularly feared that an institutionally highly developed IGA (representing the governments 'as collective') might become able to pursue goals which deviate from the sum of individual government interests. And indeed the analysis reconfirmed that such suspicions are well founded.

Nonetheless, on the macro level, the transformative impact of reform is likely to remain limited since federal dynamics remain fully subject to systemic constraints generated in lower level governments. Institutionalization matters the most when intragovernmental incentives are favourable towards strong IGAs and with it intergovernmental cooperation in the first place. In Canada IGAs need to function as a counterweight to the dominant intragovernmental dynamics which shape day-to-day interaction, while in Switzerland they function as reinforcement mechanisms for dynamics inherent in the very nature of this composite polity. Although institutionalization is by no means unimportant, the reform of intergovernmental institutions is likely to have a *reinforcing* rather than a *transformative* impact on the character of interaction prevalent in a system.

This leads us to the important distinction between potential *triggers* to set up an arrangement and the *level* of institutional development which can be sustained in a particular setting. Clearly, it is important to consider critical events which initiate the reform or the creation of an intergovernmental body such as of the Canadian Council of the Federation in 2003 or the Swiss Conference of Cantonal Executives in 1993. Strong fiscal pressure in the former context and the lack of influence in international negotiations in the latter have been crucial triggers to reform IGR. At the same time, the findings show that the potential of these two bodies to carve out a linchpin position in the intergovernmental arena varied considerably. This is where the 'corridors of adaptation' come into play. Particular events can *trigger* intergovernmental actors' *initial choices* which might contradict the incentives predominant 'at home'. We might observe deliberate efforts towards stronger institutionalization in a majoritarian context per se unfavourable to such a development. Politicians might deliberately choose to prioritize long-term effects over short-term interests and consciously counter typical intergovernmental dynamics perceived as destructive for the handling of cross-jurisdictional problems. The findings presented in this book, however, imply that the developmental potential of such structures once set up, remains subject to system-specific pressures and is thereby restricted. Thus, long-term pressures inside governments – shaping the overall level of institutional development in a system – are likely to be more decisive than an IGA's initial characteristics for the final role this IGA will be able to play in a federal system.[1] And as the findings imply, most often, initial institutional choices are located within the 'corridor of adaptation' anyway. Usually short-term interests are prioritized over potential long-term benefits.

Moving on to the second issue, the findings touch upon the debate on *how informal institutions* voluntarily set up by political actors are nonetheless able *to steer their behavioural choices* later on – a question at the very heart of institutional theory (Peters 1999: 32–3). Starting from a rational choice perspective, disaggregating IGAs into staff and members pointed to the core role of IGA staff whose strategic manoeuvring reinforces the impact of intragovernmental constraints. Once an external infrastructure is in place, intergovernmental staff start to pursue, next to the interest of their members, what they perceive as their 'institutional self-interest'. This self-interest translates mainly into maintaining the IGAs' resources and thereby their own jobs. This orientation does not necessarily violate the purpose of an IGA as initially defined by political actors supporting its foundation. Still, the two can diverge. Again reflecting the distinction between triggers for initial choices and sustainable levels of institutionalization in a particular environment, personnel of IGAs are less oriented towards the purpose which motivated the creation of a body. They consider the arrangement's role and prospects in the context of the rationale that drives member government actions which might imply a deviation from this initial purpose in the longer run.

To give one example, although the National Governors' Association in the United States was clearly set up to pursue governors' collective interests in the political arena, they developed a very strong service component (e.g. offering expertise or professional training to their members). The structural and functional convergence of IGAs with private interest groups was triggered by mutual competition between IGAs for influence on the federal government rooted in the internal fragmentation of each state. Compulsory power-sharing in the states prevented individual IGAs from 'monopolizing' the representation of 'state governments' as coherent political units. Under such conditions, the emphasis of member services actively supported by IGA staff was a rational response to

---

[1] This finding seems to reflect what is captured by the concept of path dependency developed in historical institutionalism (Thelen 1999). However, strictly speaking, the argument does not refer to mechanisms related to this concept such as increasing returns after initial institutional investments and lock-in effects leading to incrementalism over time. Instead, it refers to systemic constraints generated by stable intragovernmental incentive structures to which actors are expected to respond similarly over time and thereby produce a – on average – higher or lower level of institutionalization.

an intragovernmental fragmentation generating inter-institutional competition. Following the same rationale but facing very different intragovernmental incentives, staff of the Conference of Cantonal Executives worked towards occupying a linchpin position in the Swiss intergovernmental arena. They pushed for the stronger integration of their IGA with the older policy-specific bodies in order to secure and stabilize its position as an overall coordinator. In short, when reaching medium institutionalization, a new group of actors enters the intergovernmental arena with a strong interest in the institution's preservation, which seems to unintentionally reinforce the impact of intragovernmental constraints.

Finally, the findings point to the relevance of *modes of representation* in federal systems and their importance for the generation of voluntary commitment and engagement in non-hierarchical policy-coordination. The analysis of American IGR showed that the high institutionalization of individual IGAs is insufficient to generate lower level governments' capacity to engage in voluntary cross-jurisdictional policy-coordination. On the contrary, coupled with weak integration, it undermines the capacity of IGAs to coordinate policies between their members on a voluntary basis. Often, IGAs are vertically oriented only and engage in the lobbying of federal policies. Regarding horizontal coordination, we find either advisory bodies (e.g. proposing model laws) or interstate authorities (usually in charge of narrow regulatory issues). At first glance this seems odd; regarding the extent to which such measures bind the governments involved, they belong at opposite ends on our continuum of interaction modes. At second glance, however, this makes a lot of sense and reconfirms the inability of American IGAs to create voluntary yet politically binding commitment. By definition, advice has not a binding character and leaves state governments to unilateral choice. Interstate authorities as the opposite extreme (in the rare cases where states manage to create them) supersede individual state power and circumvent the commitment problem through legal enforcement once an agreement has been entered.

As the case studies indicated, compulsory power-sharing implies the absence of party linkages assuring the internal coherence of governments. Accordingly, the difference between American IGAs and their Swiss and Canadian counterparts is captured well by the distinction between interest groups and parties: Interest groups articulate interests, while parties aggregate collective interests into policy proposals (Lawson 2004). Correspondingly, in the United States, generalist IGAs articulate collective interests. They 'speak on behalf of' their members but do not develop binding policy-proposals for collective action. Reflecting the internal fragmentation of the states, American IGAs are organized along professional lines and represent their individual members defined by their specific function. They do not represent internally coherent government units and therefore cannot 'act on behalf of' their states. In Switzerland and Canada where governments are internally coherent, these three types of institutions remain distinct with parties as representatives of structurally anchored groups, intergovernmental bodies embracing governmental units negotiating over territorial demands, and private interest groups pushing for the special interests of professionals. The logic according to which government interests are represented and the way in which this logic becomes institutionally manifest tells us a lot about the fundamental character of a polity and its functioning (Sbragia 1993). Intergovernmental actors wishing to engage in non-hierarchical policy-coordination and to generate voluntary yet de facto binding commitment through informal agreements must effectively 'represent' their governments. They must not only speak but also act on their behalf. The following analysis of the EU will reinforce this point and demonstrate that the capacity to represent territorial interests affects policy coordination among lower level governments also outside of the national sphere.

POLICY COORDINATION IN THE EUROPEAN UNION IN COMPARATIVE PERSPECTIVE

Having guided a comparative study of federal systems, the framework put forward in this book must still face a crucial test: Can it be applied beyond the national context? The following sections suggest that the theoretical perspective developed in this book promises interesting insights when applied to the EU. Clearly, this discussion can be only suggestive when compared to extensive studies of multilevel governance and the impact of governments' internal structures and political dynamics on the Union's evolution (e.g. Moravcsik 1998; Hooghe and Marks 2001; Kelemen 2004; Schmidt 2006). Yet starting out from the study of national federal systems and 'moving up' to the EU level points to possibilities and challenges when attempting to expand federal theory to multilevel settings beyond the nation state.

It is widely acknowledged that the EU corresponds to the 'federal principle' without being a 'federal state' (e.g. Scharpf 1988; Sbragia 1993; Elazar 2001; McKay 2001; Börzel 2005*a*; Swenden 2005). Its lack of a monopoly of coercive force (as compared to the three federal states) is of minor importance for the functioning of the EU as a multilevel system. Its supranational institutions such as Commission or European Court of Justice nonetheless yield significant power of hierarchical coordination (Börzel 2007) which makes the latter directly comparable to central-level institutions involved in national decision-making in federal systems. The question of the EU's growing hierarchical steering capacity – or the challenge of centre-formation in the European integration process as Bartolini (2005) put it – is essential when thinking of the general comparability of the EU composed of nation states and federal systems which are usually historically grown nation state themselves. The theoretical framework as developed in Chapter 2 looked at federal systems from another perspective. In terms of policy making, it dealt with the exact opposite to centralized (or national) decision-making, namely the voluntary, cross-jurisdictional coordination of policies between lower level governments within their own spheres of authority. Accordingly, the analysis of the EU will focus on 'non-hierarchical' policy-coordination between member states rather than the supranational dimension of EU decision-making.[2] The assessment of modes and repertoires of policy coordination in Canadian, Swiss, and U.S. federalism and the EU will indicate in how far patterns of policy coordination are not only directly comparable using the same analytical categories but can also be accounted for by the same theoretical framework.[3]

European multilevel governance: cooperative or dual federalism?

The literature on multilevel governance has already brought forward fruitful attempts to link federalism perspectives and perspectives on European governance. These works can help us to specify core commonalities and differences and thereby substantiate why the four cases Canada, Switzerland, the United States, and EU are actually a good starting-point for analysing the various modes of policy coordination applied in each. Drawing on Hooghe and Marks, the EU belongs in the category of 'Type I of multilevel governance' characterized by general-purpose jurisdictions (2003: 236–7) as do Canada, Switzerland, and the United States. All four systems have a durable jurisdictional architecture in which competences are bundled and distributed in packages to the constituent governments. As we have seen in the U.S. case study, what the 'carriers' of these competences – intergovernmental actors– make out of this formal constellation is a different matter. The United States, with its predominantly issue-specific and functionally driven intergovernmental processes, deviates clearly from both Canada and Switzerland. While Canadian and Swiss IGR reflect their basic architecture along general-purpose jurisdictions dealing with policy in sectoral or cross-sectoral packages, the United States resembles in its practical working what Hooghe and Marks called 'Type 2 of multilevel governance' characterized by task-specific jurisdictions, multiple jurisdictional levels, and high flexibility (2003: 237–9; see also Hoornbeek 2004). This notable discrepancy of the U.S. case brings us back to the initial distinction between formal–legal framework and the nature of intergovernmental processes. Assuming that the internal nature of lower level governments affects the repertoire of policy coordination in multilevel setting more generally, we face the challenge to assess how intragovernmental relations affect policy coordination in the EU.

[2] See Sbragia (1993) for a systematic discussion of the intergovernmental or supranational character of the individual EU institutions. See Christiansen and Reh (2009) for a study on the constitutionalization of the EU.

[3] The following application draws on Bolleyer and Börzel (2007).

The formal classification of the EU polity as 'Type 1 of multilevel governance' implies that the EU can be in principle compared to any federal system since they share basic characteristics. But there are many types of federalism and a variety of proposals have been put forward about the most appropriate federal system to draw lessons from about the working or the evolution of European integration with no final answer in sight. As a general complication for any of these approaches, the EU has a much weaker centre and much stronger 'subunits' than most federal systems (Moravcsik 2001: 165; Bartolini 2005). From this perspective, federal systems with strong lower level governments such as Canada, Switzerland, and the United States seem to provide the most reasonable standard for comparison since they come closest to how power is distributed in the EU (see Chapter 2 for indicators capturing legislative and fiscal strength of lower level governments in the three systems).

The strong position of lower level governments in the three federal systems and, correspondingly, the member states in the EU also mitigates another difference between the four cases related to the particular type of federalism. Given a rather functional division of competences, in which the member states are responsible for the execution of EU laws, and the strong territorial representation in the Council of the European Union, the dynamics in the EU are often considered to resemble cooperative federalism in Germany rather than Canada, Switzerland, or United States, which in formal terms correspond more strongly to the dual federal model (Scharpf 1988; Börzel and Hösli 2003; Börzel 2005*a*). While this perspective emphasizes an important dimension of the interplay between the European and the member-state level, it tends to overlook the following. Even in highly Europeanized policy areas, the member states have far greater levy in implementing EU policies than the German *Länder* in administering federal laws. More importantly, and this brings us to the dual federal model as alternative template, the member states have retained comprehensive legislative powers. Vice versa, there remain a significant number of policy areas in which the EU has only limited competences (e.g. external security and welfare state policies). Finally, exclusive EU competences are scarce (external trade and currency), and in areas of shared competences the member states maintain their rights to enact national legislation, as long as it conforms to EU law (for the evolution of the competence distribution see Börzel 2005*b*). Thus, the legislative activities of the member states are by far more multifaceted than the model of cooperative federalism implies. Correspondingly, the lower level governments in our three federal systems engage in much more far-fetching tasks than the implementation of national policies as we have seen in Chapters 3 through 7. Given a focus on modes of policy coordination, especially the non-hierarchical, voluntary varieties (which are not centrally imposed), the comparison of four multilevel systems with lower level governments with wide legislative powers and strong fiscal resources seems to be most appropriate. In all four systems, lower level governments have wide leeway to introduce and apply the modes of policy coordination preferable to them which brings us back to the initial interest of the book stressing the crucial role of institutional choice when trying to understand federal, or more generally, multilevel dynamics.

If the framework presented in Chapter 2 holds, the modes the member states choose to coordinate their actions should be affected by the degree and type of power sharing in them. All member states are parliamentary systems which fuse executive and legislative power. They are either characterized by voluntary power-sharing (coalition governments) or, to a far lesser degree, by power concentration (one-party cabinets) (for the degree to which power is concentrated across individual countries see Lijphart 1999; and Blondel, Müller-Rommel, and Malova 2007). This leads us to a first problem which complicates capturing multilevel dynamics in the EU: The member states are not homogeneous in their degree of power sharing like the lower level governments in our three federal systems (and most federal systems in general) – an additional source of complexity which is often overlooked when comparing the EU to federal systems. While the first core hypothesis – presupposing one overall level of institutionalization equally favoured by all governments constituting a system – cannot be applied unambiguously, it still allows the formulation of systematic expectations. The hypothesis implies that most of the member states should be more willing to enter binding agreements than the power-concentrating Canadian provinces. Thus, cooperation-undermining tendencies, such as a strong orientation towards autonomy protection, should occasionally be triggered by individual member-states but not undermine the overall willingness of member states to enter legally binding agreements.

Moving on to Hypothesis 2, the member states share that none of them is characterized by compulsory power-sharing, which sets the EU apart from the United States. In absence of the fragmenting impact of compulsory power-sharing on the integration of IGR, voluntary power-sharing and power-concentrating member-states should be more effective in representing their territorial interests at the central level than the American states. Consequently, they should be able to generate voluntary commitment and engage in non-hierarchical policy-coordination. In sum, policy coordination in the EU should most closely resemble Switzerland. We should find an overall willingness on the part of member states to enter legally binding agreements as well as the capacity to engage in non-hierarchical coordination modes constituting a broad repertoire of instruments for cross-jurisdictional policy-coordination.

Evidently, we are looking at the EU in a stylized fashion insofar as we consider the member-state level as the 'lower level' in this multilevel system comparable to the regional level in federal systems. As we widely ignored the local level in the analysis of the three federal systems in the analyses, for reasons of parsimony, we now leave aside the regional level within the member states when looking at the EU. A more complete analysis of the EU would need to consider further levels, which, however, goes beyond the possibilities of this suggestive application. Yet despite the necessary analytical reduction of the EU to a 'two-level' system, the following section will show there are lessons to learn from the application of the given 'federalism framework'. The high level of abstraction might even help to highlight some of the core dynamics more clearly.

Territorial representation and policy coordination in multilevel systems

Since Hypothesis 2 can be applied more directly, we deal with its implications for policy coordination in the EU first. The focus in the section rests on the impact on the type of power-sharing in lower level (or member-state) governments on the way they represent their territorial interests vis-à-vis the central (or European) level. As the U.S. case indicated, the incapacity of lower level governments to represent territorial interests in a coherent manner (both individually and collectively) as rooted in compulsory power-sharing negatively affected the states' capacity to enter voluntary yet politically binding agreements. To put it differently, the lack of integration within the individual states and the state level undermined (institutionally channeled) voluntary policy-coordination.[4] Put in this comparative framework, the EU occurs as a particularly interesting case due to its mixed character. While compulsory power-sharing is indeed absent within the member states (on the lower level), compulsory power-sharing is dominant on the EU level (the central level). Although the prior focus of this book rests on the internal nature of lower level, thus, member-state governments and its impact on policy coordination with other jurisdictions, the external relations of the 'centre' in the international arena should be equally affected by the degree and type of power sharing inherent in central level institutions. Table 8.3 illustrates this mixed character of the EU as compared to the three federal systems which show the same incentive structures on both the national and regional level. The shaded areas indicate which governments or governmental levels can be expected to assure territorial representation in their 'external relations' due to the absence of compulsory power-sharing. The white areas indicate the latter's presence. In case of the EU, the table sums up which patterns of territorial representation to expect as a result – in EU-external relations (given compulsory power-sharing on the EU level) and in EU-internal relations (given the respective intragovernmental relations in the member states).

Since the focus rests on policy coordination within each multilevel system, here only a brief summary of the patterns on the 'upper level' shaping each polity's external relations: When comparing the 'upper level' in all four polities (the nature of national level institutions in the federal systems and of institutions on the EU level), the capacity to represent territorial interests coherently in the international arena should vary with the presence and absence of compulsory power-sharing. As Table 8.3 indicates, due to the constitutional fragmentation on the 'central level', the EU and the United States should both find it difficult to speak with one voice and act coherently in their 'external relations'.

---

[4] Note that institutionally unmediated coordination (e.g. memoranda of understanding directly mediated by executive or administrative actors) are not considered here.

TABLE 8.3. *Types of power sharing and territorial representation*

	United States	EU	Switzerland	Canada
Type of power sharing: Upper level	Compulsory power-sharing Fragmentation	Compulsory power-sharing Fragmentation	Voluntary power-sharing No fragmentation	Power concentration No fragmentation
Representation of upper level in external relations	Divided	Divided	Unified	Unified
Type of power sharing: Lower level	Compulsory power-sharing Fragmentation	Voluntary power-sharing or power concentration No fragmentation	Voluntary power-sharing No fragmentation	Power concentration No fragmentation
Territorial representation of lower level units (formal or informal institutions)	No	Yes	Yes	Yes
	Senate: territorial interests not dominant	Council of the EU/European Council: territorial interests dominant	Senate: territorial interests not dominant	Senate: territorial interests not dominant
	Also: Fragmentation of intergovernmental representation along government branches and functions	*Also*: Intergovernmental bodies inside (Open Method of Coordination) and outside (European Political Cooperation, till 1986, Bologna) the EU	*Yet*: Conference of Cantonal Executives and Conferences of Directors	*Yet*: Council of the Federation, FMC, and Ministerial Councils

Note: Shaded areas indicate governments' capacity to assure territorial representation of respective governments' 'external relations' due to the absence of compulsory power-sharing.

By contrast, this should be far less problematic for Switzerland and Canada, which are characterized by voluntary power-sharing and power concentration, respectively. The literature tends to support this argument implying similar patterns in U.S. and EU foreign relations. Due to its fragmenting impact, compulsory power-sharing on the EU level between the European Commission, the Council, and the Parliament should complicate the representation of coherent territorial interests. Indeed, it has often been pointed out that the EU's external relations suffer from serious fragmentation. Trade-related issues are dealt with under the auspices of the European Commission in the First Pillar, while security and defence are still the *domaine reservée* of the member states and subject to intergovernmental decision-making under the Second Pillar. Since policies usually have both an economic and a political dimension, problems of 'cross-pillarization' often arise. This has increased the 'capacity–expectations gap', which has plagued the EU's external relations (Hill 1993). U.S. foreign policy is characterized by similar problems of fragmentation with the President, the National Security Council, the State Department, and the Pentagon representing only the most prominent players (Risse-Kappen 1991).

Building up on the above-analysis of the three federal systems, the main interest rests on the lower part of Table 8.3 which sums up the character of intragovernmental relations in the lower level governments constitutive for the four multilevel systems and indicates whether one would expect a fragmenting effect flowing from them. As an indication of the actual patterns of representation, it lists the formal and informal institutions constructed for or meant to assure collective territorial interest representation of lower level governments vis-à-vis the central level. They indicate whether lower level governments make active efforts to speak with coherent voices and how they try to assure the representation of their collective interests by setting up particular types of IGAs, which often also facilitate self-coordination between them.[5] Thus, we arrived from where we started, the analysis of IGAs and will move on to their functional equivalents in the EU.

Talking about territorial representation in federal systems, wide parts of the literature tend to look at the second chamber of the federal legislature which is usually considered as *the* channel for representation of territorial interests of lower level governments at the national level. This presupposes, however, that lower level governments are represented in this chamber by their executives as already laid out in Chapter 2. This is neither the case in the American, Swiss nor Canadian Senate, whose members are directly elected or appointed and therefore mostly dominated by partisan interests. Thus, this line of argument does not get us very far when trying to capture channels of territorial representation or to account for the differences across informal intergovernmental institutions as Table 8.3 re-emphasizes. We still need to come back to this debate since the Council of the European Union and the European Council represent member-state governments (ministers or prime ministers). As Sbragia (1993) argues convincingly, as a consequence of the structure of these institutions, compared to federal systems, the territorial representation of member-state interests is particularly strong in the EU. However, thinking about non-hierarchical modes of policy coordination, the Council of the European Union and the European Council do not only provide a powerful representation of territorial interests at the central level, but also serve as arenas of horizontal policy-coordination among

---

[5] Whether they are actually heard, that is, whether their interests are taken into account by the central level or coordination efforts are successful is a different question. However, as Chapter 7 indicated, there is a link between a given infrastructure and the outcomes in terms of intergovernmental agreements.

the member states. We find intergovernmental bodies inside (e.g. the Open Method of Coordination) and outside (e.g. European Political Cooperation, till 1986, Bologna) the EU framework, as well as mechanisms of 'horizontal coordination' between member-state governments unmediated by supranational institutions. The latter mechanisms correspond directly to IGAs such as the Conference of Cantonal Executives and the Council of the Federation within federal systems which provide alternative, more flexible channels of territorial interest representation and policy coordination than the formal participation in national or central decision-making. Despite the presence of a central institution assuring territorial representation, IGAs for voluntary cross-jurisdictional policy-coordination are set up successfully *in addition*. A similar situation exists in Germany, where *Länder* executives are represented in the *Bundesrat*,[6] while *Länder* premiers and officials are active in informal institutions for voluntary cross-jurisdictional coordination such as the Conference of *Länder* Premiers (Scharpf 2005; Bolleyer and Bytzek 2009).

In sum, Table 8.3 implies that the nature of the second chamber involved in central-level decision-making does not tell a lot about the nature of channels set up to coordinate in spheres of competences dominated by lower level governments, neither in federal systems, nor in the EU. The nature of their executive–legislative relations in interacting governments, however, seems to shape their capacity to handle coordination pressure through less formalized modes of interaction. In particular, the presence of compulsory power-sharing on both governmental levels of the United States as well as the 'central level' of the EU weakens this capacity. Despite the U.S. Senate's weakness in terms of territorial representation, states were not able to establish informal institutions which would have effectively supported voluntary policy-coordination and the use of formal interstate compacts is rarely achieved. In Canada, Switzerland, and the EU, by contrast, the absence of compulsory power-sharing allows for territorial representation – although Canada and Switzerland represent most different cases regarding the degree of power sharing in their lower level governments and the EU member-states are a mix of the two. The *absence of compulsory power-sharing* allows for the representation of individual lower level governments as coherent units within all three multilevel systems. Although IGAs are institutionalized to a very different extent in Canada and Switzerland and collective activities are less effective in the former than the latter, in both systems lower level executives can speak on behalf of their governments in the intergovernmental arena.

While it is widely acknowledged in European studies that territorial interest representation is strong on the EU level due to the Council, Table 8.3 has interesting implications for the comparative study of multilevel systems. First, it is the United States, not the EU, which deviates in terms of a lower level representation in the four multilevel systems. This finding reconfirms that an

---

[6] Note that this construction of a second chamber in, contrast to the Senate model, forms an exception among the long-lasting federal systems.

analysis of the EU by using tools developed in comparative federalism is fruitful (e.g. Sbragia 1993; McKay 2001). We might gain more by starting out from the parallels between national, intergovernmental, and supranational multilevel regimes than by engaging in 'sui generis' debates of some sort. Second, the theoretical framework highlights the effects of different types of power sharing on the two core governmental levels constituting the European polity which, with its help, can be specified and disentangled. Depending on the point of reference, the European level, or the member-state level, the EU most closely resembles either the United States or, alternatively, Switzerland. Doubtlessly, the EU remains a peculiar mix of elements. Yet each of these elements can, once disentangled, be comparatively studied. Thus, using the abstract notion of the type of power sharing capturing intragovernmental relations dominant on different governmental levels as analytical tool allows us to deconstruct the EU's mixed character and analyse its consequences in a systematic way to, hopefully, arrive at the end at a more complete picture.

The internal life of lower level governments and modes of policy coordination

Having discussed the implications of the type of power sharing in lower level and central governments for territorial representation, this section looks at the interplay of the strong representation of territorial interests (due to the absence of compulsory power-sharing) and the dominance of voluntary power-sharing governments (instead of power concentration) within the EU member-states. This final section contrasts the internal dynamics in the four systems' lower level governments and its consequences for modes of policy coordination applied by them. Taking the implications of the dominant type (Hypothesis 2) and degree of power sharing (Hypothesis 1) together, the repertoire of institutionally supported policy-coordination modes used by the EU member-states can be expected to be broad. While modes of voluntary policy-coordination are available as laid out above, unlike the power-concentrating Canadian provinces, member states should be open to enter collectively binding agreements as well.

Albeit applicable to IGAs fulfilling different types of functions, not only policy coordination,[7] the categories used to capture the dominant interaction mode in the three federal systems widely overlap with categories introduced to characterize policy coordination in the European polity (Scharpf 2001: 4–9; Börzel 2007).[8] Both sets of categories evolve along the *relative constraints on individual government action* imposed on individual participants as the main

---

[7] For instance, we found co-decision in Switzerland and the United States, yet only in the former context IGAs were strongly involved in policy coordination.

[8] Note the focus on coordination modes channelled through collective arrangements. Unmediated ad hoc coordination between individual governors or premiers leading, for instance, to memoranda of understanding is not considered.

ordering dimension.[9] Simply put, in order to solve boundary-crossing problems, lower level governments can choose between modes of policy coordination that leave governments next to no leeway for individual action, or those that grant them maximum autonomy. Thus, in a final conceptual step, the two schemes are brought together to assess policy coordination in multilevel systems within and beyond the nation state.

The most 'collectivist answer' to coordination challenges is *centralized decision-making* based on hierarchical coordination. In the analysis of federal systems above with its focus on the interaction of lower level governments, this has not been a major focus. *National policy-making* in federal systems and *supranational centralization* and *joint decision-making by qualified majority voting* in the EU belong in this category. Lower level governments decide to delegate the power to make collective policies to the central level, be it to national agencies or legislatures. Although they might participate indirectly or directly in central and supranational decision-making processes, they do not have an individual veto. As a result, lower level governments can be bound without their consent and against their individual opposition. The clearest expression of this situation occurs in federal systems in which the second chamber is de facto controlled by the federal executive as in the Canadian situation. Centralized decision-making is also present in the EU despite the fact that the member states are still the 'Masters of the Treaties', thus treaty negotiations operate under unanimity. Leaving constitutional change aside, the European Commission has – like any national executive – been empowered by the member states to make authoritative decisions, for example, in competition policy, in which the member states have no say. The same is true for decisions of the European Central Bank (monetary policy) and rulings of the European Court of Justice (the entire First Pillar). Next to supranational centralization, individual member-states can also be obliged against their will when the Council decides by qualified majority and they are outvoted (supranational joint decision-making by qualified majority voting).

Moving on to the next less constraining mode, in *joint decision-making*, each participating government retains a veto. These decisions are legally binding either for all those governments which are willing to agree (consensus) or if all governments in the system agree (unanimity). No lower level government can be bound to new provisions without its consent. As we have seen in the Swiss and American case studies, we find legally binding intergovernmental agreements, such as concordats or interstate compact which can be struck in areas of lower level competence. Once governments have entered these, they are legally enforceable. Any infringements can be brought before a court. The corresponding mode we find in EU decision-making under the First Pillar when European laws are adopted

---

[9] The classification as laid out in Table 8.4 is based on Bolleyer and Börzel (2007).

by the Community Method. Laws are passed with unanimity of member-state governments in the European Council without a veto of the European Parliament as supranational chamber. At the same time, however, these laws can be made subject to review by the European Court of Justice.

Non-enforceable joint decision-making under the Second and Third Pillar is different and constitutes a mode one does not find in federal systems. The member states can unanimously agree on external and internal security policies, which are legally binding. However, these agreements lack the supranational nature of decisions taken under the First Pillar, that is, Council decisions are neither supreme to national law nor do they have direct effect. They are not subject to the judicial review of the European Court of Justice. If member states refrain from transposing them into national law, litigation before national courts is not possible either. In other words, intergovernmental agreements adopted in the area of Common Foreign and Security Policy, European Defense Policy, and Justice and Home Affairs provide member states with an exit option since there is no third-party authority that can *legally* force them into compliance. Here, the EU functions like any international organization whose decisions need to be ratified at the domestic level in order to come into force.[10] The Second and Third Pillars constitute a considerable area of intergovernmental policy-coordination in the EU. Therefore, this separate category is included although it has no equivalent in federal states. It emphasizes a feature of the EU which is systematically distinct from national multilevel systems given its origin as international organization operating in a space in which legally binding treaties without effective legal enforcement are rather the rule. In federal states, by contrast, legal enforcement can be taken as a given. The monopoly of power assures that, within the national sphere, legally binding intergovernmental treaties are also enforceable.

With *intergovernmental collaboration*, we arrive at political agreements that are neither legally binding nor legally enforceable, a category which covers both co-decision and ad hoc coordination as observed in federal systems. As Chapter 7 indicated, the relative capacity of informed agreements to bind individual lower level governments is affected by the relative institutionalization and integration of IGAs. In Switzerland, highly institutionalized IGAs assure *co-decision*, regularized processes of cross-jurisdictional coordination leading to precise and substantial agreements in core areas of cantonal competence. *Ad hoc coordination* leading to rather vague and less reliable agreements was the dominant practice among the autonomy-striving Canadian provinces operating within weakly institutionalized IGAs. These two categories correspond to those areas in the EU where the Open Method of Coordination is applied, such as labour

---

[10] Exceptions are countries with a monistic legal culture according to which international law can take direct effect.

or health policy, where the member states wish to cooperate without transferring competences to the EU.[11]

Finally, *policy emulation* is the mode of policy coordination which restricts the authority of individual governments the least. It refers to the voluntary and unilateral adoption of measures observed in other jurisdictions as a result of learning processes without direct interaction between government units.

Table 8.4 sums up the modes of policy coordination structurally supported in each of the four multilevel systems. It further indicates which types of agreements the governments in each multilevel system are able to generate. Drawing on the second core hypothesis of the book specifying the impact of compulsory power-sharing, one core aspect refers to whether institutions support governments to enter collective commitments able to bind the individual participants on a voluntary basis. A further issue is the presence and actual use of legal mechanisms for cross-jurisdictional policy-coordination. Compulsory power-sharing undermines territorial interest representation. It diminishes the repertoire because the absence of government units assuring territorial representation and formulating a collective interest between them renders policy coordination difficult. With power-concentrating governments, we should find the opposite. While lower level governments are capable of speaking with coherent voices, their repertoire of policy coordination remains narrow because they fear autonomy losses incurred by legally binding and enforceable agreements between them. As a result, they engage solely in voluntary policy-coordination. Voluntary power-sharing in lower level governments, by contrast, ensures effective territorial representation, while autonomy losses are minor since lower level governments are already sharing power internally. Therefore the repertoire of coordination modes is expected to be broadest.

Table 8.4 indicates that due to the pervasiveness of compulsory power-sharing, the United States is the only system incapable of generating support structures for collective commitment among states and the centre without resorting to legally binding and enforceable agreements. Canada, by contrast, is the only system without legally binding and enforceable instruments of interprovincial or central–provincial cooperation. The strong orientation towards autonomy protection of the power-concentrating Canadian provinces has so far precluded the introduction of such a mechanism through constitutional reform. Instead, the central and lower level governments enter informal agreements, which are voluntary and ad hoc in nature. As indicated by the theoretical framework, Switzerland and the EU end up as most similar. Both display a wide repertoire of modes of policy coordination. Both engage more intensively in joint decision-making than the United States, where the set-up and ratification of interstate compacts fails regularly. The EU member-states heavily rely on non-enforceable joint decision-making which is legally binding. This mode combines a certain level of effectiveness without imposing too many constraints on the participating member states. In Switzerland,

---

[11] In line with the common terminology in the EU literature informal agreements are called soft law in Table 8.4.

TABLE 8.4. *Modes of policy coordination in four multilevel polities*

Repertoire	United States	EU	Switzerland	Canada
Centralized decision-making (legally binding and enforceable)	Narrow National policy-making (national law): a. Authoritative decisions of national courts, regulatory agencies, and President b. National laws adopted by bicameral legislature	Broad Supranational centralization and supranational joint decision-making by qualified majority (European law): a. Authoritative decisions of European Court of Justice, European Central Bank, and European Commission b. European laws adopted by Community Method under co-decision (initiative Commission only, veto of European Parliament, majority rule in Council, and European Court of Justice has judicial review [First Pillar])	Broad National policy-making (national law): a. Authoritative decisions of national courts, regulatory agencies, and national executive (legislative veto infrequent) b. National laws adopted by bicameral legislature	Narrow National policy-making (national law): a. Authoritative decisions of national courts, regulatory agencies, and national executive (legislative veto unlikely) b. National laws adopted by bicameral legislature
Joint decision-making (legally binding and enforceable)	Yes Interstate Compacts adopted by state and central governments by consensus; implicit consent of Congress, ratification by state legislatures (veto credible threat), subject to judicial review	Yes European laws adopted by Community Method with unanimity of member-state governments in Council and no veto of European Parliament; and European Court of Justice has judicial review (First Pillar)	Yes Inter-cantonal Concordats adopted by cantonal governments by consensus (parliamentary ratification and/or referendum) from 2008 onwards: new instruments of inter-cantonal cooperation applied by super-majority of cantons	No

Rational Choices in Federal Systems and Beyond   223

TABLE 8.4. (Continued)

	United States	EU	Switzerland	Canada
Non-enforceable joint decision-making (legally binding and not enforceable)	No	Yes Initiative Council only or shared with Commission, unanimity in Council, European Parliament only informed or consulted; European Court of Justice has no judicial review (Second and Third Pillars); and Stability and Growth Pact (sanctions adopted by qualified majority of member-state governments)	No	No
Intergovernmental collaboration (legally non-binding and non-enforceable)	No	Yes *Open Method of Coordination*: EuroGroup; Bologna process; agreement on legally non-binding goals by unanimity of member states (no formal role of Commission, European Parliament, and European Court of Justice); and peer review (areas which are not or hardly Europeanized: labour, employment, social policy, public health, industry, culture, and education)	Yes *Co-decision in highly institutionalized IGAs*: Soft law adopted by unanimity or super-majority by Cantonal governments in Conference of Cantonal Executives or Conferences of Directors (main policy fields of cantonal competences) *Ad hoc coordination in weakly institutionalized IGAs*: Soft law adopted by unanimity in weakly developed Conferences of Directors (minor policy fields)	*Ad hoc coordination in loose arrangements*: Soft law adopted by consensus by Provincial Governments in Council of the Federation, FMCs, or Ministerial Councils
Policy-emulation/unilateral adaptation	Policy-emulation by individual governments	Policy-emulation by individual governments	Policy-emulation by individual governments	Policy-emulation by individual governments

Note: The shaded areas indicate horizontal policy-coordination without participation of federal government. Also note that the table focuses on institutionally supported modes of coordination.

no such option exists. A legally binding status is tied to legal enforcement. Thus, when concordats seem too constraining, cantons engage in intergovernmental collaboration in the form of co-decision within highly institutionalized IGAs, a mode which is entirely political. With the introduction of the Open Method of Coordination also the EU has made more extensive use of fully voluntary, intergovernmental collaboration. However, given its limited effectiveness compared to the legally binding modes, the Open Method is unlikely to reach the same prominence as joint decision-making.

What is peculiar about the EU is that unlike in the three federal systems, the Council serves as an arena for both vertical and horizontal policy-coordination. It plays a core role in central-level decision-making as well as in purely intergovernmental collaboration processes. This variegated use of the Council roots in the pillarized structure of the EU. While in the First Pillar the supranational components (the Commission, the European Parliament, and the European Court of Justice) are rather strong, they have hardly any role to play in the Second and Third Pillars where the Council is the exclusive legislator. Thus, the member states largely draw on the Council structure to coordinate their policies even when adopting legally non-binding agreements. The pillarized structure also accounts for another peculiarity of the EU which brings us to the mode of non-enforceable joint decision-making absent in our national multilevel systems. In the area of external and internal security, the EU still functions more like a traditional international organization. Member-state governments adopt legally binding decisions by unanimity, which are, however, not legally enforceable. The European Court of Justice has no power over decisions taken by the member states under the Second and Third Pillar (see above). The Treaties may provide monitoring and sanctioning mechanisms. However, any enforcement measure requires at least the consent of the majority of the member-state governments. The absence of a third-party dispute settlement body provides the member states with an exit option in the post-decision stage, which lower level governments in federal states do not have. This may explain why even autonomy-minded, one-party governments, like the United Kingdom, are willing to enter this type of legally binding agreements as an 'in-between solution'.

When entering non-binding intergovernmental agreements, member-state governments enter political commitments and create soft law and recommendations to coordinate policy, albeit to a lesser extent than the Swiss cantons. Within the EU, even voluntary coordination of member-state competences is put on formal grounds and is clearly specified for particular areas of competence in order to avoid a dynamic of 'creeping competences' (Pollack 1994). Even though the Open Method of Coordination does not entail any legal obligations, the member-state governments have made it quite clear that any policy coordination, also in an exclusively horizontal mode, requires some sort of authorization by the member states.[12] This mode is thought to prevent the European Commission from

---

[12] The Open Method of Coordination has been introduced in various policy areas by decision of the European Council. It is mentioned for the first time in the Amsterdam Treaty. The Reform Treaty

expanding its activities into sensitive areas, in which the member states want to coordinate their policies without transferring competences to the EU level. Cantonal governments follow the same rationale when engaging in horizontal policy-coordination. Co-decision among the cantons leading to the effective, collective handling of cross-jurisdictional problems prevents the federal government to interfere in cantonal competences through central regulation. In contrast to modes of intergovernmental collaboration in the EU, however, the infrastructure stabilizing these cooperation processes between the cantons lacks any formal grounds. The stronger tendency in the EU to create such formal grounds is most likely related to its status as a multilevel system 'in the making'. In contrast to long-lasting federal systems, it faces the challenge to develop a reliable institutional context in the first place – for whatever type of interaction its member governments might go for, ranging from centralized decision-making to voluntary, intergovernmental collaboration. The Swiss actors, by contrast, operate within the same constitution for decades. The level of insecurity is much lower. While constitutional reforms indeed have taken place in Switzerland, they were far less extensive than the series of treaty negotiations shaping the nature of a constantly evolving European polity, negotiations which led to the formation of a new rather than the change of an already established polity.

Reasons of efficiency played their part as well. More constraining modes of policy coordination tend to generate compliance more reliably. In fact, Swiss federalism moved towards more formalized modes of collective decision-making among the cantons reinforcing the parallels between the European and the Swiss cases. As mentioned in Chapter 4, a reform passed in 2004 established 'new instruments of inter-cantonal cooperation' applicable in nine areas of cantonal jurisdiction which are both legally binding and enforceable.[13] These instruments established an enforcement mechanism that can impose intergovernmental agreements supported by a majority of cantons on an opposing minority. Since then, a supermajority of cantons can ask the national parliament – who plays the role of a neutral arbiter – to make an inter-cantonal agreement obligatory for an opposing cantonal minority. A major reason was the limited efficiency of former efforts to set up concordats which often failed because individual cantonal blocked them. In such cases, intergovernmental collaboration, the less constraining alternative, was equally unsatisfying since those cantons blocking a concordat are equally hard to bind by political agreements. These instruments transcend joint decision-making in terms of centralization insofar they abolish an individual veto of each government and thereby strengthen the role of the cantonal level as collective actor. At the same time, they do not correspond to the centralized mode

is to provide this mechanism with a comprehensive legal base defining it as a proper mode of policy coordination and specifying the areas to which it may apply.

[13] Among them competences regarding cantonal universities, hospitals, cultural facilities of over-regional relevance, and crime control.

equivalent to national decision-making or supranational decision-making in the EU since neither the federal parliament nor any other central-level institution has independent decision-making power in this process. By inventing these new mechanisms, the cantons tried to reconfigure the balance between individual government autonomy and collective commitment, while avoiding the centralization of competences. This balancing act underlies any effort to assure effective decision-making between governments embedded in a multilevel setting without completely compromising government autonomy. Cantonal governments and EU member-states share the willingness to compromise autonomy to considerable extents to increase their collective problem-solving capacity which is by no means a matter of course.

FINAL REMARKS

This final observation brings us back to the initial question of this book: why governments establish such diverse structures to deal with boundary-crossing problems. In the course of eight chapters, the nature of intragovernmental relations was identified as a driving force, which shapes the institution-building and cooperation strategies governments choose in multilevel settings. The willingness and capacity of lower level governments to oppose central encroachment are essential to understand the power distribution in a system and its long-term evolution. At the same time, the challenge to coordinate policies in a non-hierarchical manner is important to maintain and justify those structures dispersing power – particularly in an age in which problems increasingly cross jurisdictional boundaries pressing for collective problem-solving. The concluding comparison of European multilevel governance with federal processes can only provide a first sketch of the variety of ways through which policy can be coordinated across jurisdictions within and beyond the nation state. The inventiveness of intergovernmental actors in addressing the tension between effective decision-making and maintaining the power dispersion to multiple governments as visible in Switzerland illustrates the challenges scholars face when trying to systematically account for strategies of collective problem-solving. Once having grasped and classified the range of established coordination mechanisms, intergovernmental actors might have invented new ones in the meantime. Nonetheless, we do not get around comparing and, with it, around creating concepts that are able to travel contexts. The final chapter tried to demonstrate the usefulness of analytical tools applicable within and beyond the nation state. Not only do they help to obtain a structured overview over various ways in which governments interact. They also help to pin down core conditions that facilitate or undermine the use of particular instruments. The range of available instruments to generate government compliance through collective commitment is important since it has immediate practical consequences for the problem-solving capacity of multilevel systems.

Facing pressure both to decentralize and to globalize, multilevel systems grow in number and complexity, which highlights the need for innovative comparative research. Responding to these parallel developments, a considerable number of scholars started out from the analysis of domestic politics and 'moved up' to study the EU and thereby link the two (e.g. Sbragia 1993; Hooghe and Marks 2001; McKay 2001; Nicolaidis and Howse 2001; Kelemen 2004; Benz and Papadopoulos 2006; Schmidt 2006). This book profited immensely from these works and in its final chapter, it has tried to show that in placing the EU among a range of federal systems, it does not necessarily end up as the 'odd case'. Such comparisons may not and need not lead to the negation of peculiarities. Yet they prevent us from taking these peculiarities as a premise. They help us to identify similarities and differences between the EU and national federal systems, similarities and differences as filtered through the chosen theoretical lens. The theoretical lens proposed in this book has tried to balance two conflicting goals – generalization and specificity – constituting a tension that never fully vanishes. To reach an 'appropriate' balance is and will remain a challenge for any type of comparative work – be it on federal systems or other phenomena. Each balancing act, and this is true for this study as much as for any other, necessarily generates its own virtues and weaknesses.

References

Abbott, K. W., Keohane, R. O., Movravcsik, A., Slaughter, A.-M., and Snidal, D. (2000). The concept of legalization. *International Organization* 54, 401–19.

Abderhalden, U. (1999). *Möglichkeiten und Grenzen der interkantonalen Zusammenarbeit.* Freiburg: Universitätsverlag.

Adamovich, I. B. and Hosp, G. (2003). Fiscal federalism for emerging economies: lessons from Switzerland? *Publius: The Journal of Federalism* 33(1), 1–21.

Agranoff, R. (Ed.) (1999a). *Accomodating Diversity: Asymmetry in Federal States.* Baden-Baden: Nomos.

—— (1999b). Intergovernmental relations and the management of asymmetry in federal Spain. In Agranoff, R. (Ed.), *Accomodating Diversity: Asymmetry in Federal States.* Baden-Baden: Nomos.

—— (2004). Autonomy, devolution, and intergovernmental relations. *Regional and Federal Studies* 14, 26–65.

Armingeon, K. (2000a). Swiss federalism in comparative perspective. In Wachendorfer-Schmidt, U. (Ed.), *Federalism and Political Performance.* London: Routledge.

—— (2000b). Corporatism and consociational democracy. In Keman, H. (Ed.), *Comparative Politics, New Directions in Theory and Method.* London: Routledge.

—— (2002). The effects of negotiation democracy. A comparative analysis. *European Journal of Political Research* 41, 81–101.

Arnold, D. S. and Plant, J. (1994). *Public Official Associations and State and Local Government.* Fairfax: George Mason University Press.

Auel, K. (2005). Introduction: Europeanisation of parliamentary democracy. *Journal of Legislative Studies* 11, 303–18.

—— and Benz, A. (2007). Expanding national parliamentary control: does it enhance European democracy? In Kohler-Koch, B. and Rittberger, B. (Eds.), *Debating the Democratic Legitimicy of the European Union.* Lanham: Rowan and Littlefield.

Axelrod, R. M. (1984). *The Evolution of Cooperation.* New York: Basic Books.

Bache, I. and Flinders, M. (Eds.) (2004). *Multi-Level Governance.* Oxford: Oxford University Press.

Bächtiger, A. and Hitz, A. (2006). The matrix extended: federal–municipal relations in switzerland. In Lazar, H. and Leuprecht, C. (Eds.), *Spheres of Governance: Comparative Studies of Cities in Multilevel Governance Systems.* Kingston: McGill-Queen's University Press.

Baier, G. (2002). New judicial thinking on sovereignty and federalism: American and Canadian comparisons. *The Justice System Journal* 23.

Banting, K. and Corbett, S. (Eds.) (2001). *Health Policy and Federalism: A Comparative Perspective on Multi-level Governance.* Kingston: Queen's University Press.

Bardach, E. (1998). *Getting Agencies Work Together: The Practice and Theory of Managerial Craftsmanship.* Washington, D.C.: Brookings Institution Press.

Bartolini, S. (2005). *Restructuring Europe: Centre Formation, System Building and Political Structuring between the Nation-State and the European Union.* Oxford: Oxford University Press.

References

Benz, A. (1985). *Föderalismus als dynamisches System, Zentralisierung und Dezentralisierung im föderativen Staat.* Opladen: Westdeutscher Verlag.

—— (2000). Anmerkungen zur Diskussion über Verhandlungsdemokratie. In Holtmann, H. (Ed.), *Zwischen Wettbewerbs- und Verhandlungsdemokratie. Analysen zum Regierungssystem der Bundesrepublik Deutschland.* Wiesbaden: Westdeutscher Verlag.

—— (2003). Konstruktive Vetospieler in Mehrebenensystemen. In Mayntz, R. S. and Streek, W. (Eds.), *Die Reformierbarkeit der Demokratie, Innovationen und Blockaden.* Frankfurt/New York: Campus.

—— (2004a). Multilevel Governance: Governance in Mehrebenensystemen. In Benz, A. (Ed.), *Governance: Regieren in komplexen Regelsystemen.* Wiesbaden: VS Verlag für Sozialwissenschaften.

—— (2004b). Institutionelle Regime in Bundesstaaten und in der Europäischen Union. In Marschall, S. and Struenck. C. (Eds.), *Grenzenlose Macht? Politik und Politikwissenschaft im Umbruch.* Baden-Baden: Nomos.

—— and Papadopoulos, Y. (Eds.) (2006). *Governance and Democracy, Comparing National, European and International Experiences.* London: Routledge.

—— Scharpf, F., and Zintl, R. (Eds.) (1992). *Horizontale Politikverflechtung, Zur Theorie von Verhandlungssystemen.* Frankfurt/New York: Campus.

Beyle, T. L. (1983). The governor as chief legislator. In Beyle, T. L. and Muchmore, L. R. (Eds.), *Being Governor: A View from the Office.* Durham: Duke Press Policy Studies.

—— and Dalton, R. (1983). The governor and the state legislature. In Beyle, T. L. and Muchmore, L. R. (Eds.), *Being Governor: A View from the Office.* Durham: Duke Press Policy Studies.

—— and Muchmore, L. R. (1983). Governors in the American federal system. In Beyle, T. L. and Muchmore, L. R. (Eds.), *Being Governor: A View from the Office.* Durham: Duke Press Policy Studies.

Birchfield, V. and Crepaz, M. (1998) The impact of constitutional structures and collective and competitive veto points on income inequality in industrialised democracies. *European Journal of Political Research* 34, 175–200.

Blondel, J., Müller-Rommel, F., and Malova, D. (Eds.) (2007). *Governing New European Democracies.* London: Palgrave.

Bochsler, D. (2006). Quantitative Analyse der Konkordate: Abkommen unter Nachbarn oder unter Freunden? Working Paper, Université de Genève, Geneva.

—— Koller, C., Sciarini P., Traimond, S., and Trippolini, I. (2004). *Die Schweizer Kantone unter der Lupe: Behörden, Personal, Finanzen.* Bern: Haupt.

Bolleyer, N. (2006) Intergovernmental arrangements in Spanish and Swiss federalism: the impact of power-concentrating and power-sharing executives on intergovernmental institutionalization. *Regional and Federal Studies* 16, 385–408.

—— and Börzel, T. A. (2007). Non-hierarchical coordination in multilevel settings- American, Canadian and Swiss lessons for the European Union. Paper presented at the APSA Annual Meeting, Panel in Chicago, United States, 1 September.

—— and Bytzek, E. (2009). Conflict and institutionalization in intergovernmental relations: a comparative assessment of government congruence in six countries. *Regional and Federal Studies.*

—— and Thorlakson, L (2008). Beyond decentralization: measuring the interlocked state. Paper presented at the MPSA 66th Annual Conference in Chicago, 3–6 April.

Börzel, T. A. (2000). From cooperative regionalism to cooperative federalism: the Europeanization of the Spanish state of autonomies. *Publius: The Journal of Federalism* 30, 17–42.

—— (2001). Föderative Staaten in einer entgrenzten Welt: Regionaler Standortwettbewerb oder gemeinsames Regieren jenseits des Nationalstaates. In Benz, A. and Lehmbruch, G. (Eds.), *Föderalismus. Analysen in entwicklungsgeschichtlicher Perspektive* (PVS Sonderheft 32). Wiesbaden: Nomos.

—— (2002). *States and Regions in the European Union: Institutional Adaptation in Germany and Spain*. Cambridge: Cambridge University Press.

—— (2005a) What can federalism teach us about the European Union? The German experience. *Regional and Federal Studies* 15, 245–57.

—— (2005b). Mind the gap! European integration between level and scope. *Journal of European Public Policy* 12, 1–20.

—— (2007). EU Governance: Verhandlungen im Schatten von Hierarchie und Wettbewerb. In Tömmel, I. (Ed.), *Die Europäische Union: Governance und Policy-making* (PVS Sonderheft 40). Wiesbaden: VS Verlag für Sozialwissenschaften.

—— and Hösli, M. (2003). Brussels between Berne and Berlin: comparative federalism meets the European Union. *Governance* 16, 179–202.

Bowman, A. O'M. (2002). American federalism on the horizon. *Publius: The Journal of Federalism* 32, 3–22.

—— (2004a). Horizontal federalism: exploring interstate interaction. *Journal of Public Administration Research* 14, 535–46.

—— (2004b). Trends and issues in interstate cooperation. In Council of State Governments (Ed.), *The Book of the States 2004*. Lexington: Council of State Governments.

Braun, D. (2000). *Public Policy and Federalism*. Aldershot: Ashgate.

—— (2003). Dezentraler und unitarischer Föderalismus. Die Schweiz und Deutschland im Vergleich. *Swiss Political Science Review* 9(1): 57–89.

Braun, C. (2004). *Historisches Kantonsreferendum: Resultat der interkantonalen Zusammenarbeit?* www.bk.admin.ch.

Breton, A. (1985). Supplementary statement. *Government of Canada, Royal Commission on the Economic Union and Development Prospects for Canada* 3, 486–526.

—— (1996). *Competitive Governments: An Economic Theory of Politics and Public Finance*. Cambridge: Cambridge University Press.

Brown, D. M. (2002). *Market Rules: Economic Union Reform and Intergovernmental Policy-Making in Australia and Canada*. Montreal/Kingston: McGill-Queen's University Press.

Bryman, A. (2001). *Social Research Methods*. Oxford: Oxford University Press.

Cameron, D. R. (2005). Canada. In Griffith, A. L. (Ed.). *Handbook of Federal Countries, 2005*. Montreal: McGill-Queen's University Press.

—— and Simeon, R. (2002). Intergovernmental relations in Canada. The emergence of collaborative federalism. *Publius: The Journal of Federalism* 32, 49–71.

Camissa, A. M. (1995). *Governments as Interest Groups*. Westport: Praeger.

Cattoir, P. (1998). *Fédéralisme et Solidarité Financière: Étude Comparative de Six Pays*. Bruxelles: CRISP.

Chapman, R. J. K. (1993). Structure, process and the federal factor: complexity and entanglement in federations. In Burgess, M. and Gagnon A.-G. (Eds.), *Comparative*

Federalism and Federation: Competing Traditions and Future Directions. New York: Harvester Wheatsheaf.

Christiansen, T. and Christine R. (2009). *Constitutionalizing the European Union*. Basingstoke: Palgrave Macmillan.

Chubb, J. E. and Peterson, P. E. (1989). American political institutions and the problem of governance. In Chubb, J. E. and Peterson, P. E. (Eds.), *Can the Government Govern?* Washington, D.C.: Brookings.

Cigler, B. A. (1995). Not just another special interest. In Cigler, B. A. and Loomis, B. A. (Eds.), *Interest Group Politics*. Washington, D.C.: Congressional Quarterly Inc.

Coglianese, C. and Nicolaidis, K (2001). Securing subsidiarity: the institutional design of federalism in the United States and Europe. In Nicolaidis, K. and Howse, R. (Eds.), *The Federal Vision: Legitimacy and Levels of Governance in the United States and the European Union*. Oxford: Oxford University Press.

Conlan, T. J. (2000). Courting devolution: the U.S. supreme court and contemporary American federalism. In Schultze, R.-O. and Sturm, R. (Eds.), *The Politics of Constitutional Reform in North America, Coping with New Challenges*. Opladen: Leske and Budrich.

—— (2006). From cooperative to opportunistic federalism: reflections on the half-century anniversary of the commission on intergovernmental relations. *Public Administration Review*, September–October, 663–76.

Crihfield, B. and Reeves, C. H. (1974). Intergovernmental relations: a view from the States. *Annals of the American Academy of Political and Social Science* 416, 99–107.

Czada, R. (2000). Konkordanz, Korporatismus und Politikverflechtung: Dimensionen der Verhandlungsdemokratie. In Holtmann, E. and Voelzkow, H. (Eds.), *Zwischen Wettbewerbs- und Verhandlungsdemokratie. Analysen zum Regierungssystem der Bundesrepublik Deutschland*. Wiesbaden: Westdeutscher Verlag.

—— (2003). Der Begriff der Verhandlungsdemokratie in der Vergleichenden Policy-Forschung. In Mayntz, R. S. and Streek, W. (Eds.), *Die Reformierbarkeit der Demokratie, Innovationen und Blockaden*. Frankfurt/New York: Campus.

Dennison, D. G. (2005). Intergovernmental mechanisms: what have we learned? Retrospective on the conduct of intergovernmental relations: review of machinery and processes of relations among governments in Canada, and their evolution over the years. *Looking Backward, Thinking Forward*. Kingston: Institute of Intergovernmental Relations, Queen's University.

Derthick, M. (2001). *Keeping the Compound Republic: Essays on Federalism*. Washington, D.C.: Brookings.

Dinan, J. and Krane, D. (2005). The state of American federalism, 2005: federalism resurfaces in the political debate. *Publius: The Journal of Federalism* 36, 327–74.

Donahue, J. D. and Pollack, M. A. (2001). Centralization and its discontents: the rhythms of federalism in the United States and the European Union. In Nicolaidis, K. and Howse, R. (Eds.), *The Federal Vision: Legitimacy and Levels of Governance in the United States and the European Union*. Oxford: Oxford University Press.

Downs, W. M. (1998). *Coalition Government Subnational Style: Multiparty Politics in Europe's Regional Parliaments*. Columbus, OH: Ohio State University Press.

Downs, G. W., Rocke, D. M., and Barsoom, P. N. (1996). Is the good news about compliance good news about cooperation? *International Organization* 50(3), 379–406.

Dyck, R. (1986). *Provincial Politics in Canada*. Scarborough: Prentice Hall.

Dye, T. R. (1985). *Politics in States and Communities*. Englewood Cliffs: Prentice-Hall, Inc.

Elazar, D. J. (1984). *American Federalism: A View from the States*, 3rd Edn. New York: Harper and Row.

Elazar, D. S. (1990). Opening the third century of American federalism: issues and prospects. In Kincaid, J. (Ed.), *American Federalism: The Third Century*. Newbury Park: Sage.

——(1991). Cooperative federalism. In Kenyon, D. A. and Kincaid, J. (Eds.), *Competition among States and Local Governments: Efficiency and Equity in American Federalism*. Washington, D.C.: The Urban Institute Press.

——(2001). The United States and the European Union: models for their epochs. In Nicolaidis, K. and Howse, R. (Eds.), *The Federal Vision: Legitimacy and Levels of Governance in the United States and the European Union*. Oxford: Oxford University Press.

Esman, M. J. (1984). Federalism and modernization: Canada and the United States. *Publius: The Journal of Federalism* 14, 21–38.

Fafard, C. P. and Harrison, K. (2000). *Managing the Environmental Union: Intergovernmental Relations and Environmental Policy in Canada*. Kingston: Institute of Intergovernmental Relations, Queen's University.

Fagagnini, H. P. (1978). Die Rolle der Parteien auf kantonaler Ebene. *Schweizer Jahrbuch für Politische Wissenschaft* 18, 75–94.

Filippov, M., Ordeshook, P. C., and Shvetsova, O. (2004). *Designing Federalism: A Theory of Self-Sustainable Federal Institutions*. Cambridge: Cambridge University Press.

Fleiner, T. (2006). Swiss confederation. In Majeed, A. W., Watts, R. L., and Brown, D. M. (Eds.), *The Distribution of Powers and Responsibilities in Federal Countries*. Montreal: McGill-Queen's University Press.

Forget, C. E. (2001). Success, omissions and challenges in harmonizing Canada's social program. In Salmon, T. C. and Keating, M. (Eds.), *The Dynamics of Decentralization: Canadian Federalism and British Devolution*. Montreal: McGill-Queen's University Press.

Freiburghaus, D. and Zehnder, V.(2003). Horizontale Kooperation zwischen den Kantonen und die 'systematisch-pragmatische Zusammenarbeit' in der Zentralschweiz. *Working Paper des Institut de Hautes Etudes en Administration Publique* 4, 1–15.

Frenkel, M. (1986). Interkantonale Institutionen und Politikbereiche. In Germann, R. E. and Weibel, E. (Eds.), *Handbuch Politisches System der Schweiz*. Bern: Haupt.

Gage, R. W. (1992). Sector alignments of regional councils: implications for intergovernmental relations in the 1990s. *American Review of Public Administration* 22, 207–24.

Gerlak, A. K. (2006). Federalism and U.S. water policy: lessons from the twenty-first century. *Publius: The Journal of Federalism* 36, 231–57.

Grande, (2001). Parteiensystem und Föderalismus, Institutionelle Strukturmuster und politische Dynamiken im internationalen Vergleich. In Benz, A. and Lehmbruch, L. (Eds.), *Föderalismus. Analysen in Entwicklungsgeschichtlicher Perspektive* (PVS Sonderheft 32).Wiesbaden: Westdeutscher Verlag.

Grau I Creus, M. (2000). Spain: incomplete federalism. In Wachendorfer-Schmidt, U. (Ed.), *Federalism and Political Performance*. London: Routledge.

Gray, V. (1973). Innovation in the States: a diffusion study. *American Political Science Review* 67, 1174–85.

—— and Eisinger, P. (1991). *American States and Cities*. New York: HarperCollins Publisher, Inc.

Green-Pedersen, C. (2001). Minority governments and party politics: the political and institutional background to the 'Danish miracle'. *Journal of Public Policy* 21, 53–70.

Grees, F. (1996). Interstate cooperation and territorial representation in intermestic politics. *Publius: The Journal of Federalism* 26, 53–71.

Greif, A. (2006). *Institutions and the Path to Modern Economy: Lessons from Medieval Trade*. Cambridge: Cambridge University Press.

Grodzins, M. (1966). *The American System: A New View of Government in the United States*. New Brunswick: Transaction Books.

Grossback, L. J., Nicholson-Crotty, S., and Peterson, D. A. M. (2004). Ideology and learning in policy diffusion. *American Political Science Review* 32, 521–45.

Gunlicks, A. B. (1988). Constitutional law and the protection of subnational governments in the United States and West Germany. *Publius: The Journal of Federalism* 18, 141–58.

Haider, D. H. (1974). *When Governments Go to Washington: Governors, Mayors and Intergovernmental Lobbying*. New York: The Free Press.

Hall, P. A. and Taylor, C. R. (1996). Political science and the three new institutionalisms. *Political Studies* 44, 936–57.

Heinmiller, B. T. (2002). Finding a way forward in the study of intergovernmental policymaking. *Canadian Public Administration* 45, 427–33.

Héritier, A. (1998). Political institutions, decision styles, and policy choices. In Czada, R., Héritier, A., and Keman, H. (Eds.), *Institutions and Political Choice, On the Limits of Rationality*. Amsterdam: VU University Press.

Hickok, E. W., Jr. (1990). Federalism's future before the Supreme U.S. Court. In Kincaid, J. (Ed.), *American Federalism: The Third Century*. Newbury Park: Sage.

Hill, C. (1993). The capability–expectations gap or conceptualizing the Europe's international role. *Journal of Common Market Studies* 31, 305–28.

Hocking, B. (1999). Patrolling the 'frontier': globalization, localization and the 'actorness' of non-central governments. In Aldecoa, F. and Keating, M. (Eds.), *Paradiplomacy in Action: The Foreign Relations of Subnational Governments*. London: Frank Cass.

Hooghe, L. (Ed.) (1996). *Cohesion Policy and European Integration: Building Multi-Level Governance*. Oxford: Clarendon.

—— and Marks, G. (2001). *Multi-Level Governance and European Integration*. Lanham: Rowman and Littlefield.

————(2003). Unraveling the central state, but how? *American Political Science Review* 97, 233–43.

Hoornbeck, J. A. (2004). Policy-making institutions and water policy outputs in the European Union and the United States: a comparative analysis. *Journal of European Public Policy*, 11(3), 461–96.

Hueglin, T. O. and Fenna, A. (2006). *Comparative Federalism: A Systematic Inquiry*. Peterborough: Broadview Press Ltd.

Jans, T. M. and Tombeur, H. (2000). Living apart together: the Belgian intergovernmental cooperation in the domains of environment and economy. In Braun D. (Ed.), *Public Policy and Federalism*. Aldershot: Ashgate.

Johns, C., O'Reilly, P. L., and Inwood, G. J. (2006). Intergovernmental innovation and the administrative state in Canada. *Governance* 19, 627–49.

—————— (2007). Formal and informal dimensions of intergovernmental administrative relations in Canada. *Canadian Public Administration* 50, 21–41.

Joumard, I. and Kongsrud, P. M. (2003). Fiscal relations across governmental levels. *OECD Economic Studies* 36, 155–229.

Judge, D. (2003). Legislative institutionalization: a bent analytical arrow? *Government and Opposition* 38, 497–514.

Kaiser, A. (1997). Types of democracy: From classical to new institutionalism. *Journal of Theoretical Politics* 9, 419–44.

Katz, R. S. (1994). Party organizations as empty vessels: parties in American politics. In Katz, R. S. and Mair, P. (Eds.), *How Parties Organise: Change and Adaptation in Party Organizations in Western Democracies*. London: Sage.

Kelemen, R. D. (2004). *The Rules of Federalism, Institutions and Regulatory Politics in Europe and Beyond*. Cambridge, M.A.: Harvard University Press.

Kelly, J. B. and Murphy, M. (2005). Shaping the constitutional dialogue on federalism: Canada's Supreme Court as meta-political actor. *Publius: The Journal of Federalism* 19, 217–43.

Kennett, S.A. (1998). *The Courchene Proposal. Securing the Social Union: A Commentary on the Decentralized Approach*. Kingston: Institute of Intergovernmental Relations.

Kenyon, D. A. and Kincaid, J. (Eds.) (1991). *Competition among States and Local Governments, Efficiency and Equity in American Federalism*. Washington, D.C.: The Urban Institute Press.

Keohane, R. O. (1982). The demand for international regimes. *International Organization* 36, 325–55.

Kincaid, J. (1990). From cooperative to coercive federalism. In Kincaid, J. (Ed.), *American Federalism: The Third Century*. Newbury Park: Sage.

Kincaid, J. (2001). Devolution in the United States: rhetoric and reality. In Nicolaidis, K. and Howse, R. (Eds.), *The Federal Vision: Legitimacy and Levels of Governance in the United States and the European Union*. Oxford: Oxford University Press.

—— (2003). Globalization and federalism in the United States: continuity in adaptation. In Lazar, H, Telford, H., and Watts, R. L. (Eds.), *The Impact of Global and Regional Integration on Federal Systems: A Comparative Analysis*. Montreal/Kingston: McGills-Queen's University Press.

Krause, G. A. and Bowman, A. O'M. (2005). Adverse selection, political parties, and policy delegation in the American federal system. *The Journal of Law, Economics & Organization* 21, 359–87.

Laakso, M. and Taagepera, R. (1979). Effective number of parties: a measure with application to West Europe. *Comparative Political Studies* 12, 3–27.

Ladner, A. (2001). Swiss political parties: between persistence and change. *West European Politics* 24,123–44.

Lawson, K. (2004). Five variations of a theme: interest aggregation by party today. In Lawson, K. and Poguntke, T. (Eds), *How Political Parties Respond, Interest Aggregation Revisited*. London: Routledge.

Lazar, H. (2000). The social union framework agreement and the future of fiscal federalism. In Lazar, H (Ed.), *Canada: State of the Federation, 1999/2000: Toward a New Mission*

Statement for Canadian Fiscal Federalism. Montreal/Kingston: McGill-Queen's University Press.

——and McIntosh, T. (1998). *Federalism, Democracy and Social Policy: Towards a Sectoral Analysis of the Social Union*. Project Methodology for Governance Aspects of the Social Union, Institute of Intergovernmental Relations, Queen's University, Kingston.

Lazar, H. and McLean, J. (2000). Non-constitutional reform and the Canadian Federation: the only game in town. In Schultze, R. O. and Sturm, R. (Eds.), *The Politics of Constitutional Reform in North America: Coping with New Challenges*. Opladen: Leske + Budrich, 149–76.

——Telford, H., and Watts, R. L. (2003). Divergent trajectories: the impact of global and regional integration on federal systems. In Lazar, H., Telford, H., and Watts, R. L. (Eds.), *The Impact of Global and Regional Integration on Federal Systems: A Comparative Analysis*. Montreal/Kingston: McGill-Queen's University Press.

Lecours, A. (2004). Moreno's multiple ethnoterritorial concurrence model: a re-formulation. *Regional and Federal Studies* 14, 66–88.

Lehmann, W. (2002). Attribution of powers and dispute resolution in selected federal systems. *Constitutional Affairs Series* AFCO 103. Luxembourg: European Parliament.

Lehmbruch, G. (1976). *Parteienwettbewerb im Bundesstaat*. Stuttgart: Kohlhammer.

——(1978). Party and federation in Germany: a developmental dilemma. *Government and Opposition* 13, 151–77.

——(1991). Das konkordanzdemokratische modell in der vergleichenden analyse. In Michalsky, H. (Ed.), *Politischer Wandel in Konkordanzdemokratischen Systemen*. Vaduz: Liechtenstein Politische Schriften.

——(1993). Consociational democracy and corporatism in Switzerland. *Publius: The Journal of Federalism* 23(2), 43–60.

——(2003). Das deutsche Verbändesystem zwischen Unitarismus und Föderalismus. In Mayntz, R. S. and Streek, W. (Eds.), *Die Reformierbarkeit der Demokratie, Innovationen und Blockaden*. Frankfurt/New York: Campus.

Leibfried, S. and Pierson P. (1995). *European Social Policy*. Washington, D. C.: Brookings.

Lijphart, A. (1971). Comparative politics and the comparative method. *American Political Science Review* 65, 682–93.

——(1999). *Patterns of Democracy. Government Forms and Performance in Thirty-Six Countries*. New Haven: Yale University Press.

Linder, W. (1994). *Swiss Democracy: Possible Solutions in Multicultural Societies*. London: Macmillan.

——(1999). *Repräsentation, Artikulation und Durchsetzung kantonaler Interessen im Ständerat und im Nationalrat, Studie im Auftrag der Parlamentsdienste der Schweizerischen Bundesversammlung*. Bern: Universität Bern.

Lowi, T. J. (1964). American business, public policy, case-studies, and political theory. *World Politics* 16(4), 677–715.

Maioni, A. (2002). Health care in the new millenium. In Bakvis, H. S. and Skogstad, G. (Eds.), *Canadian Federalism, Performance, Effectiveness and Legitimacy*. Oxford: Oxford University Press.

Máiz, R., Beramendi, P., and Grau, M. (2002). La federalización del Estado de las automonías: evolución y déficit institucionales. In Subirats, J. and Gallego, R. (Eds.),

Viente Anos de Autonomías en Espana: Leyes, Políticas Públicas, Instituciones y Opinión Pública. Madrid: CIS.

Majeed, A. W., Watts, R. L., and Brown, D. M. (Eds.) (2006). *The Distribution of Powers and Responsibilities in Federal Countries*. Montreal: McGill-Queen's University Press.

March, J. G. and Olsen, J. P. (1984) The new institutionalism: organizational factors in political life. *American Political Science Review* 78, 734–49.

—— (1989). *Rediscovering Institutions*. New York: The Free Press.

—— (1995). *Democratic Governance*. New York: The Free Press.

McDowell, B. D. (1997). Advisory commission on intergovernmental relations in 1996: The end of an era. *Publius: The Journal of Federalism* 27, 111–27.

McKay, D. (2001). *Designing Europe: Comparative Lessons from the Federal Experience*. Oxford: Oxford University Press.

McRoberts, K. (1985). Unilateralism, bilateralism and multilateralism: approaches to Canadian federalism. In Simeon, R. (Ed.), *Intergovernmental Relations*. Toronto: University of Toronto Press.

—— (1993). Federal structures and the policy process. In Atkinson, M. M. (Ed.), *Governing Canada, Institutions and Public Policy*. Toronto: Harcourt Brace.

Meekison, P. J., Telford, H., and Lazar, H. (2002). The institutions of executive federalism, myths and realities. In Meekison, P. J., Telford, H., and Lazar, H. (Eds.), *Canada: The State of the Federation, 2002. Reconsidering the Institutions of Canadian Federalism*. Kingston: Institute for Intergovernmental Relations.

Menon, A. and Schain, M. (Eds.) (2006). *Comparative Federalism: The European Union and the United States in Comparative Perspective*. Oxford: Oxford University Press.

Minger, T. (2004). Die Geschichte der Konferenz der Kantonsregierungen. In Konferenz der Kantonregierungen (Ed.), *10 Jahre KdK, Standortbestimmung und Ausblick*. Bern.

Morata, F. (1991). The Spanish regions and the 1993 challenge. Working paper 34. Institut de Ciencies Politiques I Socials, Universitat Autónoma de Barcelona. http://www.recercat.cat/bitstream/2072/1449/1/ICPS34.pdf

Moravcsik, A. (1998). *The Choice for Europe: Social Purpose and State Power from Messina to Maastricht*. London: UCL Press.

—— (2001). Federalism in the European Union: rhetoric and reality. In Nicolaidis, K. and Howse, R. (Eds.), *The Federal Vision: Legitimacy and Levels of Governance in the United States and the European Union*. Oxford: Oxford University Press.

Moreno, L. (1999). Asymmetry in Spain: federalism in the making? In Agranoff, R. (Ed.), *Accomodating Diversity in Federal States*. Baden-Baden: Nomos.

—— (2000). *The Federalization of Spain*. London: Frank Cass.

Muchmore, L. R. (1983). Science advice to governors: non-politics in the policy process. In Beyle, T. L. and Muchmore, L. R. (Eds.), *Being Governor: A View from the Office*. Durham: Duke Press Policy Studies.

Nathan, R. P. and Lago, J. R. (1990). Intergovernmental fiscal roles and relations. *Annals of the American Academy of Political and Social Science* 509, 36–47.

Neidhart, L. (1970). *Plebiszit und Pluralitäre Demokratie: Eine Analyse der Funktion des Schweizerischen Gesetzesreferendums*. Bern: Francke.

—— (2001). Elementare bedingungen der entwicklung des schweizerischen föderalismus. In Benz, A. and Lehmbruch, G. (Eds.), *Föderalismus. Analysen in Entwicklungsgeschichtlicher Perspektive* (PVS Sonderheft 32). Wiesbaden: Nomos.

Nice, D. S. (1987). State participation in interstate compacts. *Publius: The Journal of Federalism* 17, 69–83.

Nicolaidis, K. and Howse, R. (Eds.) (2001). *The Federal Vision: Legitimacy and Levels of Governance in the US and the EU.* Oxford: Oxford University Press.

O'Brennan, J. and Raunio, T. (Eds.) (2007). *National Parliaments within the Enlarged European Union: From Victims of Integration to Competitive Actors?* Abingdon: Routledge.

Olsen, J. P. (1998). Political science and organization theory, parallel agendas but mutual disregard. In Czada, R., Héritier, A., and Keman, H. (Eds.), *Institutions and Political Choice: On the Limits of Rationality.* Amsterdam: VU University Press.

Opeskin, B. R. (2001). Mechanisms for intergovernmental relations in federations. *International Science Journal* 52, 129–38.

O'Reilly, P. L., Inwood, G. J., and Johns, C. (2006). Challenges to Canadian intergovernmental policy capacity: health, environment and trade. Paper read at 64th Annual Conference of the Midwest Political Science Association in Chicago, United States, 22 April.

O'Toole, L. J., Jr. (Ed.) (2000). *American Intergovernmental Relations.* Washington, D.C.: Congressional Quarterly Press.

Painter, M. (1998). *Collaborative Federalism: Economic Reform in Australia in the 1990s.* Cambridge: Cambridge University Press.

Peters, B. G. (1998). Managing horizontal government: the politics of coordination. Research Paper 21, Canadian Center for Management Development.

—— (1999). *Institutional Theory in Political Science: The 'New' Institutionalism.* London/New York: Pinter.

—— and Pierre, J. (2001). Developments in intergovernmental relations: towards multi-level governance. *Policy & Politics* 29, 131–5.

Pierson, P. (2000). The limits of design: explaining institutional origins and change. *Governance: An International Journal of Policy and Administration* 13, 475–99.

Poirier, J. (2002). Formal mechanisms of intergovernmental relations in Belgium. *Regional and Federal Studies* 12, 24–54.

—— (2004). Intergovernmental agreements in Canada: at the crossroads between law and politics. In Meekison, J. P., Telford, H., and Lazar, H. (Eds.), *Reconsidering the Institutions of Canadian Federalism.* Montreal: McGill-Queen's University Press.

Pollack, M. A. (1994). Creeping competence: the expanding agenda of the European community. *Journal of Public Policy* 14, 95–145.

Prince, M. R. (2001). Canadian federalism and disability policy-making. *Canadian Journal of Political Science* 34, 792–817.

Provost, C. L. (2003). State attorneys general: entrepreneurship, and consumer protection in the new federalism. *Publius: The Journal of Federalism* 33, 37–53.

Purcell, Edward A. (2007): Originalism, Federalism and the American Constitutional Enterprise: A Historical inquiry, New Haven: Yale University Press.

Putnam, R. D. (1988). Diplomacy and domestic politics: the logic of two-level games. *International Organization* 42, 427–60.

Quebec Liberal Party. (2001). A Project for Quebec: Affirmation, Autonomy and Leadership. Final Report, Quebec Liberal Party. http://www/plq.org/en/informez_vous/programme.html.

Radin, B. and Boase, J. P. (2000). Federalism, political structure, and public policy in the United States and Canada. *Journal of Comparative Policy Analysis: Research and Practice* 2, 65–89.

Reeves, M. M. (1990). The states as polities: reformed, reinvigorated, resourceful. *The Annals of the American Academy of Political and Social Science* 509(1), 83–93.

Rentzsch, W. (2001). Bifurcated and integrated parties in parliamentary federations: the Canadian case. Working Paper 4 IIFR, Queens University.

Rich, R. F. and White, W. D. (1996). *Health Policy, Federalism, and the American States*. Washington, D.C.: The Urban Institute Press.

Riker, W. (1964). *Federalism, Origin, Operation, Significance*. Boston: Little Brown.

Risse-Kappen, T. (1991). Public opinion, domestic structures and foreign policy. *World Politics* 43, 479–512.

Rodden, J. A. (2006). *Hamilton's Paradox: The Promise and Perils of Fiscal Federalism*. Cambridge: Cambridge University Press.

Rosenthal, D. B. and Hoefler, J. M. (1989). Competing approaches to the study of American federalism and intergovernmental relations. *Publius: The Journal of Federalism* 19, 1–23.

Rothmayr, C., Varone, F., and Montpetit, E. (2003). Does federalism matter for biopolicies? Switzerland in a comparative perspective. *Swiss Political Science Review* 9, 109–36.

Salisbury, R. H. (1992). The paradox of interest groups in Washington. In Salisbury, R. H. (Ed.), *Interests and Institutions*. Pittsburgh: University of Pittsburgh Press.

Sartori, G. (1970). Concept misformation in comparative politics. *American Political Science Review* 64, 1033–53.

Sbragia, A. M. (1993). The European community: a balancing act, *Publius: The Journal of Federalism* 23, 23–38.

——(2006). American federalism and intergovernmental relations. In Rhodes, R. A. W., Binder, S. A., and Rockman, B. (Eds.), *The Oxford Handbook of Political Institutions*. Oxford: Oxford University Press.

Scharpf, F. W. (1985). Die Politikverflechtungs-Falle: Europäische Integration und deutscher Föderalismus im Verleich. Politische Vierteljahresschrift 26(4), 323–56.

——(1988). The joint-decision trap: lessons from German federalism and European integration. *Public Administration* 66, 239–78.

——(1997). *Games Real Actors Play: Actor-Centered Institutionalism in Policy Research*. Oxford: Oxford University Press.

——(2001). What have we learned? Problem-solving capacity of the multilevel European polity. MPIfG Working Paper 01/4, 1–49.

——(2005). No exit from the joint decision trap? Can German federalism reform itself? MPIfG Working Paper 05/8.

Schlesinger, J. A. (1965). The politics of the executive. In Jacob, H. and Vines, K. N. (Eds.), *Politics in the American States: A Comparative Analysis*. Boston/Toronto: Little Brown and Company.

Schmidt, V. A. (2006). *Democracy in Europe: The EU and National Polities*. Oxford: Oxford University Press.

Schram, S. (2005). The United States of America. In Griffiths, A. L. (Ed.), *Handbook of Federal Countries, 2005*. Montreal: McGill-Queen's University Press.

Sciarini, P. (2005). *Die Interkantonale Zusammenarbeit ebnet den Weg für die Föderalismusreform*. Lausanne: University of Lausanne.

Silverman, D. (1993). *Interpreting Qualitative Data: Methods for Analysing Talk, Text and Interaction*. London: Sage.

Simeon, R. (1972). *Federal-Provincial Diplomacy: The Making of Recent Policy in Canada*. Toronto: University of Toronto Press.

—— (2001). Adaptability and change in federations. *International Science Journal* 52, 145–52.

—— (2005). Plus ça change: intergovernmental relations then and now. *Policy Options* March/April, 84–7.

—— and Papillon, M. (2006). Canada. In Majeed, A. W., Watts, R. L., and Brown, D. M. (Eds.), *The Distribution of Powers and Responsibilities in Federal Countries*. Montreal: McGill-Queen's University Press.

Simmons, J. (2004). Securing the threads of co-operation in the tapestry of intergovernmental relations: does the institutionalization of ministerial conferences matter? In Meekison, P. J., Telford, H., and Lazar, H. (Eds.), *Canada: The State of the Federation, 2002: Reconsidering the Institutions of Canadian Federalism*. Kingston: Institute for Intergovernmental Relations.

Skogstad, G. (2000). Canada: dual and executive federalism: ineffective problem-solving. In D. Braun (Ed.), *Public Policy and Federalism*. Aldershot: Althenaeum Press.

Smiley, D. V. (1987). *The Federal Condition in Canada*. Toronto: Mc Graw-Hill Ryerson.

—— and Watts, R. L. (1985). *Intrastate Federalism in Canada*. Toronto: University of Toronto Press.

Steiner, J. (1974). *Amicable Agreement versus Majority Rule: Conflict Resolution in Switzerland*. Chapel Hill: University of North Carolina Press.

Stiftung, C. H. (2000). Jahresbericht der Konferenz der Kantonsregierungen, Berne.

Strøm, K. (1990). *Minority Government and Majority Rule*. Cambridge: Cambridge University Press.

Swenden, W. (2005). What – if anything – can the European Union learn from Belgium federalism and vice versa? *Regional and Federal Studies* 15, 187–204.

—— (2006). *Federalism and Regionalism in Western Europe: A Comparative and Thematic Analysis*. Basingstoke: Palgrave Macmillan.

Tannenwald, R. and Cowan, J. (1997). Fiscal capacity, fiscal need, and fiscal comfort among U.S. states: new evidence. *Publius: The Journal of Federalism* 27, 113–25.

Thelen, K. (1999). Historical institutionalism. *Comparative Politics: Annual Review of Political Science* 2, 369–404.

Thorlakson, L. (2003). Comparing federal institutions: power and representation in six federations. *West European Politics* 2, 1–22.

—— (2007). An institutional explanation of party system congruence: evidence from six federations. *European Journal of Political Research* 46, 69–95.

—— (2009). Patterns of party integration, influence and autonomy in seven federations. *Party Politics* 15(2), 157–77.

Trees, P. (2005a). Die regionalen Regierungskonferenzen in der Schweiz – Stand und Entwicklung. University of Bern, Bern.

―――(2005b). Zusammenarbeit der Direktorenkonferenzen mit den Regierungskonferenzen, Analyse verschiedener Modelle. Unpublished MA Thesis, University of Bern, Bern.
Trench, A. (2006). Intergovernmental relations: in search of a theory. In Greer, S. L. (Ed.), *Territory, Democracy and Justice: Regionalism and Federalism in Western Democracies*. Basingstoke: Macmillan.
Tsebelis, G. (1995). Decision making in political systems: veto players in presidentialism, parliamentarism, multicameralism and multipartyism. *British Journal of Political Science* 25(3), 289–325.
―――(2002). *Veto Players: How Political Institutions Work*. Princeton: Princeton University Press.
―――and Money, J. (1997). *Bicameralism*. Cambridge: Cambridge University Press.
Vatter, A. (2002) *Kantonale Demokratien im Vergleich: Entstehungsgründe, Interaktionen und Wirkungen politischer Institutionen in den Schweizer Kantonen*. Opladen: Leske and Budrich.
―――(2004). Challenges to intergovernmental relations in Switzerland and Japan. *Swiss Political Science Review* 10, 77–102.
Wälti, S. (1996). Institutional reform of federalism: changing the players rather than the rules of the game. *Swiss Political Science Review* 2(2), 113–41.
―――(2003). L'effet des rapports financiers sur la dynamique federale: la qualité mediative du federalisme Suisse. *Swiss Political Science Review* 9, 91–108.
―――(2004). How multilevel structures affect environmental policy in industrialized countries. *European Journal of Political Research* 43, 599–634.
Watts, R. L. (1999a). *Comparing Federal Systems*. Montreal: Mc Gill-Queen's University Press.
―――(1999b). *The Spending Power in Federal Systems: A Comparative Study*. Kingston: Institute of Intergovernmental Relations.
―――(2005). Comparing forms of federal partnership. In Karmis, D. and Norman, W. (Eds.), *Theories of Federalism: A Reader*. London: Macmillan.
Wheare, K. C. (1951). *Modern Constitutions*. London: Oxford University Press.
Wibbels, E. (2005). *Federalism and the Market: Intergovernmental Conflict and Economic Reform in the Developing World*. Cambridge: Cambridge University Press.
Winfield, M. S. (2002). Environmental policy and federalism. In Bakvis, H. and Skogstad, G. (Eds.), *Canadian Federalism, Performance, Effectiveness and Legitimacy*. Oxford: Oxford University Press.
Wolpe, B. C. and Levine, B. J. (1996). *Lobbying Congress: How the System Works*. Washington, D.C.: Congressional Quarterly Inc.
Wright, D. S. (1982). *Understanding Intergovernmental Relations*. Monterey: Brooks/Cole.
Zimmerman, J. F. (1990). Regulating intergovernmental relations in the 1990s. In Kincaid, J. (Ed.), *American Federalism: The Third Century*. Newbury Park: Sage.
―――(2001). *Interstate Cooperation, Compacts and Administrative Agreements*. Westport: Praeger.
―――(2002). *Interstate Relations: The Neglected Dimension of Federalism*. Westport: Praeger.

Index

Note: page numbers in *italics* refer to Figures and Tables.

Accords 171
Ad hoc coordination 19, 20, 21, 35, 180, 206, 221, 222
Advisory Commission on IGR 112–13
Agenda-setting 208
Agreement of Internal Trade (Canada 1992) 62–3
Agreements, Precision 26–7
Alternation 54–5, *57*
  Canada 86
  Switzerland 97
Annual Premiers' Conference, Canada 76, 182
Atlantic Provinces Special Education Authority (APSEA) 80
Autonomy losses 7, 36–7, 54
Autonomy protection
  Canada 81, 87, 89, 222
  Switzerland 97, 98, 99, 108–9
  United States 158

Behavioural assumptions 31–2
Belgium, IGR evolution 20
Bifurcated party system, Canada 57
'Big 7' 157
Bilateral agreements, Canada 71, 73–4, 75, 90
Binding agreements 172
Blame-shifting 36, 37, 54
  Canada 72, 78, 89
  Switzerland 107
Block grants 46
Blueprints
  Canada 62–4
  Switzerland 65–6
  United States 66–8
Boundedness of arrangements 24, 25
British Columbia–Alberta Cooperation Agreement 71

'Calculus approach' 30, 32
Canada
  Ad hoc coordination 221, 222

Alternation rate 54–5
Blueprint 62–4
Expectations 59
Federal grants 45–6
Federal system 7
Fiscal equalization 179
Fluctuation of meetings 183
Government structure 46
Integration 145–6, 166–7, *169*, *205*
  Competitive regional representation 144–5
  Horizontal 142–4
  Vertical 139–42
Interaction mode *207*
Intergovernmental agreements 174, 175, *176*
  Generalist *187*–90
  Policy-specific 191, *192*, 194–5, 198
Intergovernmental arrangements (IGAs) 69, *70*, 71
  Regional 104
Intergovernmental institutionalization 71, 88–91, 180, 181, *205*
  Horizontal dimension 76–9
  Policy-specific 80–8
  Regional IGAs 79–80
  Vertical dimension 71–5
Lower level government characteristics *56*, 57
Material examined 183, *185*
Policy coordination 222, *223–4*
Power-concentrating 34, 39
Power-sharing, Relationship to territorial representation *216*, 218
Senate 50
Supreme Court rulings 48
Canada-Wide Accord on Environmental Harmonization (1998) 195
Canadian Intergovernmental Conference Secretariat 73
Capacity–expectations gap, European Union 217

Categorical conceptualization 23–4
Caucuses, United States 41
Center for Best Practices 114, 118
Centralization 3
Centralized decision-making 220, 223
Circularity, US federal system 68
Co-decision 19, 21, 180, 206, 221
　United States 119, 120
Coalitions 6–7
　Interest configuration stability 36
　Switzerland 39–40, 107
　Use of vetoes 38
Coercive cooperation, United States 66
Coercive federalism 45
Collaborative federalism, Canada 62
Collective statements 178–80
Committee on Education of National Governors' Association *192*
Communiqués, Canada 85, *176*
Compact commissions, United States 125–9
Compacts 121, 122–5, 132, 171, 175, *176*, 180
Competence distribution, Relationship to institutionalization
　Canada 83, *84*
　Switzerland 88, 94, *95*
　United States 127–8
Competition, U.S. IGAs 118
Competitive pressure
　Canada 64
　Measurement 54–5
Competitive regional representation, Canada 144–5
Complete alternations 55
Compliance 177, 179
Compulsory power-sharing 7, 38–9, 204
　Effect on integration 205, 210
　Relationship to territorial representation *216*, 222
　United States 111, 118–19, 128, 131–2, 165
Concordats 96, 171, 174–5, *176*, 180
Conditional grants 44–6
Conference of Atlantic Premiers 186
Conference of Cantonal Executives 8, 101–4, 105, 117, 154, 167, 183, 210
　Analysis of output *187*–90

Executive composition 150
　Functions 133, *134*
　Horizontal integration 149, 150–1
　'House of Cantons' project 151–2
　Vertical linkages 147, 148–9
Conference of Central Switzerland 106, 107
　Integration 152, 153
Conférence des Gouvernements de Suisse Occidentale 106
Conference of Directors for Education 93, *192*, 193
Conference of Directors for Environment and Planning 197
Conference of Eastern Switzerland 105, 106–7
　Integration 152
Conference of Finance Directors 197, 198
　Horizontal integration 149
Conference of Northwest Switzerland 106, 107
　Integration 152
Conferences, Canada *176*
Conferences of Cantonal Directors (Direktorenkonferenzen) 93–9, 108, 151, 154
　Inter-departmental coordination 99–101
　Vertical linkages 146
Conflict potential, Policy fields 51–2
Conflict prevention, United States regional IGAs 162
Conflicts 31
　Canada 74, 75, 82, 89
　United States 158
Consensual power-sharing democracies 38
Consensus democracy 16, 34
　Switzerland 65
Consociationalism 65
Constitutional courts 46–8
Constitutional framework 31
Constitutional make-up 8
Constitutional power-sharing democracies 38
　United States 41–2
Constitutionalization 31
Constraining capacity of agreements 178, 180
　Effect of incentives *181*–2
　Effect of institutionalization *181*
Continuous conceptualization 23–4

Cooperative federalism 4, 31
  Canada 62
  European Union 213
  Switzerland 65, 107–8
  United States 66
Coordination 1
Coordination initiatives 177–8, 179
Coordination pressure 22
Coordination problem, US states 68, 116–17
'Core NGA' 114
Corridors of adaptation 22–3, 61, 204, 208, 209
Council of Atlantic Minsters of Education and Training 80
Council of Atlantic Premiers 70, 71, 79–80, 144
Council of the European Union 216, 218, 225
Council of the Federation (CoF), Canada 7, 70, 71, 72, 76–9, 140–2, 144, 166–7, 182
  Functions 133, 134
Council of Maritime Premiers 69, 79
Council of the Ministers of Education 191, 192
Council of the Ministers of the Environment 143–4
Council staff, role in CoF 78
Council of State Governments 111, 114, 121–2, 159
  Functions 133, 134
  Integration 157
  National Center for Interstate Compacts 123
  Service provision 118
  Support of policy diffusion 130
Country size differences 49
'Cross-pillarization' problems, European Union 217
Cultural accounts of IGR 31

Decentralization, Canada 81, 88
Deficit reduction policy, Canada 72
Delegation 178
Democratic Accountability 9
Density of exchanges 22
Directors, Switzerland 93
Direktorenkonferenzen *see* Conferences of Cantonal Directors
Disability policy, Canada 81

Dual federalism 34, 35
  Criteria 43
  European Union 213–14

Economic and trade policy 52
  Canada *84*, *144*
  Switzerland 95
  United States *126*, 127
Education Commission of the States 125, 127
Education policy 52
  Canada *84*, 142, *144*
  Percentages of precise and substantial agreements *192*
  Switzerland *95*, 105
  United States *126*
EEC Treaty 62–3
Elected officials short-term goals 30
Enforcement mechanisms 177
Environmental Council of the States 122
Environmental policy 52
  Canada 83, *84*, 143–*4*
  Switzerland 94, *95*
  United States *126*, 127
European Central Bank,
  Decision-making 220
European Council *216*, 218
European Court of Justice 225
  Decision-making 220
European Union (EU) 10, 211–12
  Internal dynamics of lower level governments 219–27
  Multilevel governance 212–15
  Policy coordination *223*–4
  Territorial representation 215–19
Ex ante mandating, Canada 74
Exchanges 18–19, *21*
Executive, Conferences of Cantonal Directors 94–5
Executive committee, Conference of Cantonal Executives 102
Executive IGAs, Access to U.S. federal government 116
Executive–legislative relations 2
  United States 111, 124, 131
Expertise provision, U.S. IGAs 117–18
External differentiation 24
External forces 1

Facultative referendum, Switzerland 40, 42

Federal encroachment, U.S. 115
Federal grants 44
  Conditional 44–6
  United States 67
Federal guests, Conferences of Cantonal Directors 94
Federal principle, EU 211
Federal systems 2–3
  Adaptation to global and regional integration 4–5
Federal–cantonal communication 146–8
Federal–provincial conflict, Canada 74, 75, 82
Federal–state integration *169*
  United States 156, 158–9
Federalism, Definitions 12–14
Federalism dialogue (Föderalismus-Dialog) 148
First Ministers' Conferences (FMCs) *70*, 71–2, 73, 74, 139–40, 166–7
  Analysis of output *187*–90
  Functions 133, *134*
Fiscal policy 52
  Canada 83, *84*, *144*, 198, 199
  Conflict potential 51
  Switzerland *95*, 197, 198, 199
  United States *126*, 127, 198–9
Fiscal power, lower level governments 44
Fiscal equalization, Canada 179
Formal–legal definitions of federalism 12–13
Fragmentation
  European Union 216–17
  United States 117, 128–9, 131, 132, 159–63, 210
Free-riding, Cantons 98
Functional capacity of IGAs, Effect of institutionalization 200
Functional federalism, Switzerland 66
Functional orientation of IGAs 133–*4*
  Relationship to institutionalization 200
Functional rationale, United States 129

Generalist agreements, Analysis 186–91
Generalist IGAs 17
  Comparison with policy-specific IGAs, Switzerland 193–4
  Interaction with policy-specific IGAs 190
  Material examined *185*
  United States 114–20

Germany
  Federal system 12, 35
  Joint decision-making 16
  Territorial representation 218
Globalization, adaptation of federal systems 4–5
Goals of agreements 179
  Generalist agreements 187–8
Governmental constraint, Non-binding agreements 177–80

'Hall of the States' 157, 161
Harmonization problems, Precision of agreements 26–7
Health policy 52
  Canada *84*, 86, 142, *144*, *192*, 196
  Switzerland *95*
  United States *126*
High institutionalization *see* Strong institutionalization
Historical accounts of IGR 31
Horizontal coordination mechanisms, European Union 218
Horizontal federalism
  Memoranda of understanding 129–30
  United States 120–2, 131–2
    Interstate commissions 125–9
    Interstate compacts 122–5
Horizontal integration *169*, 210
  Canada 142–4
  Switzerland 149–52
  United States 156–8, 159
Horizontal interactions 2, 3, 69, 137
  Analysis of integration 138
  Canada 76–9, 89, 90
  Cantons 97
'House of Cantons' project 151–2
Howard government, Canada 72–3

Ideological congruence 6, 36, 55–6
Incentives 5–6, 8, 35–7, 208–9
  Impact on constraining capacity of agreements *181*–2
Independence
  In definition of federalism 13–14
  Intergovernmental programs, Canada 81
Initiative-taking 208
Institutional choice 1–10
'Institutional culture' 30
Institutional emancipation 157
Institutional reform 207–8

Index

Institutional self-interest 209–10
Institutionalization of IGAs 6–7, 8, 9, 23, 204, *205*–6
  Canada 71, 89–91
    Horizontal dimension 76–9
    Policy-specific 81–8
    Regional IGAs 79–80
    Vertical dimension 71–9
  Comparisons between countries 133–5
  Conceptualization 24
  Distinction from Integration 37
  Effect on nature of agreements 180–2, 199–201
    Generalist agreements 186–91
    Policy-specific agreements 191–9
  Importance 25
  Levels 24–7, *25*
  Rational choice 29–33
  Switzerland 107–9
    Conferences of Cantonal Directors 94–9, *95*
    Regional IGAs 104–7
  United States 111–14, 131–2
    Generalist IGAs 114–20
    Policy-specific *126*
Integration of IGAs 7, 8, 137, 204–*5*, 206
  Analysis 138–9
  Canada 145–6
    Competitive regional representation 144–5
    Horizontal integration 142–4
    Vertical integration 139–42
  Comparison between countries 166–9
  Conceptualization 24
  Effect of majoritarianism 37
  Effect of power-sharing 38–9
  Indicators of 138
  Levels *27*
  Switzerland 154
    Horizontal integration 149–52
    Mechanisms of intra-regional and national-regional interrogation 152–4
    Vertical integration 146–9
  United States 155, 163–6
    Fragmentation 160–3
    Inter-branch divides 156–9
Inter-branch divides, United States 156–9
Inter-cantonal agreements 96, 98–9

Inter-party cooperation, Switzerland 99
Interaction modes 19, 206–7
Interdependence, intergovernmental programs, Canada 81
Interest aggregation, Canada 146
Interest configurations 55
  Canada 78, 79, 83, 87, 89
  Stability 35–6, 54
  Switzerland 109
Intergovernmental Affairs Office, Canada 74
Intergovernmental agreements 2–4, 171–2, *176*
  Classification *69*
  Definition 172–3
  Effect of institutionalization 180–2
    Generalist agreements 186–91
    Policy-specific agreements 191–9
  Functions 176–80
  Variety 173–5
Intergovernmental arrangements (IGAs) 1, 20–1
  Institutionalization and integration 6–8, 9, 23–8
Intergovernmental cooperation 221, 222, *224*
Intergovernmental officials 30
Intergovernmental relations (IGR) 18
  Exchanges 18–19
  Patterns 19, 20–1
  Structures 20–1
Internal differentiation 26
Internal forces 1
Internal goals 29
Internal institutional development 24
Internal Trade 183
  Canada 195–6
International agreements 176, 177
International arrangements, Canada 79
Interprovincial conflict, Canada 82
Interstate compacts, United States 121, 122–4, 132, 175, *176*, 180
Interstate relations 2
  United States 166
Interviews 53
Intra-country variance, Policy-specific agreements *192*, 195–6
Intra-ministerial bodies, Canada 88
Intra-regional integration, Switzerland 152–3
Intra-state federalism 50

Intragovernmental incentives, Effect on institutionalization 133–5
Intragovernmental processes 29

Joint decision-making 220–1, *223*
Judiciary, United States 112
Jurisdiction allocation 43–4
Justice and Crime control policy 52
  Canada *84*, *144*, *192*, 195
  Switzerland *95*
  United States *126*

Kelowna Accord 73

Laasko–Taagepera index 55–6
Legislative competences 12, 52
Legislative Exchange Council 112
Legislative IGAs, United States, Independence 163
Levels of institutionalization 24–7
Levels of integration 27
Liberal government, Canada 72
Lobbying, United States 111, 114, 164
Long-term changes in IGR 61
Loose coupling 43
Lower level governments 4
  Characteristics 57–9
  Internal dynamics 219–27
  Number of 49

Macro approaches 204
Majoritarianism
  Canada 64, 86–7, 90–1
  Effect on IGA development 37–8
Mandating, Conference of cantonal Executives 103
Manitoba–New Brunswick Memorandum of Understanding 71
Martin government, Canada 72
Material examined 183–6
Medium institutionalization *25*, 26
  Canada *84*, 85
  Switzerland *95*
Medium integration 27, 138
Memoranda of understanding 129–30, 173
Micro-incentives 5–6
Micro-level processes 16, 17
Modes of representation 210–11
Monitoring 3–4
Multilateral agreements 69
  Canada 62, 75

Multilevel governance, European Union 212–15
Multilevel systems 2–3
Multistate Tax Commission 127

National Association of Attorneys General 112
National Center for Interstate Compacts 123, 159
National Conference of Commissioners on Uniform State Laws 130–1, 159
National Conference of State Legislatures 111–12, 114, 116, 118
  Autonomy protection 158
  Functions *134*
  Infrastructure 115
  Integration 157
National Council of State Legislatures 194, 199
National Governors' Association 7–8, 111–12, 114, 116, 209
  Analysis of output *187*–90
  Founding myth 157
  Functions *134*
  Infrastructure 114–15
  Integration 157
  National–regional relations 160–3
National–regional integration *169*
  Switzerland 153
Networking practices, United States 164–5
Neuer Finanzausgleich (NFA) 98–9
New England Governors' Conference 120
Non-binding agreements 172, 173, 176, 225–6
  Canada 174
  see also Intergovernmental agreements
Non-dualist elements, Swiss federal constitution 66
Non-enforceable joint decision-making, European Union 221, *224*
'Non-interactive' coordination, Canada 89
Non-political profile, U.S. IGAs 117
Non-overlapping governments 56, *57*, 58, 59
Norms 32
Number of lower-level governments 49

Obligation 178
One-party governments 6–7
  Characteristics 56, *57*

Open elections, Switzerland 40–1
Open Method of Coordination, European Union *224*, 225
Oral agreements 173
Overlapping governments 55–6

Parliaments, role of 9–10
Partial alternation 54
Party organization
    Switzerland 40–1, 58
    United States 41–2, 58
Path dependency 209
Patterns of interaction 18, 19, 20–*1*
Pensions, Canada *84*
Period of examination 182–3
Plenum
    Conference of Cantonal Executives 102
    Conferences of Cantonal Directors 94–5
Policy coordination 220–7, *223–4*
    Canada 80, 85
    Conferences of Cantonal Directors 95–7
    Switzerland 188
    United States 121, 188–9
Policy diffusion 173
    United States 130
Policy emulation 222, *224*
Policy fields 51–2
Policy-oriented perspective 15–16, 17
Policy resolutions, United States *176*
Policy-specific agreements
    Analysis 191–9
    Canada 80–8
        Horizontal integration 142–4
    Comparison with generalist IGAs, Switzerland 193–4
    Interaction with Generalist IGAs 190
    Material examined 184, *185*
    Switzerland 93–9
        Integration 149, 153
        Regional 104–5
    United States 125–9
        Integration 159
Policy-specific IGAs 17
Political control
    Canada 82, 86, 87, 88
    Switzerland 97, 99, 103
Political dynamics 3
Polycentric democracy 34

Position taking
    Canada 85, 90
    Conferences of Cantonal Directors 95–6
Power concentration 2, 6–7, 204
Power dispersion 34
    Switzerland 64–5
Power-limiting mechanisms 33–4
Power-sharing 2, 6–7, 8, 34, 204
    Canada 63, 90–1
    Effect on institutionalization 35–7
    Effect on integration 38–9
    European Union 214
    Relationship to territorial representation *216*, 222
    Switzerland 65, 108
    United States 111, 118–19, 128, 131–2, 165
    Interstate compacts 122–5
Power shifts, United States 67
Precision of agreements 26–7, 178, 179–80
    Generalist agreements *187*–8, 189
    Policy-specific agreements *192*, 193
Premiers' Council of Health Awareness, Canada 76
Primary elections, United States 41
Private interest groups, United States 164–5
Procedural initiatives 177–8
    Substantial depth 179
Process levels 31
Professionalism, U.S. politics 118

Québec factor 77

Rational choice 30, 32, 33, 209
Recommendations, Switzerland 174–5, *176*
Regional IGAs 69
    Canada 79–80
    Switzerland 104–7
    United States 119–20
        Independence 160–3
Resource-based indicators for institutionalization 24
Revenue share 44
Routines 32

Sanctions 177
Second chambers 50

Secretariat for Information and
    Co-operation on Fiscal Imbalance,
    Canada 76
Secretariats
  Canada 85, 87
  Switzerland 94
Service provision, U.S. 117–18, 164–5
Shadow of the future 22
Short-term goals 6, 7
  elected officials 30
Size, Lower-level governments 48–9
Social policy 52
  Canada *84*
  Switzerland *95*
  United States *126*
Social Union Framework 74
Social Union Framework Agreement
    (Canada 1999) 62, 63
Societal heterogeneity 49
Spain
  Governmental system 13, 207
  IGR evolution 20
Specialists, role in United States 129
Standard Operating Procedures 30
Ständerat 47, 101
State governors, U.S. 113–14, 128
State level, United States 67
State lobbying, United States 67
Streamlined Sales and Tax Agreement
    (SSUTA) 127, 188
Strong institutionalization 25, 26, 27
  Switzerland *95*
Strong integration *27*, 138
Structural features, Assessment 53
Structure-based indicators for
    institutionalization 24
Structure-oriented approaches 33
Structures of IGR 18, 20–*1*
Substantial depth of agreements 179–80
  Generalist agreements *187*–8, 189
  Policy-specific agreements *192*, 193
Supragovernmentalism 19, 21, 126, 132,
    206
Supranational decision-making 220
Supreme Court rulings, United States 46
Switzerland 6, 93, 107–9
  Alternation rate 54
  Blueprint 65–6
  Characteristics of lower level
    government 57, 58–9
  Co-decision 221

Competences 88
Conference of Cantonal
    Executives 101–4
Conferences of Cantonal
    Directors 93–9
  Inter-departmental
    coordination 99–101
Constitutional courts 47–8
Constitutional reforms 183
Cultural-historical accounts of IGR 31
Expectations 59
Federal grants 45
Federal system 7
Institutionalization *205*, 107–9
  Conferences of Cantonal
    Directors 94–9, *95*
  Regional IGAs 104–7
Integration 154, 166, 167, *169*, *205*
  Horizontal 149–52
  Intra-regional and
    national–regional 152–4
  Vertical 146–9
Interaction mode *207*
Intergovernmental agreements 174–5,
    176
  Generalist *187*–90
  Policy-specific *192*–4, 197, 198
Intergovernmental arrangements
    (IGAs) 69, *70*
Joint decision-making 220–1
Material examined 183, *185*
Party organization 40–1
Policy coordination 222, *223*–4, 225,
    226–7
Power-sharing 34, 39–40
  Relationship to territorial
    representation *216*, 218
Regional IGAs 104–7
Relative autonomy loss 54
Senate 50
Size 49
Systemic perspective 15, 16–17

Territorial representation, European
    Union 215–19
Trade-offs 10
Transportation policy 52
  Canada 83, *84*, *144*
  Switzerland 94, *95*
  United States *126*, 127
Treaties, European Union 225

Triggers for IGA development 208–9
Trust, lack of, Canada 82
Two-party systems, Competitive pressure 36

Unemployment insurance, Canada *84*
Unfunded mandates, U.S. 115
Unified government 54
Unilateral adaptation 19, 20, 21, 206
    United States 132
Unilateral withdrawal of competences, Prohibition 12
United States
    Alternation rate 54
    Blueprint 66–8
    Characteristics of lower level government *57*, 58
    Expectations 59
    Federal grants 45
    Federal system 7
    Fragmentation 117, 128–9, 131, 132, 159–63
    Government structure 46
    Horizontal federalism 120–2
        Compact commissions 125–9
        Flexible mechanisms 129–31
        Interstate compacts 122–4
    Institutionalization 111–14, 131–2, *205–6*
        Generalist IGAs 114–20
    Integration 155, 163–6, 167–8, *169*, *205*
        Fragmentation 160–3
        Inter-branch divides 156–9
    Interaction mode *207*
    Intergovernmental agreements 175, *176*
        Generalist *187–90*
        Policy-specific 191–*2*, 194, 198–9
    Intergovernmental arrangements (IGAs) 69, *70*
    Joint decision-making 220–1
    Material examined 183–4, *185*

Multilevel governance 212
Party organization 41–2
Policy coordination 222, *223–4*
Power-sharing 34, 39, 97
    Relationship to territorial representation *216*, 218
Relative autonomy loss 54
Senate 50
Studies of IGR 17
Supreme Court rulings 46–7
United States Conference of Mayors 112

Vernehmlassungen 96
Vernehmlassungsverfahren 66
Vertical integration
    Canada 139–42
    Switzerland 146–9, 154
    United States 156, 158
Vertical interactions 69, 210
    Analysis of integration 138–9
    Canada 71–9
Vertical power dispersion, Federal systems 12
Veto players 38–9
Voluntary nature of IGR structures 42–3
Voluntary power-sharing, Relationship to territorial representation *216*
Voluntary power-sharing structures 7, 38–9, 204
    Effect on integration 205
    In Switzerland 39–40

Watts' classification, competences 83
Weak institutionalization *25*, 26
    Canada *84*, 85–6, 87, 90
Weak integration *27*, 138
Western Premiers' Conference *70*, 71, 79, 144, 186
Western Switzerland, Integration 152–3

'Zero-sum games' 36